D

S

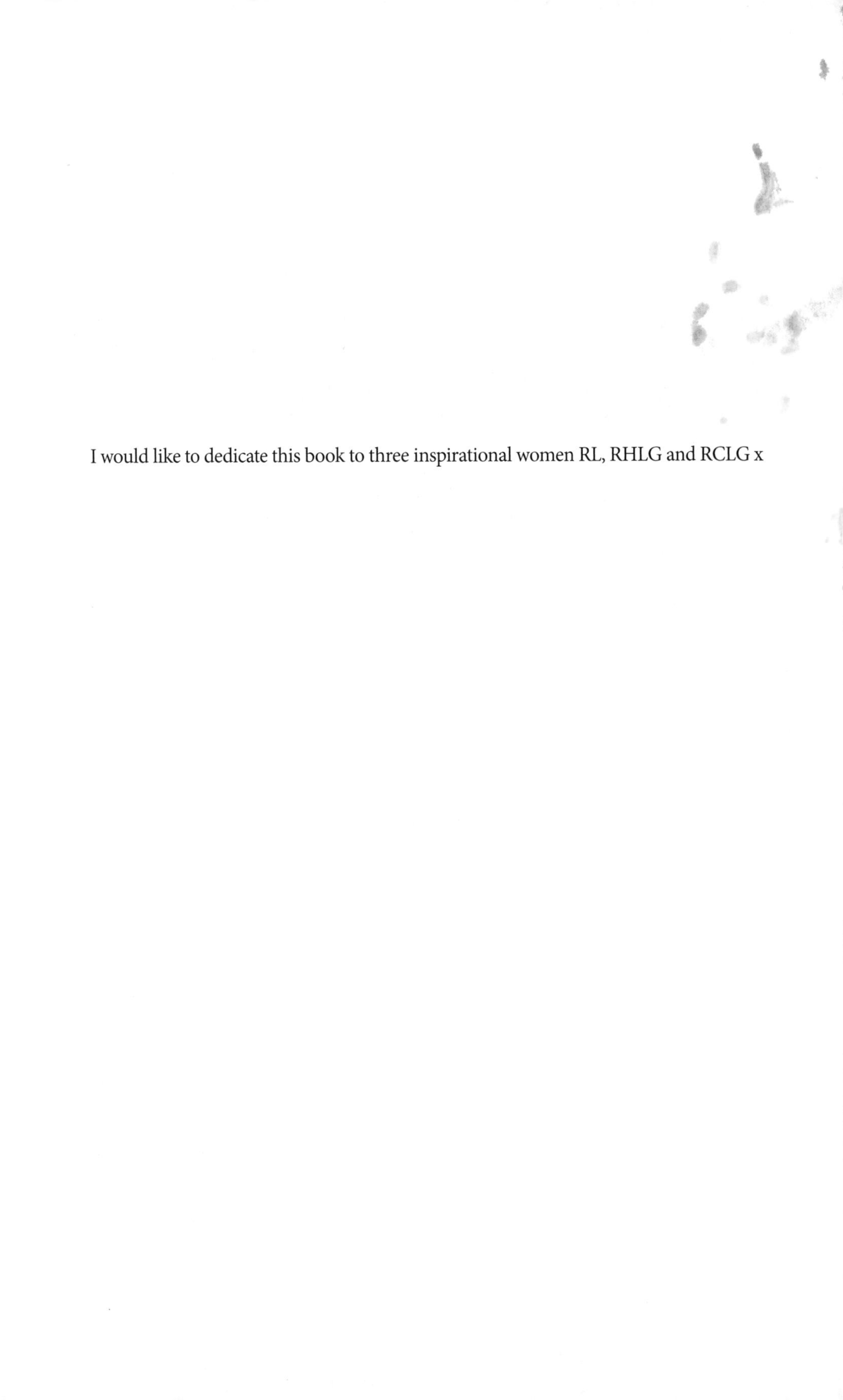

I would like to dedicate this book to three inspirational women RL, RHLG and RCLG x

'Students who are serious about improving the lives of disabled people will be richly rewarded by Goodley's ground-breaking book and challenged to engage with the content through regular questions and exercises requiring their active engagement with both text and wider literature. By critically examining diverse theories and perspectives Goodley's book meets head-on areas often glossed in the literature and in doing so provides a sophisticated transdisciplinary synthesis of contemporary critical disability theories and perspectives. Riveting to read, brimming with new ideas and challenging to students this book will take pride of place on many a disability studies student bookshelf.'
Paul Ramcharan, Co-ordinator of Research and Public Policy at the Australian Centre for Human Rights Education at RMIT University, Melbourne, Australia

'Dan Goodley has written a book that injects new energy into Disability Studies in the UK. He breaches disciplinary walls embracing, *inter alia*, sociology, critical psychology, cultural studies, inclusive education and psychoanalysis. He makes lucid practical and theoretical connections with queer, feminist, class and postcolonial standpoints that prefigure his concluding case for a version of Disability Studies that is critical and transformative. The book is driven by an eclectic pulse and a dynamic curiosity that cuts through orthodoxy. It takes the infant discipline to places it rarely ventures, into the territories of the Empire, the hybrid and the cyborg, into the emerging sites where new forms of disability activism are developing, into theories that open up new possibilities for research. A special commendation must go to the scholarly scope of the text. Professor Goodley plunders literature far and wide to produce the first introduction to Disability studies that is both global and cosmopolitan.'
Bill Hughes, Dean of the School of Law and Social Sciences, Glasgow Caledonian University

'*Disability Studies: An Interdisciplinary Introduction* provides what undergraduate and graduate students need in an introductory text. The structure of the text draws in the reader, maintains engagement with the text, and gives student and instructor numerous resources such as thinking points, student activities, seminar ideas, and discussion questions. Dr. Goodley's use of online resources makes the text contemporary and interactive. Dr. Goodley has attended to content as well as structure. He makes connections between chapters by referring the reader to previous chapters with questions for reflection and points of interest. The content covered is expansive and thorough. I intend to use this exceptional book in my doctoral level disability studies seminar.'
Susan L. Gabel, Professor National College of Education at National-Louis University

'In *Disability Studies: An Interdisciplinary Introduction,* Goodley's research is both sweeping and comprehensive. The book shows the depth of Disability Studies informing concerns while providing the reader with a substantive discussion of differences across discursive communities in the UK, Australia, Scandinavia, the US, and Canada. In taking up this comparative methodology, Goodley explains how the field analyzes the politics of human variation from a variety of standpoints, social goals, and disciplinary emphases. It breaks up a common misunderstanding that Disability Studies issues from a single orthodoxy rather than a multiplicity of approaches that complement as well as deepen each other.'

David Mitchell, Temple University

DISABILITY STUDIES

An Interdisciplinary Introduction

****

DAN GOODLEY

Los Angeles | London | New Delhi
Singapore | Washington DC

First published 2011
Reprinted 2011

SAGE Publications Ltd
1 Oliver's Yard
55 City Road
London EC1Y 1SP

SAGE Publications Inc.
2455 Teller Road
Thousand Oaks, California 91320

SAGE Publications India Pvt Ltd
B 1/I 1 Mohan Cooperative Industrial Area
Mathura Road, Post Bag 7
New Delhi 110 044

SAGE Publications Asia-Pacific Pte Ltd
33 Pekin Street #02-01
Far East Square
Singapore 048763

Library of Congress Control Number 2010920840

British Library Cataloguing in Publication data

A catalogue record for this book is available from the British Library

ISBN 978-1-84787-557-0
ISBN 978-1-84787-558-7 (pbk)

Typeset by C&M Digitals (P) Ltd, Chennai, India
Printed in the UK by the MPG Books Group, Bodmin and King's Lynn
Printed on paper from sustainable resources

Contents

Acknowledgements

Thank you to Jai Seaman and Chris Rojek at Sage for supporting this project and Rannveig Traustadóttir, Nick Watson, Paul Ramcharan and Susan Gabel for constructive feedback on proposals and drafts. I would like to express my gratitude to my mentors Michele Moore, Len Barton and Tim Booth. The ideas of Rebecca Lawthom and Katherine Runswick-Cole have hugely influenced this text. Cheers to:

- Griet Roets, Rebecca Mallett, Nick Hodge, Colin Barnes, Tom Shakespeare and Laurence Hopkins for critical debate and conscientisation.
- the *Disability, Discourse and Psychology seminar* series posse: Stephen Hodgkins, Mike Shamash, Barbara Stewart, Donna Reeve, Cassie Ogden, Brett Smith, Paul Duckett and Karl Nunkoosing.
- all at the *Cornwall Disability Research Network*, including Phil Bayliss, Theo Blackmore, Claire Tregaskis, Liz Ellis and Debs Phillips.
- under/postgraduate psychology students at Manchester Metropolitan University for discovering, among other things, that 'psychologisation' really is a word.
- the *Disability Studies Association* conference organisers for creating spaces to shout and be shouted at, particularly Hannah Morgan, Carol Thomas and Bob Sapey.
- colleagues in other climes: Andrew Azzopardi, Kristjana Kristiansen, Tsitsi Chataika, Geert Van Hove, Bjarne Bjelke Jensen, Kenji Kuno, Fiona Kumari Campbell, Swee Lan Yeo, How Kee Ling, Shaun Grech, Nagase Osamu, Simo Vehmas, Margrit Shildrick and Anita Ghai.

I would also like to thank the Economic and Social Research Council for their funding of my recent research projects, which have given me space and time to reflect on many of the issues addressed in this book (Grant No. RES-062-23-1138: *Does Every Child Matter, Post Blair? The Interconnections of Disabled Childhoods* and Grant No. RES-000-23-0129: *Parents, Professionals and Disabled Babies: Identifying En-abling Care)*. Many thanks to *Huddersfield People First* for constant reminders about the liberation of a politics of disability from the dregs of normalising society and to my inspirations Ruby Haf Lawthom Goodley and Rosa Cariad Lawthom Goodley. Girls *are* better than boys. Finally, I would like to express my gratitude to Clifford

Maurice Lawthom (1930–2009) for allowing me to loot his bookshelves and rediscover the power of C. Wright Mills and psychoanalysis. Cheers Maurice.

A small section of the following publication is reproduced with permission of the publishers Continuum, copyright © 2002, Continuum Press and co-author (Rapley), from Chapter 7, Goodley, D. and Rapley, M. (2002). Changing the subject: postmodernity and people with learning difficulties. In M. Corker and T. Shakespeare (eds), *Disability/Postmodernity: Embodying Disability Theory* (pp. 127–142). London/New York: Continuum.

Figure 1.1 is reproduced with permission from the author Copyright © 2009, Grech, from Grech, S. (2009a). Disability in the folds of poverty: exploring connections and transitions in guatemala: Draft chapter 2. Unpublished doctoral thesis, Manchester Metropolitan University.

Figures 4.1 and Tables 4.1 and 4.2 are reprinted by permission copyright 2005 ©, Taylor & Francis Group, from Goodley, D.A. and Lawthom, R. (2005a). Epistemological journeys in participatory action research: alliances between community psychology and disability studies, *Disability & Society*, 20 (2), 135–151.

Table 6.3 is reprinted with permission Copyright © 2003, American Psychological Association, from Olkin, R. and Pledger, C. (2003). Can disability studies and psychology join hands? *American Psychologist*, 58(4), 296–304.

Preface

Disability studies are a broad area of theory, research and practice that are antagonistic to the popular view that disability equates with personal tragedy. While we may identify people as having physical, sensory, cognitive or mental health impairments, disability studies place the problems of disability in society. This book views disability studies as a paradigm shift; from disability as personal predicament to disability as social pathology. If we locate disability in the person, then we maintain a disabling status quo. In contrast, by viewing disability as a cultural and political phenomenon, we ask serious questions about the social world. Undoubtedly, societies subject people with impairments to discrimination. Disabled people have been hated, made exotic, pitied, patronised and ignored. Disability also evokes admiration, curiosity, fascination and sympathy. Disability studies respond to these acts of political and cultural life. This book has been written with undergraduates and postgraduates, lecturers, researchers and professors, practitioners and activists in mind. New readers will be introduced to some key debates. Experienced readers will find new perspectives. It is anticipated that readers will come to this book from the social sciences, health, social care and the humanities, and from professions such as psychology, social work, education, counselling, medicine, nursing, therapy, community and youth work. It is assumed that we share a commitment to ending racism, heterosexism, homophobia and prejudice against disabled people. The hope is that this book is in spirit with those disabled activists and scholars who, across the globe, have challenged their marginalisation.

This book was written from a base in England but with international disability studies in mind. At the time of writing, the world was entering uncertain economic times. We know from history that when societies struggle to maintain their wealth then disabled people are among the first to suffer.[1] It is therefore paramount to develop *social* theories of disability that address the socio-economic, cultural and political conditions of disabled people's exclusion. Disability studies are held together by a community of scholars in which orthodoxies are produced through relations of power (Fox-Keller, 1962; Kuhn, 1968). One task of this book is to identify, but also question, these orthodoxies.

Some words about the title. This is a text that works with social scientific and cultural analyses of disability. *Disability studies* take – as given – the ideological and material exclusion of people with labels of physical, sensory or cognitive impairments. Disability and impairment are not synonymous. Indeed, throughout, we will make reference to terms such as 'disablism' and 'disablement' that acknowledge the marginalisation of people with impairments. The subtitle, *an interdisciplinary introduction*, conveys an attempt to span a host of disciplines, including sociology, critical psychology, cultural studies, psychoanalysis and education, to analyse three overlapping layers of everyday life: *psyche, culture and society*. *Culture* and *society* are perhaps easy to explain because they are analysed through the interdisciplinary – or, more properly, as we shall see, transdisciplinary – focus of the various chapters. We will unpack the kinds of cultural selves that are produced in a society that disavows (i.e. that rejects but is fascinated by) differently able people. The term *psyche* is used for three reasons. First, the psyche is an artefact of contemporary society that individualises social problems. We will remain sceptical about society's preference to locate social problems in the heads and bodies of (disabled) people. This leads to the commonly held view that (disabling) society is not the problem: (disabled) people are. This book rejects this idea. Second, psyche acknowledges the complex ways in which the social world is produced through individuals. Psyche recognises the tight knot of the person and the social word, the self and other people, the individual and society. Third, we critically borrow the notion of psyche from psychoanalysis, to indicate that external processes of domination, ideology and oppression shape our inner worlds. We will explore some of the ways in which a disabling society is experienced subjectively and emotionally. And crucial to this is the need to explore the psychical functions of *non*-disabled people and disabling culture. Our concern is not with the psychological health of disabled people; our focus will be on the kinds of psychology that are reproduced in a society that, for various reasons, marginalise disabled people. We will explore the ways in which non-disabled people (and disabled people for that matter) symbolise, characterise, construct, gaze at, project, split off, react, repress and direct images of impairment and disability in ways that subjugate and, at times, terrorise disabled people.

The emergence of disability studies over the last 40 years has been assisted by other radical writings. Feminists laid foundations for political change and explorations of the self and culture through the notion of 'the personal is political' and this maxim holds true for disability studies. Theories from Black civil rights, working-class and queer movements had clear relevance to the lives of disabled people. Disability is complex and calls into question a web of discourses and institutional practices. It says much about those versions of humanity that are valued and upheld by contemporary culture and society. The hope is that this book encourages you to engage with disability studies, alongside other transformative writings, in ways that remain aligned to the demands of disabled people's political organisations and responsive to emerging insights in theory, practice, research and policy.

The book is broadly split into three sections. Chapters 1–3 contextualise the book. Chapters 4–9 develop the core analyses of disability studies. Chapter 10 summarises and sets out future ideas for development. Each chapter includes a number of key readings (for you to follow up) and a smattering of 'thinking points' which disrupt the arguments made in order to pose questions to encourage an interaction with this text, provide possible essay titles, give ideas to stimulate individual and class reflections, suggest seminar activities to focus attention on critical questions and debates.

Chapter 1 sets the scene by exploring the global nature of disability. We will tentatively define what we mean by disablism, impairment and disability, and introduce different explanatory approaches. Social, minority, cultural and relational models are introduced as responses to dominant moral, medical and individual models. Chapter 2 tees up some of the debates explored in the book, such as the role of disability research, the place of impairment in theories of disablism, disability studies as a transdisciplinary place and the role of non-disabled researchers. Chapter 3 makes a simple but important point: disability cannot be considered independently of age, ethnicity, sexuality, class and gender. In this chapter we will focus on the last four of the social markers.

Rather than considering them as additive phenomena to the experience of disability, we will use this chapter to introduce some themes that intersect black, feminist, queer, class and disability studies perspectives, which we will revisit in the book.

Chapter 4 examines four distinct sociologies of disability in order to explore particular conceptions of society and the contrasting – at times complementary – ideas that they produce. It questions how different sociological disability studies make sense of the complex relationship between non/disabled people and society. Chapter 5 considers why the disabled individual is such a problem for society. It explores how social and human sciences have contributed to common sense and everyday conceptions of what it means to be 'an individual'. The chapter tackles a specific social practice that is damaging to disabled people – psychologisation. This concept, under-used in disability studies, helpfully challenges the tendency of the contemporary social world to de/value particular kinds of individual.

Chapter 6 zones in on the relationships between non-disabled and disabled people and asks: what is the psychological impact of living with impairment in a disabling society? How do disabled people deal with demanding publics? Why does society react to disabled people in the ways that it does? In answering these questions we will excavate some psychological components of disablism. Chapter 7 also asks a number of questions, including to what extent are common sense understandings of disability and impairment influenced by professional and scientific ideas? In a rapidly developing knowledge society, what possibilities are there for disrupting disabling ideas and offering more enabling alternatives? These queries are addressed through reference to the notion of discourse: ideas and practices that are re/produced through key institutions of society, including family, school, workplace and hospital.

Chapter 8 moves analysis up a notch to consider culture. We will employ ideas from psychoanalysis to make sense of some of the cultural responses of dominant society to disabled people. We will also consider some of the reasons behind the mundane and everyday disablist reactions to impaired bodies and minds. It is suggested that disabled people become both a source of fascination and rejection because cultural ideals of autonomy and wholeness are both precarious and false. In Chapter 9 we ask: how do the approaches of special and inclusive education understand disabled children? How can educators respond in enabling ways? We explore the possibilities and challenges for inclusive education in a time when schools are under increasing pressures to perform. We seek ideas for good practice from the literature of critical pedagogy.

Chapter 10 wraps up the book by pulling out some cross-cutting themes which connect disability studies with other important political agendas of feminist, queer and black studies. Such intersections are at the heart of what we might term *critical* disability studies: where disability links together other identities as a moment of reflection that Davis (2002) coins as dismodernism; that foregrounds the significance of disability to everyday life.

Note

1 An article by Ainsworth (2009) and reports from organisations such as Voluntary Service Overseas (www.vso.org.uk) indicate that in January 2009 the drop in the rate of sterling and the dollar meant that international aid organisations were facing at least a 20% budget deficit in their projects, with HIV and disability projects in Africa being among the first to be affected and, in some cases, terminated.

ONE

Introduction: *Global Disability Studies*

****

Introduction

Disability studies understand their subject matter as social, cultural and political phenomena. In defining terms, describing positions and laying foundations, we will interrogate the literature in ways that encourage us to think about where we sit/stand in relation to pan-national and cross-disciplinary perspectives on disability that have the potential to support the self-empowerment of disabled people. This first chapter sets the theoretical tone.

The global nature of disability

The word 'disability' hints at something missing either fiscally, physically, mentally or legally (Davis, 1995: xiii). To be disabled evokes a marginalised place in society, culture, economics and politics. It is concentrated in some parts of the globe more than others, caused by armed conflict and violence, malnutrition, rising populations, child labour and poverty. Paradoxically, it is increasingly found to be everywhere, due to the exponential rise in the number of psychiatric, administrative and educational labels over the last few decades. Disability affects us all, transcending class, nation and wealth. The notion of the TAB – Temporarily Able Bodied – recognises that many people will at some point become disabled (Marks, 1999a: 18). Most impairments are acquired (97%) rather than congenital (born with) and world estimates suggest a figure of around 500–650 million disabled people, or one in ten of the population (Disabled-World.com, 2009), with this expected to rise to around 800 million by the year 2015 (Peters et al., 2008). Currently, 150 million of these are children (Grech, 2008) and it is estimated that 386 million of the world's working-age population are disabled (Disabled-World.com, 2009). 88% live in the world's poorest countries and 90% of those in rural areas (Marks, 1999a). For example, India has a population of one billion and approximately 70 million are disabled (Ghai, 2002). A 1987 survey in China conservatively accounted for 51.64 million disabled people (Shen et al., 2008). In the USA, 19.3% or 49.7 million of the 'civilian non-institutionalised population of five years or older' are disabled (Quinlan et al., 2008). This makes disabled people the largest minority grouping in an already crowded theatre of multiculturalism (Davis, 1995). We know that there are global discrepancies and intra-national differences. There are more disabled people in the Southern hemisphere (Stone, 1999) and you are more likely to be labelled as schizophrenic if you are black than if you are non-black in Britain (Beresford and Wilson, 2000a). Disabled people are more likely to be victims of rape and violence, less likely to receive legal protection, more likely to be excluded from mass education, be underrepresented in positions of power and more reliant on state benefits and/or charity (Meekosha, 2008). As children they remain underrepresented in mainstream schools, work, leisure and communities (McLaughlin et al., 2008). As adults, disabled people do not enjoy equitable access to human, economic and social capital resources (Priestley, 2001). If we accept Marx's view that charity is the perfume of the sewers of capitalism, then disabled people are subjected to the bitter/sweet interventions of charity. Of the 200 or so countries in the world, only a third have anti-discriminatory disability legislation and many of these laws are questionable in terms of their legislative potency (United Nations Department of Public Information, 2008).

Thinking point: Identify, via the Internet, disability-related social policy or anti-discriminatory legislation in your own country. What areas of public life are addressed by these documents?

Disabled people are likely to suffer socio-economic hardship. In rich countries, the expanse of the free market, the proliferation of human, welfare, social, educational services and professionals and the increasing need to be 'intellectually able' and 'physically fit' for work, makes disabled people economically vulnerable (Barnes and Roulstone, 2005). Impaired foetuses are eradicated everyday as a consequence of antenatal tests and reproductive technologies (Kittay, 2006). Alive, people with impairments are ignored, pitied, patronised, objectified and fetishised. Their very presence raises questions about the 'right to die' and 'assisted suicide' (Shakespeare, 2006a). And while impaired bodies and minds have always been part of everyday life, demeaning societal responses to impairment – which we can define as 'disablement' (Oliver, 1990) or 'disablism' (Thomas, 2007) – are historically and culturally relative. Disability studies aim to make sense of this relativity.

The politics of disability

Disabled people have challenged their social exclusion through their politics and disability studies have developed to accompany this politicisation: to assist disabled people in their fight for full equality (Thomas, 2004: 571). Pinpointing the exact origins of disabled people's politics is impossible (Shakespeare, 2006b). We know that over the nineteenth and twentieth centuries, disabled people's experiences of institutions, eugenics and the Holocaust galvanised many to organise collectively against the oppressive regimes of medicine, science and professional control (Wolfensberger, 1981; Barnes, 1991; Noll and Trent, 2004; Longman and Umansky, 2001; Snyder and Mitchell, 2006; Gabel and Danforth, 2008a). The rise of new social movements, such as feminist, queer, working-class and black civil rights movements in the 1960s, enhanced the radicalisation of disabled people (Boggs, 1996). Disability studies developed, for Meekosha (2004: 724), in similar ways to Women's and Black Studies as a new interdisciplinary sphere of scholarly work. People with intellectual disabilities (previously 'mental retardation') demanded a rethink of their status through pioneering the self-advocacy movement (Goodley, 2000), while survivors of mental health hospitals and services (hitherto 'the mentally ill') demonstrated against psychiatric labelling (Sayce, 2000). Together, disabled people have exposed the material conditions of exclusion magnified through capitalism (Oliver, 1990), while also developing personal and political responses to normalising society (e.g. Morris, 1991, 1992, 1996; Shakespeare et al., 1996). The depth of activism is captured through reference to the (admittedly loose and Anglo-centric) typology adapted from Oliver and Zarb (1989) and Oliver (1990). Historically, disabled people were supported via *patronage* and *charity*, through organisations *for* disabled people which provide specialist services, consultation and advice from professional agencies (e.g. Royal National Institute for the Blind, Spastics Society). In time, *economic* and *parliamentarian* organisations *for* disabled people lobbied governments for changes in legislation to protect the rights of disabled people (e.g. Disablement Income Group, Disability Alliance, Disability Rights Commission). Such pressure was enhanced through the expanding *activist* network, where organisations *of* disabled people campaigned for collective action and consciousness raising (e.g. Direct Action Network, Sisters Against Disablement, Not Dead Yet). As these groups grew, so too did the number of *co-ordinating* organisations *of* disabled people at (inter)national levels (e.g. Disabled People's International). Disability politics, particularly activist and co-ordinating forms, have been felt by nation states and supranational organisations. The United Nations Department of Economic and Social Affairs (2009) reports how disability was placed on the radar of United Nations' policies and programmes by a raft of developments, including the 1981 International Year of Disabled Persons, the adoption of the United Nations World Programme of Action Concerning Disabled People (1982) and the release of the *Standard Rules on the Equalisation of Opportunities for Persons with Disabilities* (1993), all of which set in place systems for the regular collection and dissemination of information on disability and the promotion of disability-focused programmes. National responses are evidenced in the constitution of anti-discriminatory legislation, including the 1990 Americans with Disabilities Act, Disability Discrimination Acts of 1992 and 1995 (in Australia and the UK, respectively) and Malaysian Persons with Disabilities Act (2007). Over the last couple of years, (some) countries have ratified the UN Convention on the Rights of Persons with Disabilities. We have seen growing recognition of the need for inclusive forms of education (www.inclusion-international.org) and support for poorer countries in relation to their disabled members (www.worldbank.org/disability/gpdd). The Decade of Disabled Persons (1983–1992) was a fitting testimony, not simply to a widening participation agenda on the part of nations, but to the growing influence of disabled people's own organisations (Barnes, 2002).

The Disabled People's Movement has revolutionised global understandings of disability. By raising the personal experience of disabled people as the primary source of knowledge and identifying disability as a social problem that should be addressed by socio-political interventions, the Disabled People's Movement has politicised disability (Vehmas, 2008: 21). We can trace many inter/national stories of disability politics. The first Disabled People's International (DPI) World Congress was held in Singapore in 1981. Organisations came together from their national contexts to work towards a global political response. Since this time DPI has provided an essential hub for the sharing of campaign successes and the raising of transnational issues such as inclusive education and human rights. The historical legacy of the Disabled People's Movement can be found across the globe through the presence of Centres for Independent Living that offer not only services to disabled people, but also work with their struggles for equity (Charlton, 1998; Barnes and Mercer, 2006). We have seen the development of regional organisations such as Asia-Pacific Development Center on Disability (www.apcdproject.org) that responds to local issues facing disabled people in some of the poorest countries, such as community-based rehabilitation, basic literacy programmes and support for families. In rich parts of the world, such as the Nordic countries, Canada and the USA, the Disabled People's Movement has been heavily influenced by the self-advocacy movement organised by people with the label of intellectual disabilities (Williams and Shoultz, 1982). Organisations of the Blind were particularly strong in India, participating in hunger strikes to push for anti-discriminatory legislation (Chander, 2008). Britain saw the establishment of the United Kingdom's Disabled People's Council (formerly the British Council of Organisations of Disabled People), which has grown from the early political impact of organisations such as *UPIAS* (*Union of the Physically Impaired Against Segregation*) in the 1960s and 1970s (Campbell and Oliver, 1996). On the ground, disabled people's organisations have enacted institutional change through the delivery of disability equality training courses (Barnes, 2002), which seek to educate organisations to adopt more enabling philosophies and practices. This has created a new form of labour for disabled people.

? *Thinking point: Disabled trainers offer expert advice on eradicating the conditions of exclusion in areas such as education (www.diseed.org.uk; www.openroad.net.au/access/dakit/welcome.htm) and employment (www. breakthrough-uk.com; www.independentliving.org/indexen.html). On personal matters, disabled people have organised around inclusive play and leisure, social and sexual relationships (www.outsiders.org.uk/home). And culturally, disabled people have contributed immeasurably in the areas of arts, literature, music and performance (e.g.www.disabilityartsonline.org.uk/home). Visit these websites. How do you think these organisations have influenced wider ideas around disability?*

While a plethora of helping professions have grown around disability, disabled people have themselves had a huge impact on professional, cultural and political life. Disabled people were specifically mentioned in Barack Obama's President-elect victory speech in 2008 and there is a growing historical awareness of their contribution to politics (e.g. Rosa Luxemburg, Antonio Gramsci, Woodrow Wilson) and culture (e.g. Frida Kahlo, Helen Keller, Christopher Nolan, Ian Dury, Kurt Kobain). This book is not the place for a detailed exposition of disability activism (for examples, see instead Chamberlin, 1990; Priestley, 1999; Meekosha, 2002; Barnes and Mercer, 2006; Gabel and Danforth, 2008). What is important to keep in mind is the breadth of disability activism that continues to influence debates within disability studies. The mantra 'Nothing about us, without us' (Charlton, 1998) asks pertinent questions about the ownership of disability studies. Across the globe, the priorities of disabled people's organisations say much about their nation's (lack of) welfare system, view of the citizen (Dwyer, 2004), cultural ideas around disability (Watson et al., 2003) and the perceived importance of disability in comparison with other socio-economic inequalities (Armstrong et al., 2002).

Thinking point: Blackmore (2009) gathered information from the British Charity Commission for 2007–2008 financial years. All voluntary sector organisations have to complete and submit annual reports by law to the Commission. These annual reports are therefore legally binding and accurate. He found the following figures:

Organisations for disabled people (traditionally charities):
Leonard Cheshire = income £149,655,000; spending £146,046,000; surplus £3,609,000
Mencap = £183,456,000; spending £176,901,000; surplus £9,615,000

Organisation of disabled people (traditionally activist organisations):
UKDPC = income £167,920; spending £187,082; deficit –£19,162
People First = income £288,236; spending £274,197; surplus £14,039

What do these figures say to you about the contemporary status of charity and patronage in the lives of disabled people in Britain?

Defining disability: from pathology to politics

Official definitions of disability reflect the organisational requirements of governments, their institutions and key welfare professionals. In Britain, for example, the Disability Discrimination Act (DDA) (HMSO, 1995: section 1.1) describes a disabled person as 'anyone with a physical or mental impairment, which has a substantial and long-term adverse effect upon their ability to carry out normal day-to-day activities'. This includes *physical impairments* (weakening of a part of the body caused through illness, by accident or from birth, including blindness, deafness, heart disease or the paralysis of a limb); *mental impairment* (such as learning disabilities and all recognised mental illnesses); that the disability is *substantial* (does not have to be severe, but is more than minor or trivial), with a *long-term adverse effect* (more than 12 months) and influences normal *day-to-day activity* (your mobility; manual dexterity; physical co-ordination; continence; ability to lift, carry or otherwise move everyday objects; speech, hearing or eyesight; memory or ability to concentrate, learn or understand; or perception of the risk of physical danger). These administrative definitions allow nation states to identify those who qualify for welfare. Simultaneously, though, these definitions individualise the problems of disability. The DDA definition says something very simple: impairment, whether it be physical or 'of mind', results in and creates disability. Hence, impairment and disability are collapsed together as synonymous concepts.

Societies are predisposed to understand disability as a personal tragedy inflicting damage upon the mind and body, requiring treatment, rehabilitation or (at its most logical extreme) cure (Barnes, 1990). Following this, impairments *lead to* a myriad of disabilities – disabled childhoods, disabled learning, disabled personal relationships, disabled sex lives, disabled parenting, disabled psychologies and so on. 'The disabled' are dependent on state and professional intervention (Morris, 1993b) and their only hope is to adjust to a lacking body or mind. Drawing on the work of Olkin and other disability scholars it is possible to identify two complementary worldviews that situate the predicament of disability firmly within the individual (Table 1.1).

Disability studies are critical responses to these two cultural extremes, presented in Table 1.1, of supernatural vision and/or medical specimen (Snyder and Mitchell, 2001: 380). The moral position views disability as a sin (a punishment from God forgiven through divine intervention), while the medical perspective views disability as pathology (a physical, sensory or cognitive failing that tragically 'handicaps' those 'afflicted'). Following Snyder and Mitchell (2001: 379), moral positions have included disability as a reflection of God's dismay (ancient Greece), as evidence of an intimacy with God (medieval Europe) and a divine response to parental wrongdoing (Renaissance period). The medical model is a modern outlook (Christensen, 1996; Sachs, 2008). The church benefits from the moral position while the paramedical professions gain from the medical model. The eugenics movement of the early twentieth century, which accompanied the rise in the status of science and capitalism, located the burden of disability in the unproductive flawed individual (Fernald, 1912). Following Naidoo (2009), medicine has conceptualised disability as a distinct pathology (a pathogenic view) rather than a place on a continuum of dis/ease (a salutogenic position) or in terms of capacities and strengths (a fortigenic approach). The medical model becomes hegemonic – that is dominant – and encourages the disabled entity to be framed in terms of assisted suicide, euthanasia and antenatal termination. The human worth of disabled people is rendered highly questionable through the growing use of reproductive technologies. And as medicine intervenes so disabled bodies are made increasingly undesirable. For Oliver (1990), moral and medical approaches promote an *individual model of disability*, reducing the problem of disability to the flawed tragedy of individual personhood treatable through the interventions of charities and healthcare professionals.

Thinking point: The first Professor of Disability Studies in Britain, Mike Oliver, made the following observation about professionals:

> *The medical profession, because of its power and dominance, has spawned a whole range of pseudo-professions in its own image – physiotherapy, occupational therapy, speech therapy, clinical psychology – each one geared to the same aim – the restoration of normality. And each of these pseudo-professions develops its own knowledge base and set of skills to facilitate this, organising interventions and intrusions into disabled peoples' lives on the basis of claims to discreet and limited knowledge and skills'. (Oliver, 1996: 37)*

To what extent do you dis/agree with this observation?

Professionals and disability are clearly intertwined. McLaughlin et al. (2008) interviewed the parents of a one-year-old child, with the label of Down syndrome, who by that time had met with 124 professionals. Many bio-medical professions stipulate that impairment has such a traumatic physical or psychological impact upon the person that they will be unable to achieve a reasonable quality of life (Barnes, 1991: ix).

Table 1.1 Two dominant perspectives of disability (as) impairment

	Disability as a moral condition	Disability as a medical condition
Meaning	*Disability is a defect caused by moral lapse or sins.* The reification of sin or evil, failure or a test of faith. Includes myth that as one sense is impaired by disability another is heightened, i.e. the blind seer.	*Disability is a medical problem that resides in the individual* – a defect in or a failure of a bodily system that is inherently abnormal and pathological. Impairment and disability are conflated, i.e. the Down syndrome child.
Moral Implications	Shame to the person with the disability and their family. The family must address their immoral nature as evidenced through the presence of a disabled family member.	Repudiates the view of disability as a lesion on the soul but may blame person or family for healthcare habits (e.g. Type A personality leads to heart attack) and promulgates view of disability as a personal tragedy.
Sample Idea	God gives us only what we can bear. Example: (Gaelic plaque) 'May those who love us, love us. And those who don't love us, may God turn their hearts; and if he doesn't turn their hearts may he turn their ankles so we'll know them by their limping.'	Patients are described clinically (e.g. 'patient suffers from Trisomy 21/Down syndrome' or 'there is an incomplete lesion at the C4 level'). Isolation of body parts and view of people with disabilities (PWD) as atypical, abnormal and pathological.
Origins	Oldest of all disability models but, arguably, still the most prevalent worldwide.	Mid-1800s onwards. Underlies most rehabilitation facilities and most rehabilitation journals in rich countries.
Goals of Intervention	Spiritual or divine or acceptance. Increased faith and forbearance. Finding meaning and purpose in affliction.	Patients or clients are expected to avail themselves of services offered by trained professionals with the promise of cure (the amelioration of the physical condition to the greatest extent possible); rehabilitation (the adjustment of the person to their condition) or adjustment (adjust to live as a PWD).
Benefits of Model	Acceptance of being 'selected' to have a disability, feeling a relationship with God, having a sense of greater purpose. Some impairments understood as evidence of spiritual embodiment (e.g. pure simple child).	Promotes faith in medical intervention, a defined patient role and offers a label as explanation. Medical and technological advances in key services of the welfare state have improved the lives of PWD.
Negative Effects	Being ostracised from family and community, feeling profound shame, having to hide disability symptoms or the person with a disability. Disability exposes sinful (past and present) lives of family.	Paternalism, pathologisation and the promotion of benevolence. Interventions *on* PWD rather than *with*. Promotes research by outsiders and services for, but not by, disabled people.

Sources: Adapted from Oliver, 1996; Goodley, 2000; Olkin, 2001, 2002, 2009; Barnes and Mercer, 2003.

Linton (1998a) and Sherry (2006) suggest that this individual discourse creates a number of 'fault lines': disability is cast as an essentialist condition (with organic aetiologies); disabled people are treated as objects rather than as authors of their own lives; 'person fixing' rather than 'context changing' interventions are circulated; the power of health and social care professionals intensifies and the tyranny of normality is accentuated. Disabled people are infantilised, constructed as helpless and viewed as asexual (McRuer and Wilkerson, 2003: 10). For Abberley (1987: 18), presenting the disadvantage of disability as the consequence of a 'naturalised impairment' or 'biological flaw' lets exclusionary society off the hook.

For Greenop (2009), more and more people are being made aware that medicine makes promises it cannot keep, fails to fix 'the problem' of disability, creates dependency, denies individuals use of their own self-care strategies and may have iatrogenic consequences of side-effects and unforeseen complications (Greenop, 2009).[1] Indeed, across society, the growth in complementary therapies as alternatives to medicine and evidence of medical non-compliance of between 30% and 50% on the part of people in receipt of medical treatments (with £230 million worth of prescription drugs being incarcerated in the UK in 2002, due to non-usage), indicate that people are growing ever more critical of medicine (Greenop, 2009). Similarly, disabled people have offered their own criticisms of and alternatives to medicalisation. Key to these counter-views is the growing awareness of the social, cultural, historical, economic, relational and political factors that *dis*-able people. Disability studies dislodge disability from its medicalised and moral origins (Herndon, 2002: 122). 'Dis/ability' is not natural. Dis/ability is socially constructed. In Britain, the Union of the Physically Impaired Against Segregation (UPIAS, 1976: 3–4), devised the following definitions to acknowledge the role of society:

> Impairment – lacking part of or all of a limb, or having a defective limb organism or mechanism of the body.
>
> Disability – the disadvantage or restriction of activity caused by a contemporary social organisation which takes no account of people who have physical impairments and thus excludes them from mainstream social activities.

This was later adapted by the Disabled People's International (DPI) definition:

> **IMPAIRMENT**: is the functional limitation within the individual caused by physical, mental or sensory impairment.
> **DISABILITY**: is the loss or limitation of opportunities to take part in the normal life of the community on an equal level with others due to physical and social barriers. (DPI, 1982)

These definitions acknowledge impairment but politicise disability. Impairment is defined as a form of biological, cognitive, sensory or psychological difference that is defined often within a medical context and disability is the negative social reaction to those differences (Sherry, 2007: 10). Disability is understood as an act of exclusion: people are *disabled by* contemporary society. This concept is extended by Thomas (2007: 73), in her definition of *disablism* as 'a form of social oppression involving the social imposition of restrictions of activity on people with impairments and the socially engendered undermining of their psycho-emotional well being'. This is helpful because it permits disablism to sit alongside other forms of oppression, including hetero/sexism and racism. *Disability* is recognised as a phenomenon of cultural, political and socio-economic conditions (Abberley, 1987), disablism recognises the psychological, cultural and structural crimes against disabled people (Thomas, 2007) and *disablement* captures the practical consequences of disablism (Oliver, 1990).

Thinking point: The definitions of 'impairment', 'disability', 'disablism' and 'disablement' presented above are Anglocentric: they reflect the preferred terms of British disability studies scholars. In other English-speaking nations, terminology morphs and changes. 'Disabled people' (Britain) are referred to in terms of People First language in the USA as 'people with disabilities'. The North American preference for 'people with intellectual disabilities' (previously and now unacceptably 'the mentally retarded' or 'the mentally handicapped') are also related to other terms around the globe, including 'people with learning difficulties' (Britain) and 'people with developmental disabilities' (Australia). Individuals historically diagnosed as 'mentally ill', having 'psychiatric illnesses' or 'mental health problems' now more commonly use terms such as 'survivors of mental health systems'. And, while British scholars have addressed disablism, many North American writers have turned their attentions to ableism (see below). A helpful insight into some of the debates about disability language can be found in the publications coming out of Disability World (visit www.disabilityworld.org/aboutus.html#term) and Disabled Peoples' International (www.dpi.org). It is also worth reading the 'Editorial on Language Policy' of the leading international journal Disability & Society *for a snapshot overview of the changes in terminology (available to download at www.tandf.co.uk/journals/authors/cdsolang.pdf). Whatever the preferred terminology, all disability studies scholars share an interest in appropriating language that does not demean, is culturally sensitive and recognises the humanity of disabled people before disability or impairment labels.*

Disability is also a cultural concept. For Garland-Thomson (2002: 5), dis/ability is best understood as a sign system that, by differentiating and marking bodies and minds, produces dis/abled-bodies and maintains the ideal of the inherently stable non-disabled body or mind. Disability is a label, a signifier, that inaugurates consignment to an identity category, which signifies disadvantage and oppression (Jung, 2002: 179). The meaning and experience of impairment, disability and disablism morph over time, not simply because of the developments in 'scientific thinking' around the body and mind, but often because of changes in social policy, government guidelines and legislation. Disablism refers to those times when the relationship between the environment, body and psyche serves to exclude certain people from becoming full participants in interpersonal, social, cultural, economic and political affairs (Marks, 1999b: 611).

Thinking point: According to Ferguson et al. (1992), in 1973 the entire category of 'Borderline Retardation' was dropped from the Manual of Terminology of the American Association on Mental Deficiency, *as the*

manual was revised. What does this say about the biological or cultural nature of 'intellectual disability'?

Oliver (1990) records how the changes to the application criteria for mobility allowance in the UK in the 1980s significantly shifted and changed the population of those deemed eligible to qualify (and therefore defined as mobility impaired). A 'manipulative child' in the 1970s might get the label of Pathological Demand Avoidance Syndrome in the 2000s. Today's 'naughty boy' is more commonly known as a child with Attention Deficit Hyperactivity Disorder (ADHD) or Oppositional Defiance Disorder (ODD).

Disability breaks down when we start to scrutinise it (Davis, 1995). Disability speaks of society: being disabled is not simply a descriptor of an object – a person with a cane – but a social process that intimately involves everyone who has a body and lives in the world of senses (Davis, 1995: 2). For Ghai (2006: 147), disability refers to bodies that have become dis-embodied because of constructions around them, that create a total invisibility of the disabled individual. Society discriminates against disabled people when it becomes disablism. While disablism is negative, disability/impairment can be positive. Disability culture is rich in creativity and proud slogans of liberation, including 'Piss on Pity', 'Disabled and Proud' and 'People First'. A key task of disability studies is to tap into these affirmative understandings of the productive impaired body and mind, while examining how disablism is enacted at the level of psyche, culture and society. The psyche and the social are impossible to disconnect (Oliver and Edwin, 2002).

This book is written at an interesting time in the short history of disability studies. Analyses of disability have entered the curricula. This is evident in the USA in the founding of the Society for Disability Studies in 1982 (www.disstudies.org) and the constitution of special interest groups in Modern Language Association (MLA), the American Anthropological Association (AAA) and the American Educational Research Association in the 1990s (Gabel, 2006). The Nordic Network on Disability Research was established in Denmark in 1997 (www.nndr.no/index.php), the *New Zealand Journal of Disability Studies* was launched in the mid-1990s and the Canadian Disability Studies Association-Association Canadienne des Études sur L'Incapacité, held its first annual meeting at the University of Manitoba in Winnipeg in May 2004 (www.cdsa-acei.ca/about.html). The year 2003 saw the Inaugural Conference of the Disability Studies Association in Britain (www.disabilitystudies.net) and the establishment of the Japan Society for Disability Studies (www.jsds.org).

Disability studies perspectives

For Garland-Thomson (2002), disability studies is a matrix of theories, pedagogies and practices. Within this matrix are perspectives that should not be confused with theories (Oliver, 1996), nor constrain debate by masquerading as grand truths (Price, 2007), but viewed as particular knowledge positions (Goodley, 2001) from which to address and refute disablism (Thomas, 2007). Distinct responses have shot up in particular geographical locations. They have been viewed as oppositional (Barnes, 1999) and complementary (Linton, 1998b) though many have warned against exaggerating differences between them (L.J. Davis, 1997; Marks, 1999a; Barnes, 2004; Meekosha,

2004; Gabel, 2006; Thomas, 2007). As Marks (1999a: 9) suggests, concepts of dis/ability play a central, if latent, role in contemporary understandings of normality, the body and intelligence. It is therefore crucial to be respectful of the national contexts and historical times in which these new disability studies perspectives have emerged.

The social model: disability as a social barriers concern

A ***social barriers approach*** has led disability studies in Britain. Thomas (2007: 6) argues that the *social model*, as it is often referred to, remains *the* central theme around which disciplinary adherents coalesce. This is captured by Barnes and Mercer (1997a: 1–2) in the introduction to their text on disability studies research.

> The significance of disability theory and practice lies in its radical challenge to the medical or individual model of disability. The latter is based on the assumption that the individual is 'disabled' by their impairment, whereas the social model of disability reverses the causal chain to explore how socially constructed barriers have disabled people with a perceived impairment.

Up until the 1990s, disability was broadly conceived in terms of rehabilitation, medicine, psychology, special educational needs and social work. Sociologists tended to be medical sociologists (Barnes, 2004). From the 1990s, British disability studies grew and enjoyed disciplinary residencies in sociology, social policy and education. The social model was a 'paradigmatic leap' (Olkin, 2009: 12), offering a new vision of disability which, according to Barnes et al. (1999: 213), could not be dismissed as a 'minority concern' (see also Barnes et al., 2002; Barnes and Mercer, 2003). The social model followed the pioneering work of UPIAS (1976), adopted their distinction between impairment and disability and put forward an analysis of disabling barriers. The first major working up of the social model is to be found in Oliver's (1990) seminal text.[2] This built on Britain's Open University course (Brechin et al., 1981) Campling's (1981) influential collection by disabled women and the emergence of international journals such as *Disability & Society.* Social model scholars turned attention away from a preoccupation with people's impairments to a focus on the causes of exclusion through social, economic, political, cultural, relational and psychological barriers (see also Oliver and Zarb, 1989; Barton, 2001).

Thinking point: Vic Finkelstein (1981a) illustrated the disablement of modern culture by describing an imaginary community where wheelchair users were the majority and the environment was designed accordingly. In this 'disability culture' (as opposed to a 'disablist culture') able-bodied people were marked by bruises from banging their heads on lowered entrances (made for wheelchair users) and suffered backache from stooping down. They were helped by able-bodied equipment such as helmets, neck braces and, 'best of all', limb amputation, and money was collected for them in up-turned helmets with, 'Help the able-bodied', imprinted upon them.

To what extent does Finkelstein's imaginary community shed light on the cultural construction of 'disability' and the 'able-bodied'?

The social model has been debated as much by activists as academics. To observers outside Britain, these debates are seen as overly aggressive, exclusionary and in some cases anti-intellectual (e.g. Traustadóttir, 2006a; Vehmas, 2008), but might be better seen as testimony to the political roots of the social model. This model was, and remains, the British disabled people's movement's 'big idea' (Hasler, 1993). As Abberley (1987) argued, the social model originated in analyses of the political economy of disablement by disabled people's organisations.

One development of the social model has been the *affirmation model* (Swain and French, 2000). This approach, well summarised by Brandon (2008), celebrates the positive impacts of the disability community. Affirmation is most readily found in the Disabled People's Movement, disability arts and in Deaf culture (Corker, 1998). Social and affirmation models are best understood as platforms on which to develop theories (Thomas, 2008). To further complicate matters, a social model perspective has been developed by a group of psychologists in the USA (Nagi, 1976; Olkin, 2001, 2002, 2003, 2008; Olkin and Pledger, 2003; Pledger, 2003, 2004), who have worked within and against rehabilitative psychology. Nagi (1976), for example, pioneered a view of disability in which functional limitation was viewed as an expression of failure of environments to accommodate disability characteristics (Pledger, 2003: 282). What is apparent, according to Barnes (1998) and Davis (2006b), is that there is now a generation of second-wave social model theorists. For some, this has meant looking elsewhere for theoretical and political inspiration.

The minority model

While the social model was gathering momentum in Britain, North American activists and scholars were developing their own culturally applicable analyses. According to Gabel (2006), this work revolved around a social interpretation approach that coined the ***minority group model***.

Thinking point: Why might the notion of a minority approach to the framing of disability be in keeping with a North American perspective?

Clearly influenced by American Black civil rights and queer politics demands for raised social status, alongside thousands of returning Vietnam veterans (Meekosha and Jakubowicz, 1996), a number of key writers (Zola, 1982; Hahn, 1988a, 1998b; Rioux and Bach, 1994; Longman and Umansky, 2001) and disabled people's organisations in the USA (including American Coalition of Citizens with Disabilities, Not Dead Yet), asserted a positive minority identity (McRuer, 2002: 223–224). This was an identity forged under an American 'ethic of individuality and achievement' (Davis, 2002: 11). Underpinning this model, for Davis (2002) and Gabel (2006), was a clear challenge to *ableism*: social biases against people whose bodies function differently from those bodies considered to be 'normal' and beliefs and practices resulting from and interacting with these biases to serve discrimination (Wendell, 1996). The minority model demanded cultural redefinition in opposition to 'the cutthroat individualism' of the dominant North American and Canadian societies (McRuer and Wilkerson, 2003: 4). The People First language of 'people with disabilities' was coined to recognise humanity before the label (Linton, 1998b; Gabel and Peters, 2004).[3] For Gabel (2006), while the social model boasted neo-Marxist leanings, which addressed socio-structural barriers, the minority model took a more eclectic approach to the socio-cultural formations of disability (see also; Albrecht et al., 2001; Shakespeare and Watson, 2001a). By illuminating the common marginalised experiences of disabled people, African, Native and Hispanic American groups, the minority model addresses the importance of race and ethnicity in North American politics and the emergence of new activism from minority bodies, behaviours and abilities (McRuer and Wilkerson, 2003: 6).

Table 1.2. summarises the social and minority model approaches to disability studies described above and captured by writers such as Olkin and others.

Table 1.2 The minority and social barrier approach (incorporating the affirmation model) to disability studies (adapted from Oliver, 1996; Olkin, 2001, 2002, 2009; Gabel, 2006; Brandon, 2008)

	Disability as minority politics (USA and Canada)	Disability as social barriers (UK)
Meaning	*People with disabilities (PWD) constitute a minority position in society*, like people of colour, who are devalued, stigmatised, discredited and discounted. PWD comprise a minority group that has been denied its civil rights, equal access and protection.	*Disability is a social construct.* People with impairments are oppressed/ disabled by society: they are disabled people (DP). Primary impediments are discrimination, social isolation, economic dependence, high unemployment, inaccessible housing and institutionalisation.
Moral Implications	Society has devalued and marginalised disabled people to confer minority status. PWD are only offered peripheral membership of society.	Society has failed DP and oppressed them through barriers that prevent access, integration and inclusion to all walks of life, including work, education and leisure.
Sample Idea	The politics of PWD. 'Nothing about us without us', 'Not Dead Yet', 'Access Now', 'You gave us your dimes, now give us our rights', campaigning for anti-discriminatory legislation. 'PWD and proud'.	The politics of DP. 'Nothing about us without us', 'Piss on Pity', 'Civil rights, not charity', campaigning for anti-discriminatory legislation. 'DP and proud'.
Origins	Early 1900s, disappeared until 1975 protests in Washington DC and San Francisco, demanding that the 1973 Rehabilitation Act was signed. Intellectuals with disabilities (e.g. Charlton, 1998; Hahn, 1988a) followed impact of Goffman (1963) and Black civil rights movement.	Post-Second World War, DP's organisations. Disabled intellectuals (e.g. Hunt, 1966; UPIAS, 1976; DPI, 1982; Oliver, 1990; Barnes, 1991; Morris, 1993a) with strong adherence to (Neo-Marxist) materialist accounts of disability.
Goals of Intervention	Political, policy, economic, educational and social systems; increased accessibility of places and services; broad systemic change; development of Centres for Independent Living; disability arts. Promote positive sense of disabled self.	Political, policy, economic, educational and social systems; increased accessibility of places and services; broad systemic change; development of Centres for Independent Living; disability arts. Promote positive sense of disabled self.

Table 1.2 *(Continued)*

	Disability as minority politics (USA and Canada)	Disability as social barriers (UK)
Benefits of Model	Promotes integration of disability into self. Focus on how world disadvantages PWD. Sense of belonging and involvement in a disability community. Disability pride.	Promotes integration of disability into self. Focus on how world disadvantages DP. Sense of belonging and involvement in a disability community; disability pride. Clear distinction between social barriers (which can be changed) and impairment (which cannot).
Negative Effects	Feeling powerless in the face of political and economic odds. Need for strong self-advocacy skills. Blurring of impairment and disability.	Feeling powerless in the face of political and economic odds. Need for strong self-advocacy skills. Lack of acknowledgement of the effect of impairment on everyday life.

Sources: Adapted from Oliver, 1996; Olkin, 2001, 2008, 2009; Gabel, 2006; and Brandon, 2008

Unlike the two dominant individualising perspectives of 'disability as impairment' outlined in Table 1.1, social and minority models break the 'impairment → disability' causal link and, turn attention to the socio-political, structural and economic minoritisation and exclusion of people with impairments. Each developed in direct response to, and were developed by, the Disabled People's Movement. Through the rise of these perspectives, disability studies were born.

The cultural model

A distinguishing feature of North American – including Canadian – disability studies has been its interdisciplinary dispersion across the social sciences and humanities. Writers such as L.J. Davis (1995, 1997, 2002, 2006a); Garland-Thomson (1996, 1997, 2002, 2005); Wendell (1996); Mitchell and Snyder (1997, 2006); Linton (1998a, 1998b); Kittay (1999a, 1999b, 2001, 2006); Albrecht et al. (2001); Longman and Umansky (2001); Snyder and Mitchell (2001, 2006); Tremain (2001, 2002, 2005a); McRuer (2002, 2003, 2006); Michalko, (2002, 2008) and Titchkosky (2003, 2008), brought to bear cultural and literary analyses. Their work has been keen to connect analyses of disability studies with transformative ideas from feminism, queer and critical race studies (as we shall see in Chapter 3). Humanities scholars came to the study of disability with these critical lens already honed to put forward a ***cultural model of disability***. An overview is provided by Garland-Thomson (2002: 2), who posits that disability is a cultural trope and historical community that raises questions about the materiality of the body and the social formulations that are used to interpret bodily and cognitive differences. Affiliated scholars reject a firm distinction between impairment and disability because they view biology and culture as impinging upon one another. The cultural stance is read by Ware (2009) as a shift in thinking from 'viewing bodies as bad' (biological determinism and medicalisation) to 'thinking about bodies' (socio-cultural analyses). For Meekosha and Jakubowicz (1996), this allows us to attend to cultural empowerment and the saturation of bodies with cultural meaning. Disability pervades all aspects of culture. Burke (2009) and Bolt (2009) dismiss the (social scientific) view of cultural studies as 'decorative discipline', and point instead to a substantive corpus of literature around disability that deconstructs societal texts, critiques ideology and destabilises biological imperatives. Representations of disability and impairment are manufactured by charities, science and popular culture in ways that *dis*-locate disabled people (Snyder and Mitchell, 2006: 19). Key sites of analysis include novels, film, performance, art and drama. These cultural artefacts act as cultural vents. One strong analytical theme is disability as metaphor (Mitchell and Snyder, 1997; Snyder and Mitchell, 2001, 2006; Danforth, 2008). Far from being excluded by popular culture, the disabled person is ubiquitous, used as a metaphor for sinister, evil, ungodly, lacking, brave, fragmented and unviable. Disabled people have a perpetual place in cultural representations, reflecting deep-seated cultural conflicts (Snyder and Mitchell, 2001: 376–377). Mitchell and Snyder (2006) term this *narrative prosthesis*: disabled people are everywhere, functioning in literary (and other) discourses as a stock feature of characterisation or opportunistic device to signal social or individual collapse and disruption. Disability is used by popular culture to uphold dominant ideas as the crutch upon which narratives (and cultural practices) lean for representational power.

Thinking point: List five movies in which disability is portrayed. Now visit www.disabilityhistory.org/dwa/edge/curriculum/cult_contenta3.htm. Following Barnes (1993), to what extent do films portray disabled characters as 'to be pitied', 'tragic', 'sinister' or 'super-human'?

Cultural critique overturns disabling modes of cultural production (Barker, 2008). The work of Mitchell and Snyder, Davis and Garland-Thomson has been especially influential in exposing the myth of the 'disabled/abnormal body' – and its needed opposite 'the able/normal body'. The cultural analyst turns her gaze on to 'normal society' and considers how it promulgates its own precarious position through demonising dis/abled bodies. Cultural analysts explore how today's treatment of disabled people reflect the phantoms of the past, including eugenics, institutionalisation and science. For Mallett (2007), such theorists add a necessary cultural mix to the barriers and minority politics analyses of other disability studies thinkers. The maintenance of 'normate culture' relies heavily on its relationship with disabled people, a cultural reality defined as *dis*modernism by Davis (2002) and cultural *dis*location by Snyder and Mitchell (2006), ideas we will revisit in this text.

The relational model

While Anglo-American disability studies have developed in the social sciences and humanities, Thomas (2007: 7) observes that interdisciplinarity is more overtly felt in the Nordic countries. Disability researchers such as Bjarnason (2002, 2004), Tøssebro (2002, 2004), Gustavsson (2004), Kristiansen and Traustadóttir (2004), Traustadóttir (2004a, 2006a), Kristiansen et al. (2008), and Björnsdóttir (2009) (see also *Scandinavian Journal of Disability Research*, 6 (1), 2004) from Denmark, Finland, Iceland, Norway and Sweden counter the dominance of Anglo-North-American theories through the development of the ***Nordic relational model of disability***. Through 'writing back' from their own contexts, they have highlighted the positive influence of services and professionals on the lives of disabled people. Traustadóttir (2004a, 2006a) draws on the work of writers such as Gustavsson (2004) and Tøssebro (2002, 2004) to map out the theoretical terrain in relation to Nordic disability studies. Since the 1950s, Nordic countries have expanded disability services in ways that have been championed as some of the world's best. A strong welfare state functions in the same way as a good home (Nes, 2004). Unlike social and minority perspectives, Nordic disability studies are less connected to the Disabled People's Movement, with leadership often being found in the academy (Vehmas, 2008). Instead, disability studies developed in the context of welfare and, specifically, were influenced by the principles of normalisation (Stromstad, 2004). This philosophy originated in Denmark (with the work of Bank-Mikkelsen), Sweden (with Nirje), Britain (with O'Brien) and the USA (following Wolfensberger), and aimed to promote the community participation of disabled people. Early normalisation principles informed the beginnings of self-advocacy, and this movement remains a strong component of Nordic disability activism to this day. Being more of a guiding philosophy than a service technique, normalisation (later renamed social role valorisation) marked a radical departure in terms of professional and policy values with respect to disabled people, particularly people with intellectual disabilities (Brown and Smith, 1992). Wolfensberger (1972a, 1972b, 1987) and O'Brien (1987) set out to make ordinary available patterns of everyday living that were as close as possible to the regular circumstances of life in society.

Thinking point: Visit www.socialrolevalorization.com and outline five key components of social role valorisation. What positive effects could this approach have on the ways in which communities and professionals respond to disabled people? With reference to Table 1.2 above, how does normalisation fit with minority and social perspectives?

Normalisation was adopted as a method for assessing services, the practice of professionals and the impact of social policy.[4] For example, in the Icelandic context, Björnsdóttir (2009) argues that the 1979 Act on Support to Individuals with Intellectual Disabilities, which enforced the rights of individuals with intellectual disabilities to lead normal lives, created an 'integrated generation' of disabled people. The focus on community has led Nordic scholars to embrace feminism (see, for example, Bjarnason, 2002, 2004, 2008; Kristiansen and Traustadóttir, 2004; Traustadóttir, 1991, 1995, 1999, 2004b, 2006b) and this work has been highly influential in other countries (e.g. Read, 2000; McLaughlin et al., 2008). Traustadóttir (2004a, 2006a) informs us that the lack of unity within the Nordic languages means that the distinction between 'disability' and 'impairment' does not translate. A relational understanding of disability/impairment had to be devised through empirically-driven work and multiple approaches in order to speak across the Nordic countries. The Nordic relational model approaches the study of disability with three main assumptions: (1) disability is a person–environment mis/match; (2) disability is situational or contextual; and (3) disability is relative (Tøssebro, 2002, 2004). For Campbell (2009: 95), a relational model understands disability as a phenomenon emerging out of interactivity between impairment and disabling modes of socio-economic organisation.

Table 1.3 captures some of the nuances of the cultural and relational approaches. The former has the deconstruction of normalcy and ableism in its line of fire and celebrates the emergence of counter-cultures, including disability arts. The latter excavates the interactions of bodies, minds and environments with particular focus on the dis/empowering contributions of services and their practitioners.

Table 1.3 The cultural and relational models of disability (adapted from Davis, 1995, 1997, 2002, 2006a; Garland-Thomson, 1997; Mitchell and Snyder, 1997; Tøssebro, 2002, 2004; Traustadóttir, 2004a, 2006a; Snyder and Mitchell, 2006)

	Disability as cultural construction (USA and Canada)	Disability as relational (Nordic)
Meaning	*Disability is a construction of culture and modes of production, in ways that provide a metaphorical crutch for the constitution of 'abled'.* Disability can only be understood in relation to 'the normate', normalcy and ableism.	*People with disabilities are disabled through dynamic relationships of body/mind and the environment.* Disability is created through three relational processes: (i) the person-environment mis/match (relationship/relational); (ii) disability is a situational or contextual phenomenon; and (iii) Disability is a relative construct.
Moral Implications	Cultural re/production constitutes disabled people as mere carriers of information and passive recipients of hegemony that is founded on the ambitions of 'able' people.	Disabled people are excluded from communities, services and professional practices because of a mismatch of expectations, biological needs and environmental opportunities.
Sample Idea	Deconstruction and ideology critique of film, novel and media. Reconstructing disability histories, identifying disability fantasies and offering 'crip' alternatives.	Slogans, services and practices associated with 'Empowerment now', 'Label Jars not People', 'Community-based workplaces not segregated employment'.
Origins	1960s onwards, emerging out of minority group and social models through dialogue with cultural and literary critiques and the areas of feminism, queer and postcolonial critique. Key writers include Davis (1995), Garland-Thomson (1997), Mitchell and Snyder (1995).	1960s roots in normalisation principles – the community resettlement of disabled people outside institutions and the development of expansive, responsive forms of welfare. Open minded to pan-national models of disability studies. (e.g. *Scandinavian Journal of Disability Research*, 6(1), 2004).
Goals of Intervention	Destabilise cultural performances of dis/ability and ab/normality; promotion of disability arts and subculture; subvert liberal arts agenda which often excludes disabled people. Disability is renamed as a site of resistance that critiques 'the normate' and 'the abled'.	Political, policy, economic and social systems; increased accessibility of places and services; broad systemic change; development of Centres for Independent Living; normalisation and inclusive community living; an ordinary life.
Benefits of Model	Sense of belonging and involvement in a disability community; disability pride; promotion of critical faculties in relation to the normate culture. Disability is a site of phenomenological value not purely synonymous with the process of social disablement.	Sense of belonging and involvement in a disability community; disability pride. Promotion of empowering professionals and self-advocacy informed services.

(Continued)

Table 1.3 *(Continued)*

	Disability as cultural construction (USA and Canada)	Disability as relational (Nordic)
Negative Effects	Feeling powerless in the face of cultural hegemony. Lack of explicit engagement with disability activism, professional practice and service delivery. Over-emphasis on cultural construction rather than political marginalisation.	Lack of distinction between impairment and disability might re-insert a medicalised view of the disabled body and mind. Over-emphasis on professional practice and service delivery and lack of engagement with disabled people's organisations.

Sources: Adapted from Davis, 1995, 1997, 2002, 2006a; Garland–Thomson, 1997; Mitchell and Snyder, 1997; Olkin, 2001, 2002, 2009; Tøssebro, 2002, 2004; Traustadóttir, 2004a, 2006a; and Snyder and Mitchell, 2006

In and Outside Anglo-Nordic-North-American orthodoxies

As disability studies mature the ensuing analyses become increasingly eclectic. Herndon (2002) characterises the work of American scholars Linton (1998a, 1998b) and Wendell (1996) in terms of the former being more in keeping with the British social model and the latter more in tune with the Nordic relational approach. Linton's early work has also been aligned with a minority perspective (see Barnes, 2004; Roach, 2004), though later on, her writing can be viewed as more in keeping with a cultural stance (e.g. Linton, 2006a, 2006b). The boundary busting continues. The North American scholar Charlton (1998, 2006), whose work is often assigned a minority model position, draws heavily on Marxism and ideological critique, sharing much with social modellists. While Mallett (2007) draws attention to the definition offered by Pfeiffer and Yoshida (1995: 480) of (US) Disability Studies as a discipline that 'reframes the study of disability by focusing on it as a social phenomenon, social construct, metaphor and culture utilising a minority group model'; clearly blurring minority and cultural perspectives. Recently, cultural theorists Mitchell and Snyder (2006: x) have proposed an analysis of the cultural locations of disability 'to evoke sites of violence, restriction, confinement and absence of liberty for disabled people', harking back to the early priorities of the minority model. More and more collections of disability studies transcend perspectives and transnational contexts (e.g. Albrecht et al., 2001; Barnes et al., 2002). Increasingly, researchers work across disciplines, such as the social sciences and humanities (e.g. Barnes, 1993; Watson et al., 2003), as evidenced in initiatives such as the British Cultural Disability Studies Research Network (www.cdsrn.org.uk), the International Network of Literary Disability Scholars (www.journalofliterarydisability.com/index.htm) and the *Journal of Literary & Cultural Disability Studies* (www.jlcds.lupjournals.org).[5] Right across the globe disability studies have developed in 'glocal' ways, reflecting distinct regional contexts such as, to name but a few, Australia (Gleeson, 1999a; Meekosha, 2004; Campbell, 2009), Malaysia (Yeo, 2006; Kuno et al., 2008), France (Armstrong et al., 2002), India (Mohit, 2000; Ghai, 2006; Gabel and Chander, 2008), Greece (Vlachou, 1997; Vlachou-Balafoutis and Zoniou-Sideris, 2002), New Zealand (O'Brien and Sullivan, 1997, 2005), Zimbabwe (Chataika, 2007; Badza et al., 2008; Chimedza et al., 2008), Malta (Azzopardi, 2000, 2003, 2007, 2008),

Belgium (Devlieger et al., 2003, 2006a, 2006b; Roets et al., 2004, 2007, 2008; Van Hove et al., 2005), Japan (*Disability Studies Quarterly, Special Issue*, 28 (3), 2008), Israel/Palestine (*Disability Studies Quarterly, Special Issue*, 27 (3), 2007; *Women's Asia*, 21; *Voices from Japan*, 22, April 2009), Germany (*Disability Studies Quarterly, Special Issue*, 26 (2), 2006), Russia (Phillips, 2009). Meekosha's (2004) work in Australia combines Anglocentric social model analyses of class with North American cultural studies of colonial settler communities but finds neither suitable for explaining disability in indigenous Australian Aboriginal people and Torres Strait Islanders communities. Countries at the periphery of the English-speaking world, such as Australia, India, South Africa and Asia-Pacific rim nations, require analyses of disability that reflect their own specific colonial-settler histories (Meekosha, 2004: 725). This raises questions about how the cultural specificity and local relevance of disability studies can develop in light of attempts to cultivate a supranational universal model of disability: the *International Classification of Functioning, Disability and Health (ICFDH-2)* or the *ICF model*. As Grech (2009a: 38) argues:

> with the ambitious aim of becoming a unified universal framework for defining and quantifying disability in a culturally neutral way, the ICF attempts to bridge the medical and social models by providing a biopsychosocial model, motivated by the effort 'to achieve a synthesis' and 'provide a coherent view of different perspectives of health from a biological, individual and social perspective'. (World Health Organization, 2001: 20)

In this case, disability is an umbrella term for considering the interaction of impairment, body functions and structure, activity, participation against the wider context of personal and environmental factors (see Figure 1.1).

The ICF is upheld as a universal model that captures the complexity of disability. Barnes (2006), Pledger (2004) and Snyder and Mitchell (2006) have criticised the

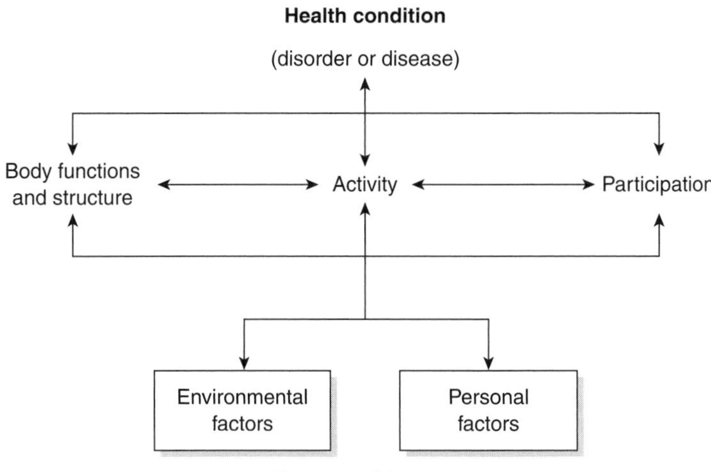

Figure 1.1 The ICF model (Word Health Organization, 2001; adapted from Grech, 2009a)

ICF for being a vague catch-all model that fails to capture the complex meanings of 'impairment',[6] simplistically placing it alongside social and relational factors like participation and ignoring definitions developed by disabled people's organisations. Wendell (1996: 14) is sceptical about universal definitions:

> Failure to recognise that standards of structure, function, ability and participation are socially relative could be dangerous to disabled people. If the standards employed are generated by people in highly industrialised societies, many people in less industrialised societies and rural areas where there are fewer technological resources will be considered non-disabled when they are in fact in need of special assistance to survive and participate where they are.

In searching for universalism, definitions such as the ICF are in danger of ignoring the culturally-specific foundations on which impairment, disability and disablism are created. Similarly, disability studies devised in Anglo-Nordic-North-American contexts may have limited value in the rest of the world.

Conclusion

This book poses a challenge: How can disability provide *the* focus for a consideration of citizenship, rights, personhood, difference and diversity at the start of the twenty-first century? This book will demonstrate that disability provides a central core around which to organise considerations of theory, methodology, politics and practice.

Further reading

Campbell and Oliver (1996). Draws on interviews with some of the key founding figures in the British Disabled People's Movement.

Gabel (2006). An accessible introduction to the development of disability studies in America.

Longman and Umansky (2001). A renowned historical text in disability studies.

Meekosha (2004). An Australian perspective on minority, cultural and social models of disability.

Mitchell and Snyder (2006). A brief though informative introduction to a key area of analysis in cultural approaches to disability: the metaphor.

Olkin (2002). An accessible introduction into social, minority and medical approaches to disability.

Tøssebro (2004). Introduces Nordic responses to disability and models of disability.

Notes

1 A recent example of the waning trust in medicine (and the values we attached to impairment foetuses) is proffered by the front-page headline '146 healthy babies lost every year due to poor Down's syndrome test' (The *Guardian*, 15 May 2009: 1), due to a test giving a 'false positive' result: assessing women as 'at risk' of having a Down syndrome when they were, in fact, carrying children without this label.

2 Though, as we shall see later in Chapter 6, it is also possible to see early ideas around the social model in Oliver et al. (1988) and early thoughts on models in Oliver (1983).

3 Such definitions paralleled the affirmative identities of Black civil rights groups as well as Gay and Lesbian groups, of which the latter offered more productive identities to the pathological labels of the medicalisation of homosexuality (Richardson, 2005).

4 For a reflection of the debates for and against normalisation, see Meekosha and Jakubowicz (1996: 81), who consider it 'paternalistic reform clothed in the language of liberation', and Race et al. (2005), who offer a more sympathetic reading.

5 An excellent overview of the emergence of cultural and literary disability studies analyses is offered by Bolt (2009).

6 Indeed, as McKenzie (2009) shows, the World Health Organisation's ICD-10 *International Classification of Diseases*, which is used by health professionals as a complementary guide to the ICF, provides a definition of intellectual disabilities which is unambiguously individualistic by definition: 'a condition of arrested or incomplete development of the mind, which is especially characterised by impairment of skills manifested during the developmental period, skills which contribute to the overall level of intelligence, i.e. cognitive, language, motor and social abilities. Retardation can occur with or without any other mental or physical condition'.

TWO

Debates: *Political Disability Studies*

****

Introduction

This chapter introduces some key debates that we will revisit in subsequent chapters. First, we will explore models of research in disability studies. Second, we will consider the place of impairment. Third, we will ask questions about the potential for disability studies to include and represent all disabled people. Fourth, we will conclude by thinking about disability studies as a transdisciplinary arena.

Researching disability

Individualising moral and medical models of disability have historically dominated the lives of disabled people (Table 1.1). These ideas have also influenced research *on* disabled people, often carried out *by* non-disabled people, which have contributed to deficient understandings. Linton (1998a: 531) has argued that:

> The overwhelming majority of scholarship on disability either utilises or implies the third person plural: 'they' do this, 'they' are like that, 'they' need such and such. This contributes to the objectification of disabled people and contributes to their experience of alienation.

Alternative models of disability, posed by disability studies, have brought with them contrasting approaches to research (Tables 1.2 and 1.3). Theorists from a relational model, for example, study the complex fit between impairment and environment. Cultural theorists ask questions about ideology in the constitution of dis/ablist culture. Social model thinkers demand changes to the structural exclusion of disabled people. Following a close reading of the literature, Goodley and Lawthom (2005b) teased out a number of common questions asked by disability studies researchers:

- *Inclusion* – to what extent does research include disabled people?
- *Accountability* – who are disability studies researchers accountable to?
- *Praxis* – does disability research make a positive difference in the lives of disabled people?
- *Dialectics* – how is disability research impacting upon, and is influenced by, the social conditions in which it is carried out?
- *Ontology* – whose knowledge and experiences count?
- *Disablism/impairment* – does disability studies research focus on understanding disabling society or the meaning of impairment?
- *Partisanship* – whose side is the disability researcher on?
- *Analytical levels* – does research investigate politics, culture, society, relationships or the individual?

Clearly, there is not enough space here to visit all of these debates (see instead Taylor and Bogdan, 1984; Atkinson and Williams, 1990; Morris, 1992; Zarb, 1992; Skrtic, 1995; Stone and Priestley, 1996; Barnes and Mercer, 1997a; Oliver and Barnes, 1997; Barton and Clough, 1998; Moore et al., 1998; Priestley, 1998; Goodley et al., 2004; Kristiansen and Traustadóttir, 2004; Van Hove et al., 2008). We will, though, consider three areas of contention.

Research by whom, with whom and for whom?

As disability studies developed alongside the growing politicisation of disabled people then, this raised questions about ownership, involvement and applications of research, depicted by Figure 2.1. Each of these three positions is captured well in the exchanges of Barnes (1996), Shakespeare (1997b) and Oliver (1998). Barnes's position is one aligned to the right of the continuum. He argues that researchers must work with disability organisations to develop user-led research with and for disabled people. Social model research aims to contribute to the politics of disability: by unearthing and challenging the structural exclusion of disabled people, thus enhancing the 'catalytic validity' of research (Law, 2007). Shakespeare (1997b) provides an alternative account. He argues that while he remains personally accountable to many of the aims of disabled people (and their organisations), research can be academic, developing theory that can be used for those with emancipatory visions. He argues that researchers should, of course, be mindful of the application of their ideas, but should not be apologetic about developing new theories. For Shakespeare, the researcher can lead research as long as s/he keeps in mind that the aim of disability studies is theorising and tackling disabling society. Shakespeare is open to any theory that has utility. Oliver (1998) intervenes in an interesting way. While aligned with the position of Barnes, he worries about the exploitative tendencies of researchers who, led by an interest in capturing the experiences of disabled people, develop their own academic careers rather than the ambitions of disabled people. He argues, 'this raises the uncomfortable question of whether disability researchers are "shitting" disabled people when they write about experiences

Disability studies research can be conceived as a continuum:

Knowledge	Shared knowledge	Action research
e.g. An academic analyses the constitution of normalcy (Davis, 1995)	e.g. Researchers work with a self-advocacy group to develop inclusive research practices (Doherty et al., 2005)	e.g. Disabled people's organisations work with researchers to measure and eradicate disablism (Arthur and Zarb, 1995a)
Non-participatory	**Participatory**	**Emancipatory**
Researcher-led	Researcher invites participants into research	Co-researchers

For overview, see Special issue of *Disability, Handicap and Society*, 7 (2), 1992

Figure 2.1 Research as participatory and emancipatory

that they have no access to, save through their own research techniques' (Oliver 1998: 187). Instead, Oliver proposes, disability researchers need to change the social and material relations of research production in order to make research worthwhile. Yet, perhaps akin to the position of Shakespeare, Oliver himself concludes that his own attempts to promote emancipation in research have failed (while his own career has blossomed). While it has been argued that many disabled people are unwilling to actually contribute to emancipatory projects (Kitchin, 2001: 67), Oliver asserts that unless research works with disabled people towards their goals and ambitions then it will fail to be anything more than an academic endeavour – a time of waste and a waste of time (Oliver, 1992). Oliver (1998: 188) argues that a new epistemology for research practice must reject the discourse that sustains investigatory research and replace it with a discourse of emancipation. The debate between Barnes, Shakespeare and Oliver capture different perspectives on theory and activism.

Paradigms, priorities and methodologies

How you study disability will depend on how you define good research, the kinds of questions you ask and the methods you use. *Measuring Disablement* was a study carried out by Zarb and colleagues in Britain in the mid-1990s (Arthur and Zarb, 1995a, 1995b; Begum and Zarb, 1996; Salvage and Zarb, 1995b), which gathered statistical measurements on key indicators (such as regional employment, independent living, use of transport) to assess the extent to which disabled people were (not) marginalised. The researchers designed and implemented national and local questionnaires with the hope of assessing disabled people's ratings of their experiences of these key indicators. In a reflective piece on the project, Barnes (1995: 8) noted that while 'certain aspects of the obstacles to disabled people's participation may be amenable to measurement, physical access, for example, there are other issues which are not; namely, prejudice'. The latter is a more elusive element of disablism and calls for methodologies in tune with the meaning-making processes of everyday life. In addition, behind any question of method is the question of priority: either to assess the social conditions of disablism or measure the impacts of impairment. For example, the British government commissioned the 1984 Office of Population, Censuses and Surveys (OPCS) surveys of disability and four separate surveys of disabled adults and children in private households and communal establishments were carried out (Martin et al., 1988; Martin and White, 1988). These surveys had the potential to give a major overview of the contemporary position of disabled people. However, as Oliver (1990) and Abberley (1987) point out, the phrasing of the questions of the surveys were based upon individualistic conceptions of disability. They pull out a number of examples (from the OPCS surveys) and offer alternative questions (based upon a social model of disablism):

> OPCS: 'Can you tell me what is wrong with you?'
> Alternative: 'Can you tell me what is wrong with society?'
>
> OPCS: 'Does your health problem/disability prevent you from going out as often or as far as you would like?'
> Alternative: 'What is it about the local environment that makes it difficult for you to get about in your neighborhood?'
>
> OPCS: 'Have you attended a special school because of a long-term health problem or disability?'
> Alternative: 'Have you attended a special school because of your educational authority's policy of sending people with your health problem/disability to such places?'

Disability studies do not conflate impairment and disability (as we saw in the last chapter with the moral and medical models) but instead seek more detailed understandings of the relationship between people with impairments and contemporary social arrangements (Moore et al., 1998). With these priorities in mind, it is possible to distinguish two distinct (though complementary) paradigms. Research can adopt either of these paradigmatic stances, summarised in Table 2.1, to measure or access the meaning of disablism.

You don't have to be disabled to work here (but it helps)

Can you carry out disability research if you are not disabled? This question recalls second-wave feminism (e.g. Oakley, 1981; Stanley and Wise, 1993) when, in contrast to 'malestream' notions of objectivity (which distanced the researcher from the research), feminist standpoint theory celebrated the rich experiences that women brought to research. Disability studies similarly engage with positionality. Oliver (1990) understands the early work of disability studies writers such as Hunt (1966) and Finkelstein (1981a, 1981b) as examples of 'organic intellectualism' (a phrase borrowed from the disabled Marxist Antonio Gramsci), where disabled activists develop theory. While questions remain about the role of the 'bearded feminist' in feminist theory, by contrast, disability studies have embraced the contribution of non-disabled researchers. Nordic relational models, for example, were heavily influenced by (non-disabled) academics rather than disabled activists (Vehmas, 2008). In Britain, non-disabled people have been conditionally welcomed into the fold (Duckett, 1998). Those from a cultural

Table 2.1 Researching disablism

Research and science	Research and meaning
Positivism – an objective deductive engagement with observable real things.	Hermeneutics – a subjective inductive engagement with the processes of meaning making.
How are people with impairments included or excluded by society?	*How do disabled people experience contemporary society?*
Operational definitions – a specific definition of the real thing we observe.	Emergent understandings – we come to understand disablism through the meanings at play in the social world.
A high rate of unemployment is indicative of the economic exclusion of disabled people.	*Unemployment reflects society's views around the validity of disabled people's lives.*
Validity – are we measuring what we set out to measure?	Authenticity – are we capturing our research participants' meaning making?
Do the OPCS surveys measure socio-economic exclusion or personal incapacity?	*Do our methodologies give voice to disabled people's view of their socio-economic life chances?*
Reliability and generalisation – the extent to which our measures are consistent in terms of their findings, which can then be extrapolated to the wider population.	Indexicality and specificity – the extent to which our findings capture the rich meanings of a particular time, place and context.
Our study gives rise to consistent findings which allow us to say some general things about wider disabling society.	*Our study is specific to one context, time and place which might resonate with other inter/national contexts.*
Quantitative – methodologies and analytic frameworks numerically measure our research findings.	Qualitative – methodologies and analytic frameworks engage with the meanings of our findings.
Questionnaires, observations, surveys and experimentation give rise to data that are analysed using descriptive and inferential statistics.	*Interviews, ethnography, narrative, discourse analysis give rise to data that are analysed using grounded theory, discourse, narrative and thematic analyses.*

model have often troubled the definite category of disability (Garland-Thomson, 2002). Davis (1995: xviii), for example, is particularly dismissive of the imperative of being disabled to be a disability studies researcher. Asking himself the question 'Are you disabled?', he retorts: 'my aim is to confound the question and by extension the category that the question begs'. Linton (1998a: 537) concedes that 'it is incumbent on non-disabled scholars to pay particular attention to issues of their own identity, their own privilege as non-disabled people, and the relationship of these factors to their scholarship'. Moreover, research with people with intellectual disabilities has a long history of collaboration between people so-labelled and non-disabled researchers (see for examples, Atkinson, 1989, 1993a, 1993b; Atkinson and Williams, 1990; Atkinson et al., 1997; Walmsley, 1997; see also *British Journal of Learning Disabilities*, Special Issue, 32 (2), 2004). These examples of participatory approaches to research synthesise distinct contributions:

> The expertise of the 'disabled participant' and the analytical and reportorial skills of the (non) disabled researcher are combined to draw out broader socio-structural, cultural, political and theoretical points. (Levine and Langness, 1986: 192–205)

Inevitably, such research has not been without its critics. In Britain, Aspis (1997, 1999) has been particularly outspoken about non-disabled people making careers on the back of 'disabled people with learning difficulties'. Instead, she argues for a more emancipatory approach to research led by people with intellectual disabilities.

In answer to the question 'Do you need to be disabled to carry out disability research?', we can identify a number of responses. First, *the John Lennon response*:[1] you have every right to speak about disability studies as any other member of the human race. Disablism should be a concern shared by all. Second, *the postmodern response*: you might choose not to self-disclose a disabled identity because (a) you're not disabled; (b) its not anyone else's business; (c) you don't accept the unitary, atomistic concept of 'dis/abled' (see Chapter 5); or (d) you don't think it's important to be disabled to speak of disability. Third, *the partisan response*: you think it is more important to articulate an alliance to the aims of the Disabled People's Movement than to self-identify as disabled. Intent might be more powerful than identity. As Goodley and Moore (2000) have argued, tensions are heightened around the divide between research driven by the ambitions of (non-disabled) academics (concerned with the development of theory and the writing of publications for assessment by government bodies such as the Research Assessment Exercise in Britain) and research driven by the aims of disabled people (focused on structural and attitudinal change rather than the development of theory and the academy). It could be argued that one should come to disability studies with a profound desire to understand and change the conditions of contemporary society (Stone and Priestley, 1996). If not, why bother?

Table 2.2 Questions for the book about disability research

- To what extent do disability studies engage with other transformative research agendas (Chapter 3)?
- How do different sociological theories understand disablism (Chapter 4)?
- How is the non/disabled individual understood by scientific approaches to research (Chapter 5), qualitative approaches (Chapter 6), discursive approaches (Chapter 7) and cultural studies (Chapter 8)?
- In what ways can emancipatory research approaches inform inclusive models of professional practice (Chapters 9 and 10)?

Impairment and diversity in disability studies

As we have seen, splitting impairment and disability allowed many scholars – especially those in the British social model camp – to turn their attentions away from the personal tragedy model of impairment to the public problems of disablism. The distinction severed the link between the body and disablism. However, for some, this has created a number of dilemmas in relation to impairment.

The 'reality' of impairment

Some disabled scholars responded to the severed link by publicly reflecting on personal experiences of impairment. Disabled feminists such as French (1993), Crow (1996) and Morris (1992) were heretical in their attempts to articulate their experiences of impairment. Of course society was disabling, they argued, but impairment effects such as pain, inability and tiredness were also disabling in their own right. These views sparked outrage:

> Writers like Jenny Morris have elevated the importance of personal psychological experience in understanding disability. Such work encouraged a shift away from thinking about the real world. Finding insight in the experiences of discrimination is just a return to the old case file approach to oppression, dressed up in social model jargon. (Finkelstein, 1996: 11)

Similarly, Barnes (1998) dismissed impairment talk as 'sentimental biography', which was preoccupied with the medical details of a particular condition. Impairment talk creates conflict. This word symbolises social death, inertia, lack, limitation, deficit and tragedy. It references an individualised phenomenon, the currency of medics and other rehabilitation-related practitioners, hardly the focus of critical researchers engaged with the socio-cultural conditions of disablism. The 'absent presence' of impairment in (British) disability studies has been a key focus for Shakespeare and Watson (e.g. Shakespeare and Watson, 1997, 2001a, 2001b; Shakespeare, 2000, 2006a; Watson, 2002). In one of these pieces, Shakespeare and Watson (2001a) argue against the policing of debates by some disability studies academics, such as Barnes, who now use the social model as a rigid shibboleth. This strong social model, they argue, has outlived its usefulness and therefore should be put to one side so disability studies can start again. The social model has bracketed impairment in similar ways to the denial of biological difference by feminists in the 1970s. They argue that impairments are important because some are static, others episodic, some degenerative and others terminal. Some impairments are painful, others create fatigue, others threaten lives. They conclude that a social model can only explain so much before we need to return to the experiential realities of 'impairment' as object(s) independent of knowledge (Shakespeare, 2006a: 54). Impairment *is* a predicament and *can* be tragic. Meanwhile, back in the rest of the (minority) world, impairment talk is less fraught. As we saw in Chapter 1, Nordic relational theorists share interactionist views of the impairment and disability dynamic. Yet, how impairment is conceptualised has huge implications for questions about quality of life, reproductive decisions and debates around the right to die (Chapter 7).

Impairment and culture

The severed link has also been criticised for casting a simplistic understanding of impairment as natural and biological. Critics suggest that impairment is far from being natural and more an embodied experience shaped by culture (Hughes and Paterson, 1997, 2000; Hughes, 1999, 2000, 2002a, 2002b, 2004; Paterson and Hughes, 1999; Jung, 2002). Abberley (1987), for example, was an early critical voice about the atheoretical impairment label that had been left by UPIAS (1976). His solution? To call for a sociology of impairment alongside a sociology of disability: 'a theory of disability as oppression [that] recognises and, *in the present context, emphasises the social origins of impairment*' (Abberley, 1987, in Barton and Oliver, 1997: 176, my italics). Donaldson (2002) and Thomas (2004) both challenge what Meekosha (1998: 175) describes as the dangerous problem of leaving the impaired body as untouched and unchallenged: a taken-for-granted fixed corporeality. Marks (1999b: 611) goes further to suggest that the British social model's marginalisation of the personal experiences of impairment actually contributes to the maintenance of the individual model of disability. By excluding a discussion of impairment from an analysis of disability, a theoretical vacuum is left, which is filled by those who adopt an individualistic and decontextualised perspective (such as medics):

> **IMPAIRMENT**: is the functional limitation within the individual caused by physical, mental or sensory impairment. (DPI, 1982)

There is something inherently medicalised and individualised about this definition. To counter this, Marks (1999a) (following Abberley, 1987) demands that we to consider impairment on a number of levels, including when and where an impairment was first discovered; perception of and the in/visibility of the impairment; the severity of the impairment and the standards against which that severity is judged; whether or not having an impairment provides a base for the development of positive identity formation and social group membership; the relative stability and fluidity of impairment. As soon as we start thinking through the meaning, experience, treatment and enactment of the impaired body or mind we begin peeling away the socio-cultural layers of these phenomena. Impairment is understood by the words we use to describe it. And words or discourses are socially mediated. It may be possible to say there is no body or mind outside discourse (Chapter 7). Moreover, the very 'fact' of impairment cuts to the flesh and bones of what it feels to be in our bodies and heads. As we consider in Chapter 6, our bodies are felt in relation to others: what Marks (1999a: 129) defines as the phenomenology of the body. Impairment evokes deep psychological feelings about minds and bodies. The psyche is made through the cultures in which we develop (Chapter 8). Impairment, we could argue, is made by institutions, such as schools, which define children through the use of a growing array of scholastic labels (Chapter 9). The concept of impairment is predicated on the notion that some bodies/minds are flawed and others are not. And those that are not are deemed to be autonomous, able and capable. We can only know impairment in relation to that which is upheld as its opposite (Chapter 5). The meaning of impairment is culturally constructed because bodies/minds have histories, are experienced, performed and institutionally located. Finally, minds/bodies can only be understood as raced, gendered and sexed, which intersect to further complicate the 'fact' of impairment (Chapter 3).

Impairment effects

Thomas's (1999) notion of 'impairment effects' has been highly influential in British disability studies. Thomas (2008: 16) argues that disability studies need to further develop social theories of disablism and impairment inspired by the social relational ideas of founding fathers such as Finkelstein (1981a) and Abberley (1987). In any real social setting, impairment and disablism are thoroughly intermeshed with the social conditions

Table 2.3 Questions for the book about impairment

- How do impairment, gender, class, race and sexuality interconnect (Chapter 4)?
- Why do some disabled people not see themselves as disabled? Could this be associated with their relations with others (see Chapter 5)?
- What kinds of reactions does impairment engender in others (Chapter 5, 6 and 8)?
- How is impairment spoken about in professional discourses (Chapter 7) and institutions like schools (Chapter 9)?
- To what extent can we argue that impairment is relationally experienced (Chapter 6), socially constructed (Chapter 7) and cultural mediated (Chapter 8)?
- How can communities embrace and empower people with impairments (Chapters 9 and 10)?

that bring them into being (Thomas, 2007). The ways we feel the 'realness' of our bodies – the materiality – are felt in the dynamic interplay of self and the social world. While Shakespeare and Watson (2001a) appeal to the biological realities of body, Thomas calls for a more dialectical analysis of impairment and disablism, well captured in Ghai's (2006: 129) definition that 'impairment, like disability, should be a signifier of not just society's response to impaired bodies but also to illustrate how these bodies are shaped materially and culturally'. Thomas (1999) suggests that the pain of impairment is often only felt during times when 'restrictions of activity' (UPIAS's definition of disability) are imposed on people with impairments. Hence impairment is felt at the same time as disablism. These impairment effects capture impairment as a 'socially embedded and embodied phenomenon' (Ghai, 2006: 149). A realisation of the embeddedness of disability in impairment adds to an understanding of the complexities of a disabled person's identity (Ghai, 2006: 52). For as Ghai asserts, 'to negate ontological reality would imply that every issue connected with disabled existence could be resolved with a change in social conditions' (Ghai, 2006: 53).

Divisions and differences

Watson (2002) asks an important question: If disabled people do not see themselves as disabled, then do disability studies have anything of relevance to say to them? For Finkelstein and Stuart (1996: 176) the vast majority of disabled people are 'non-politicised, marinated in a disabling culture and identify themselves with repressive individual models of disability'. Watson's question raises three related queries. First is the question of identification. Clearly, people will differ in the marks of identity that they prioritise. Gender, ethnicity, age, class and sexuality might be as important as, or more important than, disability, and we will address the issue of diversity in Chapter 3. Who is to say that disability is the 'master signifier' of one's identity (Shakespeare, 2006b)? Identity work is often more complex than the essential binary difference of disabled/non-disabled (Sherry, 2006). Second is the question of why people do/not identify as disabled? This requires us to interrogate culture, society and politics for possible answers. Throughout this book we will explore some of the reasons why people might resist (or adopt) a disabled identity. Third is the question of representation. Can disability studies address the ambitions of all disabled people? While disability can be a source of pride, it also recalls a history of shame. People with the label of intellectual disabilities, for example, set disability studies a number of challenges, including making research more inclusive, theoretical ideas more accessible and fully representing their activism as it is enacted in the international self-advocacy movement (e.g. Chappell, 1992, 1998; Chappell et al., 2000; Boxall, 2002a, 2002b; Boxall et al., 2004; Doherty et al., 2005). Questions remain about how scholars understand 'intellectual disabilities'. Goodley (2001) argues that, historically, British social model writing has risked viewing intellectual disabilities in terms of deficit – as an organic impairment of intellectual functioning, social incompetence and maladaptive functioning – because of the uncomplicated essentialist notion of impairment left by the original UPIAS (1976) distinction. This is acknowledged by Aspis:

> People with learning difficulties face discrimination in the disability movement. People without learning difficulties use the medical model when dealing with us. *We are always asked to talk about advocacy and our impairments as though our barriers aren't disabling in the same way as disabled people without learning difficulties.* We want concentration on our access needs in the mainstream disability movement. (Quoted in Campbell and Oliver 1996: 97, my italics)

Pat Worth, a Canadian self-advocate, expresses similar misgivings: 'People see our disability only, they don't see our ability. We may have a handicap but *we're* not the handicap' (quoted in Yarmol, 1987: 28, italics in original). This explains the self-advocacy movement's preference for People First language: emphasising their humanity over the pathological labels that they have acquired (Gillman et al., 1997). If, by contrast, their 'intrinsic handicaps' were tacitly assumed, then one would expect disability studies to remain unconnected to their lives. Similarly, as Beresford and colleagues have argued, disability studies (at least in Britain) have been largely unresponsive to the activism of survivors of mental health systems (Beresford et al., 2002; Beresford and Wilson, 2002a, 2002b). Survivors have been involved in different fights from those of other disabled comrades. Following Chamberlin (1990) and Sayce (2000), the survivors' movement can be characterised by three main historical projects. First, the rejection of dehumanising 'mental illness' labels assigned through arbitrary, unsystematic and oppressive forms of 'scientific diagnosis'. Their fight for humanity shares similarities with comrades from the self-advocacy movement. Second, survivors have challenged the practice of, what Rose (1979, 1985) calls, the *psy-complex*: those human service and welfare institutions and assemblages of knowledge that have contributed to practices and treatments associated with 'the abnormal' (see Chapter 5 and Parker et al., 1995). Third, the multiple positions of 'madness' suggest an ever more complicated relationship with impairment than that nominally described in some of the disability studies literature. Madness can be a positive identity, a state of rebellion, a call for help and/or a manifestation of cultural impotence and political constraint (Donaldson, 2002). The extent to which disability studies respond to diverse requests and ambitions remains an ongoing debate.

Table 2.4 Questions for the book about the scope of disability studies

- To what extent do particular groups of disabled people become excluded as a consequence of their impairment label (Chapter 9)?
- Which theoretical approaches have been responsive to the needs of people with intellectual disabilities (Chapter 4)?
- In what ways do the activism of survivors of mental health systems feed into wider forms of deconstruction (Chapter 7)?
- In what ways do psychological theories aid our understandings of the day-to-day experiences of disablism (Chapter 6)?

Conclusions: disability studies as a transdisciplinary space

Tackling the debates raised above requires us to think across disciplines. It is possible to view disability studies as a *trans*disciplinary space which breaks boundaries between disciplines (Thomas, 2007) and creates in-roads into disciplines that have historically marginalised disabled people, such as medical sociology (Thomas, 2007), philosophy (Kristiansen et al., 2008) and psychology (Nagi, 1976; Olkin and Pledger, 2003). Disability studies might be seen as *paradigm busting*: subverting the normative tendencies of academic disciplines, testing respected research encounters and challenging theoretical formations. Disability studies continue to develop theoretically in ways that can and should encompass the ambitions of all disabled people. The social, cultural, minority and relational models provide philosophical and political resources from which a whole host of social theories and forms of activism can be developed. Disability studies populate an arena in which social theories of disability and impairment can be developed to promote the inclusion of all disabled people in mainstream life.

Table 2.5 Questions for the book about transdisciplinarity

- How can we connect diverse identities of gender, sexuality, race and disability (Chapter 3)?
- In what ways do academic disciplines promote or hinder critical theories of disability (Chapters 4 and 5)?
- How can we make sense of cultural conditions of disablism (Chapter 8)?
- In what ways can disability studies inform the development of more enabling approaches to education (Chapter 9) and community-based professionals (Chapter 10)?

Further reading

Barton and Oliver (1997). Includes debates about non/participatory approaches to research.

Beresford and Wilson (2002b). A critical mental health perspective on disability theory.

Goodley (2001). Explores the problematic position of intellectual disabilities in British social model thinking.

Shakespeare and Watson (2001a). A rejection of the strong social model.

Thomas (2001a). A brief exploration of impairment and disability debates.

Note

1 I have used this in honour of the great man's response to a journalist's question during the 'Bed-in protest' in Amsterdam, March 1969, when asked what 'right he had' to make such a demonstration.

THREE

Intersections: *Diverse Disability Studies*

****

Introduction

A body or mind that is disabled is also one that is raced, gendered, trans/nationally sited, aged, sexualised and classed. Disability is imbricated with other categories of difference, experiences of marginality and forms of political activism (Goggin, 2008: 1). Disability studies contribute to a growing pluralism in social theory that attends to this human diversity (Marks, 1999a: 187). Adopting the view from Marks (1999a), Thomas (2007) and Price (2007) that disability studies constitute a transdisciplinary space, we will consider the relationship of disability to other markers of gender, sexuality, race/ethnicity and social class.[1] Intersectionality is not simply about bringing together these markers and their theoretical responses, but to consider how each supports the constitution of the others. This chapter is a plea to remain mindful of the complexity of disability, particularly when it intersects with other markers of identity and oppression.

Diversely disabled

Thinking point: 'What I am rejecting is society's tendency to set up rigid standards of what is right and proper, to force the individual into a mould. Our constant experience of this pressure towards unthinking conformity in some way relates us to other obvious deviants [sic] and outcasts like the Jew in a gentile world, a negro [sic] in a white world, homosexuals, the mentally handicapped [sic]; and also to more voluntary rebels in every sphere – artists, philosophers, prophets, who are essentially subversive elements in our society' (Hunt, 1966: 151). The Disabled People's Movement has a long history of association with the women's movement, working-class trade unions and Black civil rights. But what are the similarities and differences between these social movements?

Disability studies have connected with other forms of oppression. British social model writers have long engaged with issues of race (e.g. Stuart, 1993; Vernon, 1999), feminism (e.g. Morris, 1996) and sexuality (Shakespeare et al., 1996). Some approached the study of disability with political attitudes born out of prior struggles. Vic Finkelstein came to disability studies following his ejection from South Africa for anti-apartheid activities. Jenny Morris's work emerged from her own engagements with the women's movement. North American cultural disability studies originated in part from the postcolonial/raced, feminist/gendered and queer/sexuality theoretical training of their writers. Conversely, disability studies have been sidelined by these theoretical sites. In cultural studies, the triad of race, gender and sexuality have been theorised without reference to disability (Mallett, 2007), sociological analyses of class-consciousness have marginalised disabled people (Davis, 1995: xi), feminisms have suffered a structural amnesia about the particularities of exclusion experienced by disabled women (e.g. Morris, 1996; Ghai, 2002, 2006) and critical race and postcolonial literatures have had, at best, a troubling relationship with disability (Sherry, 2007). All of this has led Olkin (2002) to ask: 'When will disabled people be allowed to board the diversity train?' For Davis (2006b: xviii), disabled people are *the* ultimate intersectional subject, the universal image, the important modality through which we can understand exclusion and resistance.

Throughout this chapter we will use terminology from queer, feminist and postcolonial literatures. In relation to postcolonialism, the terms 'Global North', 'Metropole', 'minority world' refer to national contexts oft-associated with the term 'developed country' or 'first world', or 'WENA (Western European and North American) nations'. 'Global South' and 'majority world' are employed in place of 'developing country' or 'third world'. We remain mindful of the complexity of these terms, aware that it is possible to find Global North localities in Global South contexts (and vice versa), but use them as reminders of the resonance of imperialist and globalising practices (see Spivak, 1985; Venn, 2001; Burman, 2008; Meekosha, 2008). In relation to queer, while this term has been associated with radical writings around sexuality in the areas of lesbian, gay, bi and transsexual politics, the term is appropriated here as a practice and ambition that unsettles, disturbs and challenges normative ways of living.

Gendered

Disabled feminists, including Campling (1981), Fine and Asch (1988), Morris (1991, 1992, 1993a, 1996), Lloyd (1992), Wendell (1996), Corker and French (1998), Meekosha (1998, 2002, 2004), Corker (1999, 2001), Kittay (1999a, 1999b; 2001, 2006), Jung (2002), Marks (1999a, 1999b), Thomas (1999, 2001a, 2007), Olkin (2003), Garland-Thomson (2005), Ghai (2006) and Price (2007) addressed being 'shut up and shut out' by the feminist mainstream (Quinlan et al., 2008) while tackling incidents of 'gender-blind' disability studies. Robertson (2004) attributes the latter to the privileging of public issues such as property ownership and employment (historically the remit of men) over private issues such as the domestic sphere, parenting and relationality (spaces women have been forced to occupy). Disabled women occupy a specific site of exclusion.

Thinking point: 'The Other, i.e. the disabled, is silenced because she is the Other. ... Yet, the feminist agenda, and the women's movement, have not remarked on these conditions. Possibly, the experience of disability is

imagined to be opaque, intransitive and idiosyncratic' (Ghai, 2006: 88). What other reasons can you give for the failure of non-disabled feminists to respond to issues of disabled feminists?

Meekosha (2004) fills the silence identified by Ghai (2006). Disabled women are more likely to be poor than disabled men; are less likely to have access to rehabilitation and employment; are more likely to experience public space as threatening; are more likely to live in the parental home and experience sexual abuse. Higher levels of depression are found in disabled women than men (Olkin, 2008), women are more likely to remain in abusive (often heterosexual) relationships due to a reliance on partners for personal assistance and financial support, combined with concerns about losing custody of their children (to their non-disabled partners) (see also Olkin, 2003). Disabled feminisms re-examine feminist politics of reproductive technologies and ethics of care (Garland-Thomson, 2002). As Morris (1996) demonstrates, non-disabled feminist calls for the 'right to choose' the termination of disabled foetuses and their concerns with the subjugation of women through 'unpaid care practices' (often, of disabled people) are complicated by a disability studies agenda.

Historically, disability and femininity have been coupled, as mad, bad and ill women's bodies are categorised through conditions such as premenstrual tension, hysteria, post-natal depression and Munchausen's Syndrome by Proxy (see Campbell, 2009: 100). Labels such as anorexia, hysteria and agoraphobia are feminine roles enlarged to disabling conditions that blur the line between 'normal feminine' behaviour and 'pathology' (Campbell, 2009: 120). Indeed, for Ussher (1991), no understanding of the 'disabling conditions' of women's mental health can be made without direct reference to the emergence of sexist discourses of pathology and diagnoses that grew through the merging of patriarchy, industrial capitalism and the birth of sciences such as psychology, medicine and social policy. Disability is a key feminist trope (Jung, 2002).

Garland-Thomson (2005) provides an evaluative bibliography of feminist disability studies literatures. She argues that feminist disability studies 'deeply engage with the question of what it means to have a dynamic and distinct body which witnesses its own perpetual interaction with the social and material environment' (Garland-Thomson, 2005: 1582). For Garland-Thomson, disability studies and feminisms merge around three key practices. The first, ***retrievals***, involves finding women's writings that have the potential for 'narrative recuperation'. These writings might not explicitly announce themselves as being disability studies texts (nor do disabled women have to author them), but they might nevertheless capture the disability experience. An example would be Wendell's (1996: 13) use of Iris Marian Young's observation that women are 'physically disabled' by sexist society, through the application of rigid standards of feminine body comportment, objectification and invasion, which stipulate how women should hold and act themselves (see also Silvers, 1995).

The second, ***reimaginings,*** strives to rewrite oppressive social scripts: 'because prevailing narratives constrict disability's complexities they not only restrict the lives and govern the bodies of people we think of as disabled, but they limit the imaginations of those who think of themselves as non-disabled' (Garland-Thomson, 2005: 1567). This calls for, she argues, situated theory: feminist disability sitpoint theory, a direct counter-reference to the influential work of Stanley and Wise's (1993) feminist standpoint theory. 'As a cripple I swagger … unnerving the non-crip … to demetamorphise and depathologise disability' (Garland-Thomson, 2005: 1573).

The third, ***rethinkings,*** opens up disabled feminisms to a host of theories (which we will explore in subsequent chapters), including materialism (e.g. Thomas, 1999), phenomenology (e.g. Wendell, 1996), and poststructuralism (e.g. Ghai, 2006). One concept to rethink relates to the universalised view of the functioning body as an autonomous, capable and, by definition, male body (Michalko, 2002). As we explore later in Chapter 5, the idealised individual, against which a disabled person is viewed, is an historical artefact of modern society: a *master*ful individual (see also Chapter 8). Disability is constructed through direct recourse to these gendered norms and sexist practices. To think of dis/ability we need also to be cognisant of fe/male. To explore disablism we need to remain mindful of sexism.

Raced

Thinking point: 'Race and disability share much metaphorically and politically.' Consider this statement and outline five historical common experiences of discrimination faced by people who identify as disabled and people who identify as black.

Disability and race can be understood as constructions of disabling and colonial societies (Stone, 1999; Armstrong et al., 2000a; Priestley, 2001). Following Fanon (1993), disabled people and people of colour, who have been colonised by non-European and North American countries, have been described as sinful, uncivilised, wretched, ugly, immoral, savage, innocent, sexual, exotic, im/potent and social dead. Following Shakespeare (2000), Sherry (2007) and Campbell (2009), 'disabling' and 'colonising' denote similar processes of exclusion, fascination and genocide. Hunt (1966: 154) viewed racialised ghettos and disabling long-stay institutions as similar contexts that 'salved society's conscience'. The history of public education has been predicated on the exclusion of some on the basis of their religion, colour, class and disability (Lipsky and Gartner, 1996). Black men are overrepresented in mental health statistics: twice as many African-American boys are labelled intellectually disabled than non-African-American boys (Connor, 2008) and African-American men fare worse in education and work than non-African-Americans (Lynn, 2004).

Black disabled people have been described as doubly oppressed (Stuart, 1993). Michalko (2002) refers to the cultural centre of North American society as the 'homeland'. Implicit in this description, particularly in these post-9/11 days, is White-Able-non-Arab-America that requires security and defence. Many critical race theorists, such as Lynn (2006), regard US juridical and legislative frameworks as upholding the rights of those permitted to occupy the homeland. Black and disabled citizens experience their legislative position often in terms of control and discipline rather than rights and freedom. The place of African-Americans and disabled people in this 'homeland' remains questionable.

Race and disability share tangled histories. Connor (2008) highlights 'animality theories' that historically viewed black and disabled people as less than human: the freak shows of the nineteenth century that displayed non-European and impaired exhibits as 'exotic' and 'repulsive' attractions; scientific studies of feeblemindedness that fuelled eugenicists concerns about the mingling of races, classes and abilities; segregation of slaves and 'village idiots' from the wider breeding populace. Disability is compounded by nationhood and colonialism. It is estimated that 113 million primary school-age children are not attending school, with 80 million of these living in Africa (Ngcobo and Muthukrishna, 2008), around 23 million in India (Gabel and Chander, 2008), many of whom could be labelled as disabled. Women with disabilities are denied equal access to education. Their literacy rate, worldwide, is probably under 5%, according to Disabled People's International. Olkin (2009: 18) slates WENA disability studies for alienating some women of colour through ignoring values of interdependence, extended family and religious faith. Ghai (2006) estimates that there are 35 million disabled women in India, many of whom will suffer further experiences of discrimination and familial rejection, due to complex situations of caste, tradition, dowry and familial honour. In a recent survey of Indian households, 50% of families thought that the cause of disability was a 'curse of God' (Hardy, 2008). There are many epic stories in Hindu culture that use disability as narrative prosthesis (see Chapter 2) to convey badness (such as the evil-blind king Dhritarashtra, son of Vichitravirya). Husaini (2009: 64) observes that:

> since Karma theory is so deep rooted in the religion followed by the majority of the Indian population, it has not completely disappeared. In household conversations this concept still prevails, particularly in rural India, which constitutes the pulse of the nation.

We know too that poverty hits more women in majority world contexts like India, where property ownership structures are patriarchal by design (Meekosha, 2004, 2008). The goal for many Global South disability activists has been basic survival (Ghai, 2002). Living a hand-to-mouth existence means that the birth of a disabled child or the onset of significant impairment in childhood can be viewed as fates worse than death (Ghai, 2002). Due to the traditions of dowry, based on the assumption of giving a perfect, innocent girl in the case of marriage from one family to another, disabled girls have to be compensated. This creates further socio-economic anxieties for families. Up to 10 million girls in India may have been selectively terminated in the past 20 years (Boseley, 2006: 13), with recent estimates putting that figure nearer 13 million. Girls are more expensive than boys. To understand these fertility choices requires a critical framework that is mindful not simply of Indian cultural values but of the consequences of colonialism (Ghai, 2002).

Occidentalism is described by Venn (2001) as a worldview manifestation of modernity, imperialism and colonialism. Occidentalism understands human development as unfolding in a linear 'cleansing' fashion towards an end point of civilisation (teleology), pushed along through the rational and reasoned acts of human beings (logocentrism). In the search for rational progress and the wonders of technological advance, we come to forget what Venn terms the debris of history and oppression.

Thinking point: Venn argues that the occident is 'the becoming West of life.' Outline the ways in which the world is becoming increasingly westernised

and/or Americanised? In your answer consider either (a) economic (e.g. financial, industrial, manufacturing) or (b) cultural (e.g. TV, film, music and consumption) examples.

As we shall see in Chapters 5 and 8, the age of reason gives birth to a particular type of Global North citizen (independent, solitary, self-contained, independent) – the heroic subject of modernity – that is contrasted with the 'East' and 'uncivilised' natives of 'developing' countries. The occidental individual of WENA societies is logocentric (rational and autonomous), Eurocentric (bound to the cultural and political values of European societies) and phallocentric (tied to patriarchally inscribed and masculine-centred forms of being) (Venn, 2001: 196). Modernity describes a unique period of time based on secular principles of science and positivism, intimately correlated with the emancipatory aims of reason and liberty, locked into globalised forms of rational capitalism. As Global North countries intervene in Global South regions in the name of rationality and liberty, indigenous knowledge is trampled on by imperialist logos. Grech (2009c) and Darder and Torres (2009) classify globalisation as the oppression of indigenous people; the decolonisation and formation of new nation states with the ensuing exploitation and exclusion of minority workers; violent struggles that have increased the movement of refugees[2] and racialised conflicts which have increased the difficult position of these new migrant workers. The label 'third world', which signifies underdevelopment and savagery, is a powerful signifier that masks the imperialist 'worlding' of many countries (Spivak, 1985). Spivak's discussion of the paradoxical position of 'third world' (or subaltern) women caught between a modern world, in which their traditions seemingly render them passive objects, on the one hand, and traditions that seemingly make them agents, but only of their own suicide, on the other (K. Oliver, 2007: 354). For Venn (2001), a critique of occidentalism requires a postcolonial response. As Loomba (2001) argues, postcolonialism is not a term that signifies the end of colonialism but a means of contesting its legacies. Hence, the termination of female foetuses in India can only be understood in terms of those pre/modern legacies that have left many Indians poor and bereft of material needs.

Postcolonial theories challenge the touristic/voyeuristic view of the colonised/disabled, developed by occidentalism, which required the makings of an irrational, unreasoned, propertyless, uncivilised class of people (the disabled, female, non-western, non-white) in order to promulgate its (in reality rather shaky) vision of the rational, reasonable, civilised WENA individual. Postcolonial theory is anti-Eurocentric and anti-colonial (Hardt and Negri, 2000: 143). Lavia (2007) views postcolonial theory as disturbing the subject of colonised and coloniser, interrogating occidental ideas – found in the discourses of medicalisation, rehabilitation, education and civilising practices – and their impact on colonial contexts. The inhabitants of these locations are writ-over by acceptable ideas of Eurocentric science, morality, ethics and politics. As Barker (2008) notes, colonial history leaves a legacy of colonial psychologies and forms of personhood and subjectivity. The image of the black man left by colonisation is a 'frightened, trembling negro [sic], abased before the white overlord', whom the (European) coloniser later repudiates (Fanon, 1993: 61–64):

> In the company of the white man who unmercifully imprisoned me, I took myself far off from my own presence … and made myself an object. What

> else could it be for me but an amputation, an excision, a haemorrhage that spattered my whole body with black blood? (Fanon, 1993: 112)

Similar images are left for disabled people. Sherry (2006, 2007) articulates points of overlap between postcolonial and disability studies. Shakespeare (2000) draws parallels between coloniser/helper and colonised/helped, and Barker (2008) explores the ways in which disability is offered as a metaphor for disasters of colonisation. Davis (1995) highlights connections made between race and intellectual disability (of mental slowness and racial innocence demonstrated symbolically in the case of Down syndrome/'Mongolism'). Meekosha (2008) has recently synthesised postcolonial and disability studies to propose a Global South disability studies perspective. There are 400 million disabled people in the Global South (between 66% and 75% of all disabled people, depending on which statistics one draws on). While disabled people do indeed make up the majority world, they remain excluded from global citizenship. Citing a number of resources (including www.wecando.wordpress.com/about and www.apids.org), Meekosha questions the implicit values of Northern hemisphere disability studies, including (1) claims to universality (what happens in the Global North should happen in the South); (2) a reading from the Metropole (a methodological projection of ideas from the centre into the periphery); (3) emphasis on the importance of Northern feudal/capitalist modes of production (with an accompanying ignorance and grand erasure of indigenous/traditional modes of living of the South); (4) a colonialism of psychic, cultural and geographical life of the South by the North; and (5) ignorance of the resistant – subaltern – positions of Global Southerners. For Sherry (2006, 2007), concepts of worlding, nation state and cultural/social constructions of disability/race provide opportunities for alliance. Both postcolonialism and disability studies revisit key experiences of exoticisation, ambivalence and exile. Majority-world contexts are materially subjugated through the workings of the global market (Meekosha, 2008): the exportation of pollution and contaminated waste (including pollution havens in Africa); the exploitation of sweatshops (including Internet companies data entry); the arms trade and the globalisation of the disability marketplace (such as privatised managed care proliferating in poor countries). Such material and discursive shapings of the South by the North threaten to render disabled people alienated from the emerging dominant order of their local and national contexts:

> The experience of cultural imperialism means to experience how the dominant meanings of society render the particular perspective of one's group invisible at the same time as they stereotype one's group and mark it out as other. (Ghai, 2006: 40)

To think of dis/ability requires awareness of the intersections of race and post/coloniality.

Thinking point: Outline a number of examples of global inequalities, where poor countries are becoming poorer, and rich countries are getting richer. Consider the impact of these inequalities on disabled people in the rich and poor nations of the world.

Sexed

> Disability studies … particularly those working with queer and feminist theory, are increasingly problematising the conventional parameters of sexuality, in order to explore non-normative constructions of sexual identities, pleasures and agency that more adequately encompass multifarious forms of embodied difference. (Shildrick, 2007a: 227)

Disabled people's sexualities have been ignored, controlled, denied and treated (Shakespeare et al., 1996). Disabled bodies have been conceptualised as asexual, unruly, monstrous and unattractive. A key area of activism for people with the label of intellectual disabilities has been around their sexual autonomy, fertility and their right to parent (Booth and Booth, 1994, 1998). They have clashed with professionals and service providers who, for a variety of reasons ranging from paternalism to risk-avoidance, maintain asexual and incompetent views of their clientele (Varela, 1978). When sexuality and disability are discussed, they tend to be in terms of maladaptive sexual behaviours as a consequence of abuse (Brown and Craft, 1989) or attributions of sexual dysfunction unproblematically 'caused by' impairment effects (Shuttleworth and Grove, 2008). Indeed, as Shuttleworth and Grove (2008) observe, the research corpus on sexuality and disability tends to over-emphasise psychosexual (mal) functioning; explores men's sexuality rather than women's; places a lot of store on medical rehabilitation and therapeutic interventions; and implicitly assumes heterosexual encounters.

Sex, disability and abuse do connect. Between one-third and one-tenth of the disabled population have been sexually abused at some point in their lives (Brown and Craft, 1989).[3] As Gonzalez (2004) writes, he was unable to escape a childhood of sexual abuse simply because, as a wheelchair user, he was unable to escape down the stairs of his home. That abuse is so prevalent is particularly galling in light of eugenics and institutionalisation programmes that aimed to outlaw the sexualities of disabled people. Even today, erotophobic attitudes and excessive repression suppress discussions about sex and pervade professional beliefs about disabled people. Wilkerson (2002) notes that the norm of heterosexual vaginal intercourse erases more polymorphous forms of sexuality required by those with non-normative bodies,[4] including the debate about disabled men accessing sex workers (Waterman, 2004) and the input of personal assistants to support disabled sex lives. When dis/abled men use sex workers, when disabled people are aided by personal assistants to make love with their partners, when diverse bodies rely on parts of their body for pleasure, we start to ask important questions about the polymorphous nature of desire that all dis/abled people hold potentially in their bodies and at the interface of their relationships with others. While many dis/abled people might lead fairly humdrum, normal sex lives, we should not be scared of addressing the polymorphous nature of desire:

> Polymorphousness need not be thought of as 'perverse' … polymorphousness might be viewed as a treasure rather than something dangerous. … [It] need not be thought of as a substitute for lack and hence, less than the original pleasure or less the normality. It can be viewed as pleasure itself. (Bardach, 2007: 251)

What if our different/missing/deviant bits/oozing fluids/states are the *very sources* of that desire/fetish? (Campbell, 2009: 122). A disabled body is a sexually challenging idea.

Recently, there has been a growing body of work connecting sexuality and disability – *Sexuality & Disability*; *GLQ: A Journal of Lesbian and Gay Studies* (see special issue, 9 (1), 2003); *NWSA Journal* (see special issue, 4 (1), 2002) – and also evidenced in the work of GLBT (Gay, Lesbian, Bisexual and Transsexual) and disability activist cross-over organisations (McRuer and Wilkerson, 2003). One particular theoretical thread circles around a synthesis of queer and disability theories (e.g. McRuer, 2002, 2003, 2006; McRuer and Wilkerson, 2003; Sherry, 2004; Whitney, 2006). Queer theory grew out of HIV activism and non-heteronormative sexual politics. Queer challenges heterosexism and disablism. Individuals who breach the standards of these social systems (disabled and gay, lesbian, transsexual, queer people) share a rehabilitative history, ranging from extermination in Nazi camps to the more 'humane' treatments of hypnotherapy, castration, aversion therapy and psychoanalysis. Gorman (2009) notes that queer youth (particularly young gay men) are being increasingly diagnosed using a variety of impairment labels in the USA. Sampson (1993: 1221) conceptualises homosexuality as a fundamental challenge to the heterosexist ethic. Disabled people, similarly, challenge the ethics of ableism. Non-heteronormative values link neatly to the project of disability studies. McRuer (2006) adapts Rich's (1980) concept of 'compulsory heterosexuality' to develop the notion of 'compulsory able-bodiedness': an imbricated system interwoven with the system of compulsory heterosexuality. The most successful heterosexual subject is one whose sexuality is not compromised by the 'disability' of being queer and the most successful able-bodied subject is the one whose ability is not compromised by the 'queerness' of disability. Compulsory able-bodiedness functions by covering over, with the appearance of choice, a system in which there is actually no choice.

Fortunately, the system is bound to fail: the ideal able-bodied identity can never be achieved (Chapter 8). Everyone is virtually disabled, both in the sense that able-bodied norms are intrinsically impossible to embody and the most severe bodies are the ones best placed to refute the compulsory nature of able-bodiedness (McRuer, 2003). Sherry (2004) recognises the overlap of queer and disabled. Many disabled and gay people experience family isolation (they may be the only disabled/gay member of the family), stereotyping, emotional trauma, assumed biological aetiologies for their difference (gay gene or organic impairment), and encounter displays of 'passing' as non-disabled/heteronormative.

Thinking point: Sherry (2004) suggests that we ask two questions: (1) How is queerness evoked in the construction of disability? (2) How is disability evoked in the construction of queerness? Address each of these questions with reference to the queer disability studies literature introduced to you in this chapter.

Disabled sexualities are marginalised but they are also subversive. Queer is against heteronormativity and homonormativity (McRuer and Wilkerson, 2003). Queer develops fugitive knowledges to express what it means to be a transgressive subject: of centring queer and queering the centre (Vickers, 2008). Queer contests the able individual, disputes the psychological, geographical and cultural normative centre and breaks fixed binaries of 'straight/gay', 'dis/abled' (Austin, 1999; McRuer, 2002; Sherry,

2004; Atkinson and De Palma, 2008). Disabled, female and dark bodies are no longer seen as incomplete, vulnerable or incompetent bodies. Queer inserts a productive trajectory because, following Garland-Thomson (2002: 7–8), these bodies are 'ungovernable, intemperate and threatening', gifting exciting possibilities for reconstituting social and cultural relationships, as highlighted by Shildrick and Price (2005/2006) in their use of this quote from Hardt and Negri (2000: 216):

> The will to be against really needs a body that is completely incapable of submitting to command. It needs a body that is incapable of adapting to family life, to factory discipline, to the regulations of a traditional sex life, and so forth. (If you find your body refusing these 'normal' modes of life, don't despair – realize your gift!).

Impaired bodies and minds queer – or following McRuer (2006) 'crip' – norms (Chapter 5), directly challenge narrow conceptions of what constitutes body beautiful and beautiful mind (Chapter 7), ask what we should desire (Chapter 8) and demand us to think more creatively about professional practice (Chapter 9). To be queer or crip is to be subversive. To use disability studies critique queers the norms of contemporary society.

Classed

There is overwhelming evidence to suggest that those in lower classes have lower life expectancies, higher death rates, raised infant mortality rates, less access to quality healthcare, and live in more toxic, hazardous and non-hygienic environments that render them vulnerable (Syme and Berkman, 1976). This evidence has been around at least since the twelfth century, while the relation between social class and health status has been officially and systematically assessed in France and England since the nineteenth century (Liberatos et al., 1988). Where there is poverty we will find disability. As we shall explore in Chapter 4 there is a rich vein of sociological analysis that links the economic and social exclusion of disabled people to the rise of capitalism and the impact of urbanisation, industrialisation and institutionalisation (Oliver, 1990; Barnes, 1991; Skrtic, 1995). Disability has often been understood in relation to work. 'Invalid' in Soviet Russia was defined in terms of a lost capacity to work from the nineteenth century onwards (Phillips, 2009). Measures of social stratification and class have changed markedly since Karl Marx's analyses of the bourgeoisie and proletariat and Max Weber's hierarchical notion of class, status and party. Administratively, social class is a derived classification achieved by mapping employment status to class categories, to produce distinct socio-economic groups (Rose, 1995). In Britain, the Office for National Statistics (2009) continues to draw on the British Registrar General's Scale (developed in 1911), that permits one to self-code in terms of five classes; I, managerial and professional occupations; II, intermediate occupations; III, small employers and own account workers; IV, lower supervisory and technical occupations; and V, semi-routine and routine occupations. In the USA, the 1980 US Bureau of the Census grouped occupations into 13 categories, including executives, professional specialists, technicians; administrative support, service workers (private household), protective service workers, other service workers, farm operators and managers, mechanics and repairers, machine operators, assemblers and inspectors, transportation operatives, handlers and helpers. These categorisation systems have been drawn on and correlated with a host of health issues over the years (see Liberatos et al., 1988). Yet, these measures of social class – indicative of work, education and income – are particularly problematic for those who have been excluded from education, are unemployed or 'economically inactive' (Rose, 1995: 5). Clearly, in terms of involvement in the labour market, disabled people continue to occupy a peripheral position. In Britain, 30% of adults with intellectual disabilities with 'low support needs' are in paid work, with only 3% of those with 'high support needs' finding work (Beyer, 2009). Many do not receive an adequate nor appropriate wage for their work. Furthermore, acquiring impairment labels – such as 'mental illness' – is often correlated with a 'downward drift' in socio-economic status, associated with difficulties in finding employment as a person with a 'psychological illness' (Goldberg and Morrison, 1963). Zaidi and Burchardt (2009) note that disabled people are overrepresented in three measures of economic disadvantage: low income (due to an inability to work or/and exclusion from work); additional costs (because it is more expensive to live life as a disabled person to access an exclusionary society); and constraint (denied opportunities to become economically viable). The lower the wealth, education and social class, the higher the incidence of physical impairment (Gjonca et al., 2009). Unpacking these relationships reveals that poor children rarely benefit from competitive school structures and (poor) disabled children are excluded from schools that have been historically designed for (relatively well-off) non-disabled children (Bratlinger, 2001; see also Chapter 9). Furthermore, you are more likely to be labelled as disabled if you are poor, particularly if you are from a 'minority' ethnic group (Bratlinger, 2001).

We know from Chapter 1 – and the discussion of postcolonialism above – that there is a close link between poverty and disability. Most disabled people live in the majority world and many of these nations are economically poor. A report by Braithwaite and Mont (2008) on behalf of the World Bank indicates that we are only now beginning to take seriously measures of disability and poverty. Using the poverty line measure of $1 a day or less, estimates suggest that 20% of the world's poor in developing countries are disabled. They note that when the concept of poverty is broadened, disabled people in poor countries continue to suffer in terms of material well-being (having enough food, assets and work); social well-being (being able to bring up children; self-respect and dignity; peace, harmony and good relations in the community); security (civil peace, safe environment, security in old age); freedom of choice and action (psychological well-being, peace of mind, happiness).

Shakespeare (2006a, 2009) argues that when disability studies scholars think of disabled people as an entire class of people they fail to engage adequately with the complex intersections of social class and disability. Clearly, having more access to financial and community resources will influence how well one can cope with a disabling society. That said, the relationship between class and disability remains complex. The family provides us with one microcosm of wider society through which to consider this complexity. The notion of the 'disabled family' conceives the family unit as a whole and takes this as the starting point for analysing the material, cultural and personal challenges faced by disabled children and their families. A plethora of work has emerged over the last ten years that has taken seriously the lives of disabled children and their families (e.g. Traustadóttir, 1991, 1995, 1999; Kittay, 1999a, 1999b, 2001, 2006; Read, 2000; Ryan, 2005; Runswick-Cole, 2007). Drawing on this literature, McLaughlin et al. (2008) identified a number of recurring findings:

- more and more disabled children are living longer;
- families are often reliant on benefits and those who can claim benefits often find it difficult to do so;
- benefits that families do receive often do not meet the additional outgoings associated with having a disabled child;
- families of disabled children often live in poverty, the work of parents is reduced in order to care for their children and their household incomes are lowered;
- parents' lives and the children's education are disrupted by recurring appointments and professional treatment;
- families report widespread parental stress, lack of sleep, lack of respite care and reliance upon extended family (if they are present);
- families often lack access to accessible leisure pursuits and housing and responsive respite care;
- children are excluded from friendship groups and parents from parent groups.

In short, disabled families face social, economic and cultural poverty. More recent research suggests that this picture is not changing. Children with intellectual disabilities are more likely to live in poor families and 60% of British children with the label of 'developmental delay' were living in poverty at 3 years of age (Emerson, 2009). Furthermore, changes in the occupational status of parents of disabled children are associated with escape from or entry into income poverty and hardship (Emerson et al., 2009). That said, we know too that families act as powerful networks that mediate between disabling society and the impact on disabled children (Syme and Berkman, 1976). This point relates to how we conceptualise social class. In epidemiology, for example, concepts have been used interchangeably, such as social class, social status, social inequality, social stratification and socio-economic status (Liberatos et al., 1988: 88). In sociology, the work of Bourdieu has been useful in expanding the concept of social class away from a preoccupation with economic capital, to include other forms of capital, including cultural (e.g. educational credentials, aesthetic preferences, bodily characteristics and comportment, speech dialect), social (e.g. networks, group memberships) and symbolic (e.g. role, legitimacy, authority, prestige). Thus, it is possible to view the disabled family as a rich context for the potential emergence of these various forms of capital that may well challenge the socio-economic marginalisation of disabled children (McKeever and Miller, 2004; Nind, 2008).

Thinking point: Read the following story taken from an interview with Mary, the mother of 13 year-old Debbie from the project (www.rihsc.mmu.ac.uk/postblairproject). Debbie lives with her mother and father in a town in the North-west of England.

> *Where do I start about Debbie? She's got Moderate Learning Difficulties [intellectual disabilities], speech and language problems, she's a little live wire, but happy, she's always happy, everyone calls her 'happy Debbie'. Apart from her dad, and me, who know there's 'horrible Debbie' sometimes! We've had some real difficult times, it's been the hardest journey of my life this, having Debbie. ... David and I had been trying for a baby for three years, we were just about to go for tests in January and we found out on Christmas Eve that we were expecting Debbie. And then, on Boxing Day, I fell ill and then by January 3 I had pains in my legs and by January 7 I was in intensive care with a pulmonary embolism. They told me that the baby wouldn't survive but we'd tried so hard to have her and basically I thought if Debbie is coming to us then she's coming to us and whatever disabilities may be there she has a right. ... I was told to have a termination. I was told that there was no way that the baby would survive. And I said I can't, I just couldn't. It was one thing for nature to take that choice away, but I couldn't. I'm so glad I didn't, despite her problems. I wouldn't swap Debbie for anything. I would like things to be different for her sometimes but only for herself really. She is who she is and I wouldn't have sacrificed that for anything. As hard as it has been, as difficult as it has been, it's been other people that have caused the problems, not Debbie herself.*

Now read the extracts from the researcher field notes of Katherine Runswick-Cole, which were written after the interview with Debbie's mother, Mary.

> *I'm sitting in a lay-by in the rural northwest, having just been to visit Debbie.*
>
> *I've just interviewed her mother Mary. The house is on a very 'middle class' estate on the edge of a small village. The houses look like they were built in the 1980s and look like 'executive homes'. Debbie's house backs onto countryside and has a large, bright extension on the back of it. Mary opens the door and Debbie came to greet me immediately with a 'Horrid Henry' book in her hand. Her dad David also comes to say hello. Mary brings me a cup of tea and leaves me to talk to Debbie. Debbie can't remember why I've come to see her, so I tell her that I work at a university. She says she's been to one. I say that it is a place where some people go to learn like a school and other people work there and try and find out things, and I want to find out about what children and young people do. We sit on the floor together. I show Debbie the digital recorder and microphone. Debbie is very interested in it and so we record a few words and play them back. Mary comes through with some photos and we start to talk about them. Debbie loves her cat and the dogs. She shows me a photo of the hamster that died last week. Debbie's photos show her playing in the snow with her dad, swimming in the pool on vacation with her dad, making a cake at Guides that she goes to every Thursday. There are lots of pictures of*

Debbie with her friends from school out for a curry. Debbie spots that the digital recorder isn't recording! We go back through the pictures and Debbie wants to listen to the recording. I'm a bit taken aback when she yanks the microphone out of the recorder! We share the headphones and listen back to the conversation. Debbie laughs and laughs when she hears my voice back! She doesn't think her own is so funny. We talk about meeting again and Debbie sends me off to find a date after her holiday in Disney. Debbie loves hearing herself talk on the microphone so I promise to find out how to make a video on the lap top for next time and she will bring back some photos.

David, Mary and I sit and chat in the kitchen. I can hear Debbie watching the television in the sitting room. David and Mary talk a lot about school. We sit chatting about school. They feel very unhappy about the way they've been treated. They feel that they have to be exemplary parents and Debbie is watched all the time. Everything about her is scrutinised and commented on. David and Mary feel there is a 'glass half empty' attitude to Debbie. They compare it with the States and Spain where they've been on holiday and say that there the 'glass is half full'. They feel there is less discrimination in the States in particular. David talks about taking Debbie to the football [soccer]. She started going with him this season. At the first match she cheered when both sides scored but she's learnt not to now! David says football is a great leveller; it is the only place that Debbie can truly be herself because she can cheer and shout and no one quietens her down. She is totally accepted by the people who sit around them. David says there are lots of other people with special needs there. As I leave, Debbie stands at the door shouting 'goodbye' until I shut the car door. As I drive off I turn around and wave to her, and she waves back. Mary described her in the interview as 'Happy Debbie' and I can see why. David and Mary worry for her but they are positive about her and believe other people should be too. It is still a mystery to them (and to me!) why Debbie has been bullied, why the school doesn't want her there and why people are so intolerant of her in general.

Question 1: What possible forms of capital do you think Debbie's family might have access to that contribute to making a 'good life' for Debbie?
Question 2: In what ways do class, ethnicity, gender and sexuality interact in the accounts of Debbie and her family?

Conclusions

Following Nkweto-Simmonds (1999), poor, black, disabled, queer and female bodies share a history of being lynched, raped and condemned: 'adorned and unadorned, I cannot escape the fantasies of the western imagination' (Nkweto-Simmonds, 1999: 56). Disabled bodies are denied access to the wider world, which has been designed for a young, adult, non-disabled, materially wealthy, male paradigm of humanity (Wendell, 1996: 19). Temporarily Able Bodied (TAB) people await a time of material exclusion when their bodies 'fail' to meet this paradigm. This chapter sought to intersect disability, gender, sexuality, class and race through the overlapping perspectives of feminism, queer, postcolonial class and disability studies. These perspectives unsettle what it means to be human (Chapter 5), help us to question relationships between disabled and non-disabled people (Chapter 6), destabilise discourses that we use to differentiate people (Chapter 7), turn the spotlight on how wealthy cultures are formed to reflect the insecurities of their dominant others (Chapter 8) and demand us to think imaginatively about professional responses to disability (Chapter 9).

Further reading

Garland-Thomson (2002). Feminist analyses of relevance to disability studies.

Lynn (2006). Introduces critical race theory: a framework for interrogating social inequities enshrined in law.

McRuer and Wilkerson (2003). An overview of queer and critical disability studies.

Meekosha (1998). Cyber-feminist reflections.

Sherry (2006). Postcolonial, queer and disability studies perspectives are combined into an accessible text.

Notes

1 Due to space, this chapter omits to intersect disability with age (see instead Murray and Penman, 1996; Billington, 2000; Priestley, 2001; Bjarnason 2004; Björnsdóttir, 2009; Ryan, 2005; Runswick-Cole, 2007; McLaughlin et al., 2008).
2 A further point to make about the close relationship of disability and nation, particularly in the twentieth century, is that disability services, policies and legislation have often responded to the 'war disabled'. Hence in Britain (Barnes, 1991), the USA (Meekosha, 2004) and Russia (Phillips, 2009), the nation state had to be seen to respond through welfare to its returning national heroes.
3 Kennedy (1996) goes further to suggest that one in two girls and one in four boys suffer some form of sexual abuse, with 75% of all disabled children being a conservative estimate. Olkin (2003) highlights data suggesting that disabled girls and women experience more abuse than disabled boys and men.
4 Wilkerson (2002) gives the example of staff tying sandpaper to a disabled man's legs to stop him masturbating through the movement of his legs.

FOUR

Society: *Sociological Disability Studies*

****

Introduction

Our task in this chapter is to map the theoretical landscape of sociological disability studies. Following Wright Mills (1970), by scrutinising sociology we are able to understand theoretical developments in other disciplines (such as psychology, human geography and education) because sociological debates around structure–agency, subjectivity–objectivity and consensus–conflict are key to all disciplines. We seek to clarify some of the epistemological, ontological and methodological assumptions of particular sociological theories.

Knowledge and knowing

The sociological study of disability, in Britain, is carved into two main camps by Thomas (2007): disability studies, which is often associated with the writings of the social model, and medical sociology, which is often used interchangeably with sociology of health and illness. The latter holds a number of common assumptions. Disability is viewed through a 'social deviance' lens, disability and chronic illness are fused and narratives of illness/disability are explored to see how people negotiate these life narratives. While medical sociology is now a variegated field, reflecting a growing interest in diverse theoretical ideas,[1] the 1970s saw a rise of a new sociology of disability as a countermovement to the pathologising tendencies of medical sociology (Barnes and Mercer, 1997b). Disability studies developed a social oppression perspective of disablism that countered the social deviance view. The minority, cultural, social and relational models were conceived across a host of pan-national contexts by scholars and activists to foreground disability as a socio-political, cultural and relational phenomenon. Our focus for this chapter is sociological disability studies rather than medical sociology.

A helpful place to start is C. Wright Mills' (1970: 14–16) declaration that sociology should examine two key concepts: 'private troubles' of individuals that occur in our relationships with others (often when our own values are threatened) and 'public issues' of organisations and institutions (that often arise as a crisis of institutional arrangements). In dealing with these public issues and private troubles, the sociologist asks key questions about history and biography (Wright Mills, 1970: 13): what is the structure of this particular society as a whole? Where does this society stand in human history? What varieties of men and women now prevail in this society and this period? How we answer these sociological questions will depend on the sociological perspectives we adopt.

Mapping sociological theories

Much has been written about the ontological, methodological and epistemological bases of disability studies (e.g. Abberley, 1987; Priestley, 1998; Thomas, 1999; Goodley, 2001).

Thinking point: 'An ontology is a theory of what exists and how it exists, and an epistemology is a related theory of how we can come to know these things' (Clough and Nutbrown, 2002:30). Use these two concepts to make sense of (a) the medical model; (b) the social model; and (c) the relational model of disability (see Tables 1.1, 1.2 and 1.3 respectively in Chapter 1).

A popular framework for making sense of these 'ologies' is provided by Burrell and Morgan (1979), extended in the work of Orford (1992), Gabel and Peters (2004) and Goodley and Lawthom (2005a) (Figure 4.1):

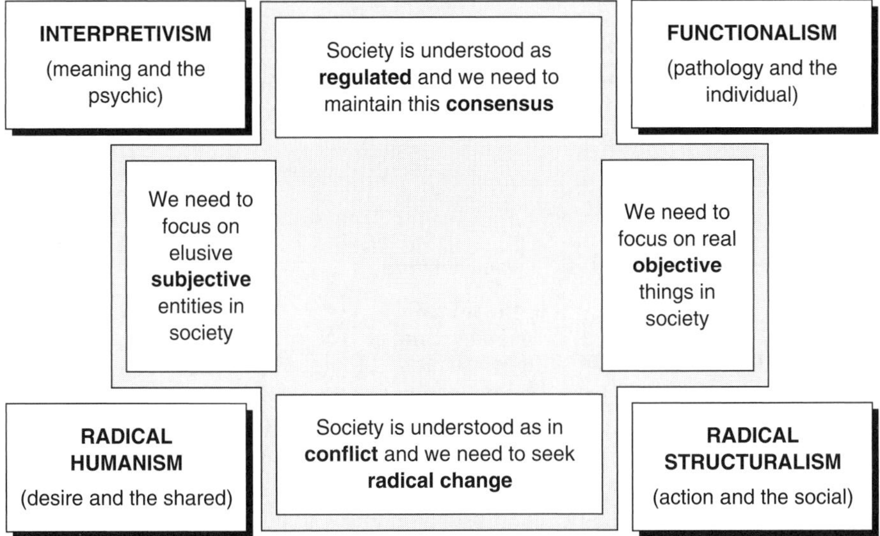

Figure 4.1 A model for mapping sociological theory (adapted from figure 3.1, 'Four paradigms for the analysis of social theory', Burrell and Morgan (1979: 22))

Following Skrtic (1995), we can understand the subjective–objective and radical change–regulation distinctions in the following ways.

Subjectivity and objectivity

Clearly, a subjectivist or objectivist position acts as a foundation on which the sociologist understands ontology, epistemology, human nature and methodology (Figure 4.2).

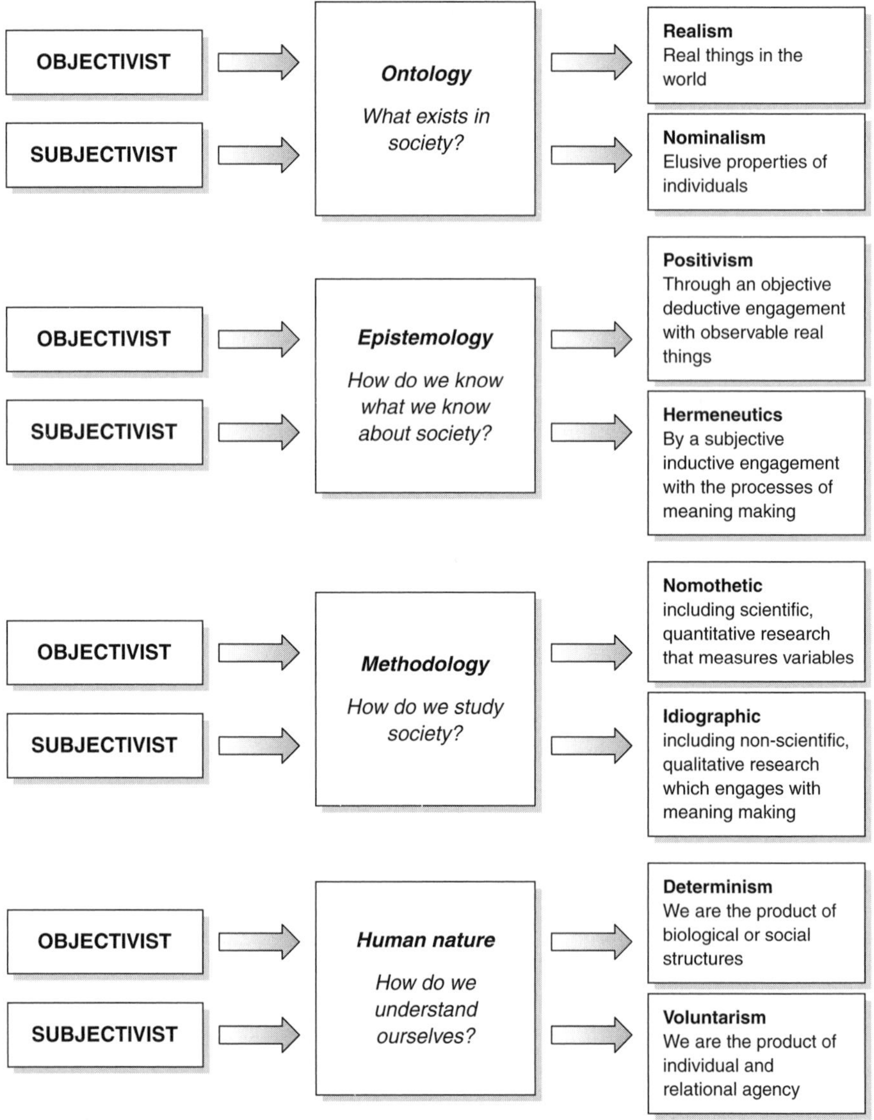

Figure 4.2 The subjectivist–objectivist divide (adapted from figure 1.1, 'A scheme for analysing assumptions about the nature of social sciences', Burrell and Morgan (1979: 3))

However, for Burrell and Morgan (1979), this is only one of the axes on which we can hang sociological theories (Figure 4.2).

Radical change (conflict) and regulation (consensus)

The second axis – the radical change/regulation distinction – conceives the social world in a number of different ways (Skrtic, 1995).

Table 4.1 The concerns of sociologies of regulation and radical change

We are what we are …	We are what we do not want to be …
A Sociology of regulation is concerned with the status quo; social order; consensus; social integration; solidarity; need satisfaction and the actuality of society	**A Sociology of radical change** is concerned with radical change; structural domination; modes of domination; contradiction; emancipation; deprivation and the potential of society

(Adapted version of Table 2.2, 'The regulation-radical change dimension' (Burrell and Morgan, 1979: 18))

We can see from Table 4.1 that a regulation position assumes that the need satisfactions of individuals are sated by existing social structures (a consensual stance). A radical change position views the status quo as depriving people of human fulfilment (a conflict stance). This distinction is a familiar one to students of sociology. Wright Mills' (1970) classic argument captures some of the debates around these binaries, emerging as it did at a time when serious questions were being asked of popular sociological theories that (a) reflected an abstracted empiricist approach to study (drawing on positivistic and nomothetic approaches, which valued technicians rather than thinkers, and produced findings that reflected their methods rather than social reality); (b) were consensual in nature (interested in finding out how things worked together rather than in opposition); and (c) directly reflected the backgrounds of their theorists, many of whom who came from white, small-town, middle-class America. Wright Mills demanded an approach to sociology that was critically aware of the *conflicts* endemic within societies and engendered an approach to research that captured private troubles and public issues.[2] Likewise, Rioux (1994b) argues that if the status quo is viewed as a process of consensual functioning, then those who disrupt society risk being subjected to practices such as segregation or corrective therapies. Such a viewpoint, for Rioux, has justified the exclusion of people with intellectual disabilities from immigration to 'New World' contexts of Australia and Canada because it aims to breed similarity, promote assimilation and, at worse, eradicate difference (see also Meekosha, 2008). A conflict position, as articulated by Althusser (1971), considers the status quo to be constantly in conflict, requiring forms of ideological apparatuses to maintain the dominance of the state over its members. Disablism is understood as one element of ideology.

The sociological terrain of disability studies can be understood in terms of paradigmatic shifts (Kuhn, 1968) from a view of disability as the product of an individual's mental functioning and behaviour (functionalism) to an engagement with the structures and institutions of society that disable (radical structuralism). Along the way, researchers have illuminated the primacy of experiences of disabled people to an understanding of the social world (interpretivism), while others have contested ideologies of disablism (radical humanism). Following Burrell and Morgan (1979) – and adapting Goodley and Lawthom (2005a) – we can define these four positions.

A *functionalist* view of the world sees society as regulated and ordered, promotes objective measures of (dys)functional mental states and behaviours and, inevitably, views disabled people as adherents of a 'sick role' (Barnes, 1998). From this worldview, disabled people have inherited pathological conditions that can be objectively diagnosed, treated and in some cases ameliorated (Gabel and Peters, 2004: 587). It is, as

Gabel and Peters note, difficult to find much resistance for disabled people in the functionalist position, perhaps only in disabled people's active appropriation or rejection of medical intervention. Disability is viewed through a distal rather than proximal lens.

An *interpretivist* stance understands the social world as an emergent social process, created by individuals and their shared subjective understandings. Disabling or enabling identities and attitudes are made by and between voluntaristic individuals in a coherent and regulated world (Ferguson et al., 1992). This position takes seriously the accounts of agents of the social world.

Radical humanism situates knowledge production in the elusive shared subjective creation of dominant disability discourses, hegemonies and social meaning-making processes of wider society. Meanings are imprisoned within ideological processes but also produced by resistant counter-hegemonic cultural practices and emergent community identities (Marks, 1999b).

Radical structuralism sees the social world as constantly in conflict, where economic and political structures can be objectively observed and in which certain social groupings are always at risk of alienation, oppression and false consciousness. This stance is acutely connected with emancipatory aims and is closely related to (Neo-)Marxist ideas.

Thinking point: Google and briefly outline what you understand by the term 'Marxism'.

Four sociologies of disability

We will now sketch out these foundational sociologies of disability; functionalism, which sets impairment and disability as synonymous concepts; interpretivism, which explores the meaning of impairment and disability as they are constructed through interpretations and actions of individuals; radical humanism, where disability and impairment are cultural signifiers constructed through culture and ideology; and radical structuralism, where disability or, more properly, disablism refers to the socio-political, economic and structural exclusion of people with impairments. In articulating these distinct perspectives we must be careful not to draw artificial boundaries. As Thomas (1999:16) warns, 'compartmentalism underplays the extent to which ideas are cumulative and cross-cutting, and can overstate the degree to which medical sociology or disability studies follow singular theoretical tracks'.

Functionalism and deficient individuals

Early sociologies of disability were heavily influenced by the structural–functionalist sociologist Parsons (e.g. 1951), whose *The Social System* 'sought a common explanatory perspective that threatened the coherence of the social system with society being conceived as analogous to a biological system – a system of social structures interacting and co-existing as a consensual web of relationships' (Thomas, 2007: 16–17). Functionalism views disability as a product of a deficient material body that 'struggles to escape the pitfalls of essentialism and biological determinism' (Donaldson, 2002: 112), and this is clearly evident in Parsons's 'sick role'. Attempts to step out of the sick role are understood as denial, maladjustment or unrealistic. This position fits with the stance of medicalisation articulated in Chapter 1 and has close alliances with psychological and sociological theories that individualise – that is *psychologise* – the problems of disability. Functionalism starts and ends with individuals and the maintenance of the social order: a problem we will explore in Chapter 5.

This view has promulgated a pathological, problem-infused victim who must place herself in the hands of authorities – such as medicine – in order to follow 'illness management regimes' (Donaldson, 2002: 112). The perfect patient is deferent, dependent and compliant (Greenop, 2009). The consensual underpinnings of this theory focus on the ways in which disabled people are managed to maintain the social order, even if this involves them being therapeutically treated (controlled) by professionals allied to medicine, such as social work (Oliver, 1983) and psychology (Goodley and Lawthom, 2005b).

C. Wright Mills (1970) demolished Parsons' theory on the grounds of conservativism and its adherence to consensual values. Wright Mills (1970: 44–45) viewed Parsons' work as legitimising institutions rather than critiquing them.[3] Wright Mills argued that 'power is often not so authoritative as it appeared in Medieval period' (1970: 45) – a key analysis developed by Foucault, as we shall see in Chapter 7 – and that it was important to examine the deeply divided nature of current society. Functionalism, based as it is on abstracted empiricism (a proposed specialisation drawing solely on the use of pseudo-scientific methods), reduces sociological phenomenon to the level of the individual living in a consensual world. Many studies of disability, up until the 1990s, followed this methodological individualism (Rioux, 1994a).[4] empowering the traditional and moral models described in Chapter 1.

Thinking point: In what ways are methodological individualism, functionalism and the medical model co-related?

Interpretivism and the myth of 'mental retardation'

> A sociology of mental retardation can be developed and applied to the field of mental deficiency if a systematic effort is made to develop the relationship between general sociological theory and the specific life experiences of mentally defective individuals. (Dexter, 1956: 16)

An interpretivist approach understands disability as the product of voluntaristic individuals engaged in the active creation of identities (Goodley, 2004: 119). Interpretivists are interested less in 'people and their moments and more in moments and their people' (Charmaz, 2004: 982). Preferred methods of key informant interviews and life hi/stories imply that one has a life to recount, presents (disabled) informants as moral agents (McRuer and Wilkerson, 2003: 11) and situates the locus of culture in the interactions of self and others (Whitemore et al., 1986: 10). This recognises the importance of subjective interpretations of social actors in a social world, a focus taken up by Goffman (1961, 1963), whose work remains an inspiration to disability researchers (Sherry, 2006; Shakespeare, 2006b; Nunkoosing and Haydon, 2008). Goffman's concepts allow us to view disabled people as subjected to stigmatisation and spoilt identities which are at the mercy of attributions of in and out groups. Taylor and Bogdan (1989), Gleeson (1999a) and Reeve (2008) relegate Goffman's work to the social psychological rather than sociological. What these critics really mean is that Goffman's consensual position leads to more interest in the status quo than wider structural inequalities. Yet, these critics fail to recognise the radical application of Goffman's work. His work on institutions (Goffman, 1961) strengthened arguments for the closure of long-stay hospitals and his work on stigma (Goffman, 1963) allowed many scholars to reposition disability as a sociological – rather than a functionalist psychological – problem (see, for example, Hunt, 1966): a problem of relationships not pathological bodies. 'Disability was not measles', as Rioux and Bach (1994) phrased it, and Goffman permitted analyses of attitude formation and the iterative processes of exclusion (Oliver, 1990: 56).

> In total institutions, territories of the self are violated. The boundary the individual places between his being and the environment is invaded and the embodiments of self profaned. (Goffman, 1961: 29)

Individuals are labelled by institutions (such as the school or hospital) and pressurised to act in ways consistent with behaviour imputed by that label (Braginsky and Braginsky, 1971). Acting 'like the retard' becomes second nature (Koegel, 1986), contributing to socio-emotional isolation and the socialisation of incompetence (Levine and Langness, 1986: 197). The work of the Syracuse Center on Human Policy has been hugely important in illuminating the social construction of intellectual disabilities (e.g. Bogdan and Taylor, 1976, 1982; Taylor and Bogdan, 1989, 1992). Their work draws on qualitative methodologies, including in-depth interviews, to represent the expert voice of disabled people. In Bogdan and Taylor (1982: 216), they re-present the stories of Ed and Pattie ('people with the label of mental retardation' [sic]), and ask:

> What then is the 'truth' about Ed and Pattie? ... The truth of Ed and Pat's condition cannot be explained by deferring to official definitions of their problems. Their compelling words require that we give them at least as much credence as we do their judges.

Interpretivism gives voice to those who are often spoken of. Ed and Pattie offer *their* opinions on intellectual disabilities:

> The word 'retarded' is a word. What it does is put people into a class. I like mental handicap better than mental retarded. The other word sounds nicer ... my day's gonna come through ... I'm gonna tell them the truth. They know the truth. All this petty nonsense. (Ed Murphy, in Bogdan and Taylor, 1982: 77)

Thinking point: In what ways does an insider perspective of disability (offered by an interpretivist sociology of disability) give a more thorough understanding of disability than an outsider perspective (proffered by a functionalist perspective)?

These insider/emic accounts contrast markedly with outsider/etic accounts of clinicians and physicians (Whitemore et al., 1986). Ambitions and experiences are made available over signs and symptoms of impairments:

> Case studies of individuals ... force us to acknowledge their *competencies*, sometimes quite hidden from public view, and the existence of which further strains the credibility of arguments purported to define or explain *the* nature of retardation. (Levine and Langness, 1986: 192, italics in original)

First-hand accounts of people have clarified the socio-cultural nature of disability. Yet, questions remain about the subjective–consensual and voluntaristic principles of interpretivism which risk presenting stigmatised roles as the responsibility of the people who enact them (Greenop, 2009). For Thomas (2007), some interpretivists identify a host of 'crisis' strategies for the maintenance of stigmatised identities. Many medical sociologists have adopted this project. The work of Frank (1994, 1995, 2000, 2005) is indicative. Frank's narrative research with ill/disabled[5] people aims to re-present their accounts of restitution (cure and overcoming impairments), quest (achieving personal growth) and chaos (tragedies without a plot). Frank (2000) draws on Goffman's view of the self: less 'self as organic being' and more as 'self-as-actor'. Frank's task is to explore how the first-person narratives of disability/illness are the performative re-creations of a 'self in jeopardy' (Frank, 2000: 136).

> Autobiographical work, then, is a performance of which the ill person becomes an effect, and the effect can be to claim a place within a separate system of honour of those who share the illness or disability. (Frank, 2000: 137)

Frank's analysis typifies interpretivism's ambivalent relationship with the concept of illness. Illness is characterised as disruptive ('the biggest of which are the disease and its effects', Frank, 2000: 139) and ontologically threatening ('To live in deep illness is to be constantly aware of one's differences from those who are not ill', Frank, 2000: 152). These claims have the potential to individualise disability: illuminating personal suffering in ways that mask structural forms of disablism. They also fail to trouble the meaning of 'illness' and its required binary opposite 'healthy'.[6]

Similarly, Charmaz (1995) typifies a sensitivity to the insider accounts of living with impairment but threatens to (re)pathologise these accounts through an analytical lens that emphasises surrendering to the sick self by 'relinquishing the control' (Charmaz, 1995: 657). Charmaz risks superimposing the illness/disability narrative 'as the story of an ordinary life interrupted by illness' on stories which in actuality are more messy or resistant than one might think (McRuer and Wilkerson, 2003: 12). This has led some disability studies scholars to reject interpretivism for storying damaged bodies in fixed regulated societies. A closer look at the work of Frank demonstrates the potential of interpretivism to challenge functionalist fixity ('deep illness itself is not necessarily brokenness', Frank, 2000: 152) and embrace the ever-developing nature of an ill or disabled identity:

> One person can never say of another, 'this is who such a person is'. One can say, at most, 'this is how I see this person now, but I cannot know what she or he will *become* … the basic recognition is that this future is *open*. In existential terms, the claim of unfinizability is a claim of freedom. (Frank, 2005: 967, italics in original)

Attending to the fluidity of narratives is demonstrated by writers such as Charmaz (1995) and Smith and Sparkes (Sparkes and Smith, 2002, 2003; Smith and Sparkes, 2004, 2005). The latter researchers' work with men with spinal cord injuries (SCI) demonstrates a willingness to take seriously not only the question of biographical disruption but also the positive identities afforded by an acquired disabled identity.

Thinking point: Think of a time in your life when you have been ill. To what extent did this experience influence (1) how you perceived yourself, and (2) how others perceived you?

A related theoretical position to interpretivism is phenomenology, which places the dilemmas and possibilities of disability at the level of embodiment. (Hughes and Paterson, 1997, 2000; Paterson and Hughes, 1999; Hughes, 2002a; Michalko, 2002; Titchkosky, 2003; Overboe, 2007a). Phenomenologists attend to the capacities of the body to be a source of self and society. This has been termed a carnal sociology, drawing on the work of such people as Merleau-Ponty (1962), to theorise the body as *the* place where self and society interact (Shilling, 2005; Landbridge, 2007). Embodiment refers to how the body operates in the world at the intersections of the corporeal and institutional (Sherry, 2006). Comportment, for example, reflects conventions. Ability is a response to environment demands. Illness is a narrative written on to and lived with through recourse to a whole host of powerful narratives, such as medicine and self-help. The phenomenology of the everyday (Turner, 2008: 12) engages with the 'lieb': the living, feeling and sensing facets of bodily experience (Crossley, 1995). Bodies are sites for subjectivity and consciousness, our active vehicles for being in the world. Practical engagements with our surroundings inform the intentionality of the body. Senses provide thickness of meaning that then constitute the world around us. We open our selves and bodies onto, and by doing so create, environments (Merleau-Ponty, 1962). The experience of disability and impairment is conceptualised through reference to the social self and its production of the life world (Hodge, 2006), where the cultural constructions of disability and impairment are played out within and through the body.

Overboe (2007a), for example, argues that the disabled self can be embraced as a unique embodied entity through which to revise how bodies should and could be lived in. While there is this potential, critics accuse phenomenology of being nothing more than an individualistic account of embodiment, from the point of individual bodies, lacking a sociological and historical context (Turner, 2008: 52). Located in a consensual foundational position, phenomenology does not develop conflict understandings of the makings of somatic relationships, which might veer from inclusion to alienation in particularly socio-cultural milieu. This has led some disability studies scholars to question the political intent of phenomenological and interpretivist researchers, who bring back impairment through their 'sentimental biography' (as we considered in Chapter 2).

Radical humanism and the cultural politics of disability

> To write a sociology of the body [or mind] is thus not to write a treatise on society and physiology. It involves the historical analysis of the spatial organisation of bodies and desire in relation to society and reason. (Turner, 2008: 40)

Radical humanism tackles the contradictions and asymmetries of culture and ideology. Methods include cultural and literary critique as well as ethnographic and anthropological study. It is plausible to view cultural model theorists, described in Chapter 1, in this vein. A radical humanist stance is interested in the politics of appearance (Garland-Thomson, 2002), the cultural *dis*location of desire (Mitchell and Snyder, 2006), the ma(r)kings of normalcy (Corbett, 1991; Davis, 1995), the socio-cultural production of bodies (Donaldson, 2002), the fiction of an idealised body politic (Price, 2007), ideological representations of dis/ability (Hevey, 1992; Barnes, 1993; Shakespeare, 1997a) and disability as a site for the reproduction for social ideologies of perversion, victimisation and fetish (McRuer and Wilkerson, 2003). All share a conviction that the world is an inherently unequal place. Dominating modes of cultural production deprive minority groups of representation. The release of desire is a crucial element: to revive creativity from its ideological imprisonment. Ideology has been described as the vocabulary of standardisation and a grammar of design sanctioned and sustained by particular social practices (McLaren, 2009: 70). Culture relates to sets of practices, ideologies and values on which groups draw to make sense of the world (McLaren, 2009: 65). The ideas of cognitivism, nativism and ableism underpin a contemporary ideology of individualism in which self-contained, productive, pliant and isolated individuals are valued and re/produced (Chapter 5). Radical humanism identifies and challenges these disabling ideologies. Inspirations include early humanist Marx (1845) and the Frankfurt school that included scholars such as Adorno, Marcuse, Horkheimer, Habermas, Fromm and Reich (see Frosh, 1987; Parker, 1997). These scholars aspired to question the 'nature' of human essence, unpick ideology as a form of false consciousness, challenge practices of excessive repression that served the aims of capitalism (for example, in relation to the arts, creativity or sexuality), explored the contradictory maxims of Marx ('life determines consciousness') and Freud ('anatomy is destiny'), struggled with the conflict between individual desire/creativity and social prohibition/management, recovered bodily pleasures (including original sensuous child-like polymorphous perversity of our bodies) from the normalising pressures of labour, and celebrated alternative forms of institutional and relational arrangement (matriarchal rather than patriarchal society). Many of the Frankfurt school theorists saw themselves as damaged because society was (Davis, 1995: 14), and all writers shared the aim of synthesising the sociology of Marx and the psychology of Freud in the name of radical social theory (Giroux, 2009; Goodley et al. 2011).

Giroux's (2009) account of the Frankfurt school captures the shared ambitions of this group of writers to rescue reason from technocratic rationality and positivism. Naïve positivism informs capitalist ideologies through the fetishisation of facts and the sidelining of subjectivity. In contrast, the radical humanism of the Frankfurt school, views theory as ever-present, and dialectical, with the potential to inform emancipatory practice: to subvert ideology.[7] Dialectical theory reveals incompleteness where completeness is claimed and views culture as colonised by ruling ideas and hegemonic practices. For example, an ideology of ableism underpins contemporary culture (Campbell, 2009) and schools reproduce culture in ways that exclude learners who fail to match up to the ideological imperative of achievement and success (Chapter 9). Disabled people are cast as other and able-bodied subjectivities are built on this othering (Chapters 5, 6 and 8). Questions are asked about the kinds of national and local cultural capital that exist around disabled people (Chapter 10). 'Disability' and 'impairment' are pulled off their functionalist foundations and recast as ideological categories that are culturally produced and negotiated (Klotz, 2003).

The anthropological studies of Groce (1992), Langness and Levine (1986a), Koegel (1981, 1986) and Whitemore et al. (1986) exemplify an analysis of disability/impairment – as related to intellectual disabilities – where the 'objective truth' of this phenomenon is dispelled and its ideological make-up revealed. The category of intellectual disabilities is the product not only of labelling (Scheff, 1974), but also of wider cultural constructions of in/competence, mal/adaptive behaviour and intelligence (Goodley, 2001). This work has been heavily influenced by the UCLA Mental Retardation Research, particularly the work of Edgerton (Edgerton, 1967, 1976, 1984a, 1984b; Edgerton and Bercovici, 1976). Langness and Levine (1986b) point out, following Edgerton (1967), that US estimates suggest that 75–85% of all 'retarded' individuals are considered 'mildly retarded', and therefore lack an organic basis to the 'condition'. Underpinning these cultural formations is a testing culture based around a spurious (at worst), culturally relative (at best), concept of (low) intelligence.

Thinking point: In 1970, the North American President's Committee on Mental Retardation produced a report entitled The 'six-hour mentally retarded child: A Report' *which concluded that between 9am and 4pm, five days a week, a whole host of children were defined and reacted to as 'retarded children' purely on the basis of their IQ scores (Langness and Levine, 1986b). That most of these children were Puerto Rican, African-American, Mexican-American and Hawaiians raised significant questions about the objectivity of scores and the cultural insensitivities of schools to educate children of colour. Why do you think Puerto Rican, African-American, Mexican-American and Hawaiian children were overrepresented in the intellectually disabled population?*

The testing, measurement and sifting of children has been linked to the increased marketisation of education, which calls for ever more performances on the part of schools and pupils and, in contrast, the growth in the identification of students who do not achieve. As we shall see in Chapter 9, this has created schools that are hostile to difference, particularly difference that disrupts the performance of schools. To ignore these socio-cultural and economic factors 'renders the complexity of retardation into an over-simplified "condition" – something that one has or does not have that may be referenced to some underlying medical or cognitive deficiency' (Levine and Langness, 1986: 203). For Koegel (1986: 47), a socio-cultural understanding of intellectual disabilities is a necessary antidote to the ideological dominance of medicalisation and functionalism:

> However much we pay lip service to the influence of socio-cultural factors, we *do* primarily see mentally retarded people as a biomedical phenomenon and we *do*, as a result, tend to attribute incompetent behaviour to physiologically causes. (Italics in the original)

In contrast, radical humanism offers cultural critique.

Thinking point: 'Mental retardation [sic] is, in fact, a socio-political not a psychological construction. The myth, perpetuated by a society which refuses to recognise the true nature of its needed social reforms, has successfully camouflaged the politics of diagnosis and incarceration' (Bogdan and Taylor, 1982: 15). Discuss.

Similarly, Levine and Langness (1986: 191) conclude:

> Mental retardation [sic] is as much or more a social and cultural phenomenon as it is a medical – genetic or cognitive – psychological one. … The definition of retardation [sic], then, and some of the consequences of being thus labelled are concomitants of social life.

Intellectual disabilities are understood as an ideological construction – a creation of culture, politics and society – a category of mass education, differentiation, testing and auditing. In similar ways to the study of racialisation, in which race becomes made through the processes of culture, disablism is related to the procedures of individualism, psychologisation and medicalisation that rank a population in terms of traits or cultural signifiers. Racism and disablism are complex ideological apparatuses of domination that are intricately linked to the conservation of power and control over resources and material wealth (Darder and Torres, 2009: 159). Moreover, by studying deviance we can learn something about normalcy (Edgerton, 1976) and through analysing normalcy we can understand the ideological necessity for abnormalcy (Davis, 1995). The nature of sanity evokes cultural constructions of insanity (Levine and Langness, 1986). We are reminded of the work of Gramsci (see Oliver, 1990) with its focus on the makings of dominant culture: hegemony. The 'normal' is a hegemonic idea crucial to the esoteric progress of industrialisation: an ideological consolidation of the power of the bourgeoisie (Davis, 1995: 49) and resultant preferred cultural practices:

> The notion of disability reveals the epistemological bases and dialectical relations inherent in any notion of aesthetics … [we need a study of] the complex interactions between the body, the text and the world. (Davis, 1995: 124–125)

The problems of contemporary society are those that deviate from middle-class, small-town ways of living, that threaten the stability of the precarious ideal of normal living (Wright Mills, 1970: 99). The disabled body, then, becomes a cultural container for all the baggage of the precious normal body. The disabled body provides a metaphorical crutch for the sustenance of 'abled' culture: it becomes a body that sparks cultural fascination but also rejection (Fox and Lipkin, 2002). In order to cherish the hegemonic (the able), we make abject the alternative (the disabled). Individuals and their bodies become the anchor for stability of self and the immutable nature of the normal. Highly individualistic and self-absorbed tendencies underpin hostile cultures of disablism and contribute markedly to the exclusion of disabled people. As we shall see in later chapters of the book, the cultural construction of disability relies on the idealisation of the individual – and related personhood, self and subjectivity – that are demanded and interpolated by contemporary culture. The ideal individual of contemporary culture is productive and normal. The individual is a key aspect for the reproduction of ideology which:

> takes every child at infant-school age, and then for years, the years in which the child is most 'vulnerable', squeezed between the family state apparatus and the educational state apparatus, it drums into them … a certain amount of 'know-how' wrapped in the ruling ideology. … Somewhere around the age of sixteen, a huge mass of children are ejected 'into production'. (Althusser, 1971: 174)

Ghai (2006) suggests that a radical humanist perspective critically analyses beliefs, values and cultural understandings, to free us from the bondage of disablism.

Thinking point: Read the following extract:

2 February 2008
Down's syndrome bombers kill 91
Baghdad's fragile peace was shattered yesterday when explosives strapped to two women with Down's syndrome were detonated by remote control in crowded pet markets, killing at least 91 people in the worst attacks that the capital had experienced for almost a year. (www.timesonline.co.uk/tol/news/world/iraq/article3287373.ece)

How would you explain this incident in relation to sociological theories of disability?

Regardless of how we might view the war in Iraq, what emerges here is a particular view about the value of disabled bodies. As we shall explore in Chapter 6, social psychoanalytic theorists might understand the sacrifice to traditional law of undesirable women as their last attempt at redemption: 'their difference can only be forgiven through their sacrifice as a form of purification ritual' (K. Oliver, 2007: 353). As we saw in the last chapter, ideologies of dis/abl(e)ism are closely tied to ideologies of heterosexism, racism and colonialism. And in a critique of ideology we attempt to find spaces for resistance (Giroux, 2003, 2004, 2009).

Radical structuralism and the materialist social model

Radical structuralism – specifically historical materialism – has heavily influenced British disability studies (e.g. Finkelstein, 1981a, 1981b, 1981c, 1996, 2001; Abberley, 1987; Ryan and Thomas, 1987; Barnes, 1990, 1991, 1998; Oliver, 1990, 1996; Zarb, 1992; Morris, 1993b; Gleeson, 1999a, 1999b; Thomas, 1999, 2007; Barton, 2001). This perspective is the foundational principle of the social model introduced in Chapter 1, reflecting the influence of Marxist sociologies in the 1970s, through which issues such as illness and disability were understood as products of capitalism. Key units of analysis include material conditions of labour, transport and leisure (Gleeson, 1999b). Power is centred in the external, material world, not in people's heads. Ideology is therefore a tool of ruling class structures that maintain unequal means of production. Radical structuralists seek to resurrect militant democratic socialism as a basis for imagining a life beyond the dream world of capitalism (Giroux, 2004: 32). The work of Marx and Engels (e.g. 1832/1962, 1845) and neo-Marxists such as Althusser (1971) and Illich (e.g. llich et al., 1977) were influential in conceptualising the disability professions as key practitioners of the state: maintaining their status through reproducing ruling ideologies that reduced disabled people to passive recipients of state intervention. The imperialist tendencies of medicalisation were viewed as practices that upheld class inequalities, spawning anti-psychiatrists such as R.D. Laing, whose work combined an interest in destabilising psychiatry and Marxist ideas of emancipation. As survivors of mental health systems have long pointed out, 'mental illness' is closely tied to the capitalistic necessity for healthy, pliant workers (Sayce, 2000).

Materialist analyses view the categories of disability/impairment as essential to a capitalist system's exclusion of certain social groups from participating in economic activity (Erevelles, 2005: 433). Disabled people become ever more excluded by capitalism as it develops modes of production that make labour a commodity to be bought and sold in the market. As Gleeson (1999a, 1999b) argues, rather than changing attitudes (a position associated with interpretivism) or cultural imagery (oft-linked to radical humanism), the materialist social model gave a political-ethical dimension to the study of disability through addressing material needs via increased socio-political participation and socio-spatial inclusion (Gleeson, 1999a: 150). As Apple (1982: 165) puts it, 'material and ideological conditions provide the conditions of existence for a good deal of our social formation'. Finkelstein's (1981b) analysis of the changing position of disabled people from feudal society to three phases of capitalist society presents a classic materialist analysis of disablement (adopted and developed by such luminaries as Barnes, Oliver and Gleeson). Feudal societies offered at least some opportunities for work in small communities. Disabled people had, to varying extents, community belonging supported by families and church (Phillips, 2009). While feudal/peasant societies created work regimes which matched, to some extents, bodily capacities of members, from the sixteenth century onwards labour became increasingly a commodity to be bought and sold in employment markets outside the home, village or community (Gleeson, 1999b).

Thinking point: A Marxist account of disability. Finkelstein (1981b) argues that while early capitalism (phase 1) offered some inclusion in the community through disabled people's involvement in small-scale cottage industries, the rapid growth of manufacturing and machinery supplanted their contribution to a growing labour force. Phase 2 saw manufacturing industries such as coal and steel expanding. Mass migration from rural to urban areas increased exponentially. Industrialisation deskilled and impoverished disabled people who had previously worked in agrarian communities (Slee, 1996: 99). Many disabled people, deemed incapable of offering labour, quickly joined the unemployed in the cities.

> *Industrialisation demanded fit workers. Factories exposed uncompetitive workers. Institutionalisation provided a means of controlling non-viable workers and, in contrast, developed new forms of labour for those working in them (Barnes et al., 1999: 14–20). Phase 3, late capitalism, offers more opportunities for consumer groups and disabled people's organisations to challenge their exclusion from mainstream life. What are the strengths and weaknesses of this account? What is missing from this analysis? To what extent is it possible to explain the politics of disability through reference to economic modes of production?*

Questions remain about the inclusion of disabled people in the labour market (Barnes and Roulstone, 2005). Late capitalism has spawned a knowledge economy that might include some disabled people, for example through the use of enabling technologies (Roulstone, 1998; Meekosha, 2002), though this will also exclude many others too (for example, those with the label of intellectual disabilities). Add to this the rapid rise in numbers of helping professions and disabled people are increasingly the objects of professional intervention rather than the active subjects of the labour market.[8] Historical materialists explore the conditions of material exclusion and social marginalisation (rather than psychological discrimination) that occur as a consequence of people's direct experience of the physical world. Materialists, as Meekosha (2004: 11) puts it, share the common aim of accounting for disability in ways that stress the systemic nature of the social order and its reinforcement of powerful institutions and their capacity to enact and impose definitions and allocate resources. The economic value of disabled people is inevitably tied to economic rationalism. As Oliver (1990: 44) contends:

> The requirements of the capitalist economy were for individuals to sell their labour in a free market and this necessitated a break from collectivist notions of work as the product of the family and group involvement. It demanded nothing less than the ideological construction of the individual … the isolated, private individual appeared on the historical stage.

Radical structuralism politicises disability: shifting the problem from the interiority of the functionalist body to the exteriority of capitalist structures and modes of domination. The institutions of the family, education, care and welfare are viewed as organisationally structured and tuned to the purposes of international capitalism (Bratlinger, 2004). Mass education provided control of disintegrative and anarchistic forces, thought to be latent in unsocialised and uneducated people, and sought to grade and upgrade the labour force to better support an expanding capitalist system (Gerber, 1996: 160). To contend that disablism is a matter of cultural production, identity formation or bodily deficiency ignores the deeply divisive nature of capitalist economies that render disabled people open to exploitation. To this end, then, radical structuralism excludes the individual, their subjective accounts and the body, in favour of a macro-sociological focus on the social system (Turner, 2008: 34), with all the dis/advantages this entails.

Post-conventional sociologies

In reality, sociologies of disablism cast their net across the bows of many different perspectives. The social and minority models of disability, developed respectively in British and North American contexts, are testimony to the privileging of personal accounts of disabled people (interpretivism) that, as a consequence of their telling, have troubled material structures (structuralism) and normate cultures (humanism) of disabling society. As we shall see in Chapter 6, feminists straddle materialist (structuralists) and idealist (radical humanist and interpretivist) positions through their interest in the psychological experiences of disablism. It is possible to read Hunt's (1966) classic personal attack on the stigmatisation of disabled people as a piece that combines subjective qualities of a personal account (interpretivism) with a hardened neo-Marxist understanding of the social world (radical structuralism) that says much about the exclusionary culture of disabling society (radical humanism). Indeed, in Goodley et al. 2011, it is suggested that Hunt's work can be read as a piece of cultural critique synonymous with psychoanalytic ideas (a stance we develop in Chapter 8 of this book). The work of Edgerton, Bogdan and Taylor can be seen as straddling storytelling (interpretivism) and ideology critique (radical humanism). Davis (1995, 2002), writing from cultural and literary disability studies, articulates a strong radical humanism position heavily influenced by critical theories from radical structuralism. McRuer and Wilkerson (2003: 14) combine radical humanist, queer and radical structuralist analyses when they argue that 'too much disability threatens to disrupt or halt the system, so even as capitalism has desired disability to define able-bodiedness or to maximise profit, it has disavowed it, or institutionalised it, or left it to die in the streets'. Finally, one might occupy different sociological positions in the short space of time of a research journey, as articulated by Goodley and Lawthom (2005a).

Such boundary breaking might explain why sociologies of disablism are increasingly more in tune with post-conventional or postmodern debates. Contributions from, for example, Corker and French (1998), Corker and Shakespeare (2002), Price and Shildrick (1999), Davies (2002), Tremain (2005a) and Ghai (2006), capture the methodology of postmodernism – poststructuralism – that shares much with a radical humanist position, but goes further to disrupt and explode epistemological positions. As we shall see in Chapter 7, disability is constructed and replenished through the use and enactment of discourses, ideas and practices, tied to various institutions of society (Goodley, 2004: 121–122).

Thinking point: Gabel and Peters (2004: 587) argue that a postmodern position negates the likelihood of objective reality, assumes that ambiguity is at play in the world, and destabilises notions of oppositional power relations by revealing the tensions and paradoxes of the social world. This postmodern attitude has placed sociological theory in disability studies in a creative position of 'snagging ideas, blurring paradigmatic lens and breaking distinction between subjectivism/objectivism and post/structuralism' (2004: 591). What are the potential pitfalls of this approach to the study of disablism?

Freed from a firm foundationalist position, post-conventional theories allow us to ask questions about the constitution of impairment, dis/ability and dis/ablism, not simply in terms of ideas, words and meanings, but also in relation to theories of the human and social sciences and practices of the social world. Anti-foundationalism should not be equated with 'anything goes', but considered as a strategy – to gather sociological ideas from a number of foundational positions in order to theorise and challenge disablism. This might aid us in the analysis of what Christensen (1996) defines as the 'bivalent social injustice of disablism': the socio-economic and cultural oppression of disabled people. This allows us to ask questions about the makings of dis/ability in contemporary society. Who benefits from conceptualising disability in functionalist ways? To what extent can we argue that a materialist/radical structuralist view of disablism implicitly holds on to a problematic conception of the materially impaired body and mind? If disability is culturally constituted, is the impaired body also a cultural construction? How is the self made through its relationship with others – including small others (people) and big others (discourses and ideology)? What does a study of disability tell us about the rest of society? What similar challenges do disabled people, women, people of colour, poor people and those with non-normative sexualities face? Who is producing the sociological knowledge in disability studies and who benefits? What kinds of sociological theory can be developed in disability studies that are in tune with the damaging impacts (and perhaps potentiality) of globalisation? Scholars from distinct positions will be able to provide specific answers to these questions, but it is helpful to think across perspectives in order for you to develop responsive and explanatory sociological theories.

Conclusions

Sociology has played a huge role in the development of disability studies. The extent to which it allows discussion of psychological, individual, relational, educational and community concepts remains questionable. While we will interrogate these psychical and socio-cultural realms in this book – drawing in ideas from outside sociology – the sociological attitude of ensuring a critical and political view of disability will be maintained. It is impossible to interrogate the politics of disablism without at least some grasp of the wealth of analyses offered from sociology. Indeed, if we keep disablism as a sociological problem through and through, then we lessen the risk of individualising the problems of disability, impairment and disablism.

Further reading

Gabel and Peters (2004). Scans across different epistemological positions towards an argument for the use of theories that attend to resistance of disabled people.

Goodley and Lawthom (2005a). Develops further the Burrell and Morgan typology of theory and applies it to community psychology and disability studies.

Oliver (1996). A collection of ideas from the man some believe is the 'Godfather' of disability studies in the UK.

Priestley (1998). Excellent account of epistemological positions occupied by disability scholars.

Thomas (2004). Takes a couple of positions in disability studies and teases out their sociological merits.

Notes

1 As Thomas (2007) shows, medical sociology has always been pulled in a number of directions, some more radical and politicised than others. She suggests that contemporary medical sociologists are open to reconceive their work in light of the maturing sociological theories emerging from disability studies.
2 This debate was to fuel discussions around the use of qualitative research in sociology. Work by Nisbet (1976) and Bertaux (1981) championed the promotion of critical, idiographic approaches to the study of sociological problems at a time when pseudo-positivistic approaches were the preferred methodology.
3 Greenop (2009) offers a more sympathetic reading of Parsons, suggesting that his theories at the very least understand the sick role as one intimately related to social expectations about a social role and trajectory: the sickness career. This offers a less reductionist view of the sick role by situating it in terms of social expectations.
4 Shield (1992) makes a similar point about the dominance of functionalism in psychology that has helped contribute to a deficit view of 'woman'.
5 Frank, like many other medical sociologists, often uses 'ill' and 'disabled' interchangeably.
6 This view of the ill body as a tragic body is evidenced in a narrative from Charmaz (2004: 990): 'Cynthia [an informant with an acquired impairment] had an earlier view of herself as possessing the bodily attributes of invincibility, agelessness, unceasing functioning, and strong personal control. She had possessed valued identities; she saw valuable attributes that reflected a vital self . . . it stood in stark contrast with how she viewed having a diagnosis of Parkinson's disease. Cynthia recalled her thoughts and feelings when she received her diagnosis as "disaster. The end. Kaput."'
7 Parker (2007: 116–117) describes the critical theory of the Frankfurt school, and other radical humanists, as opposing positivist neutrality; a shift from crude economics to consciousness; a view of individualism as destructive and a shared ambition to recover human potential from the oppressive and dialectical markings of capitalist life.
8 Radical structuralists such as Oliver and Barnes, have clearly demonstrated the direct relationship between the rise of capitalism and the emergence of 'scientific' theories such as Social Darwinism, through which 'industrial' and 'evolutionary' development were fused as one.

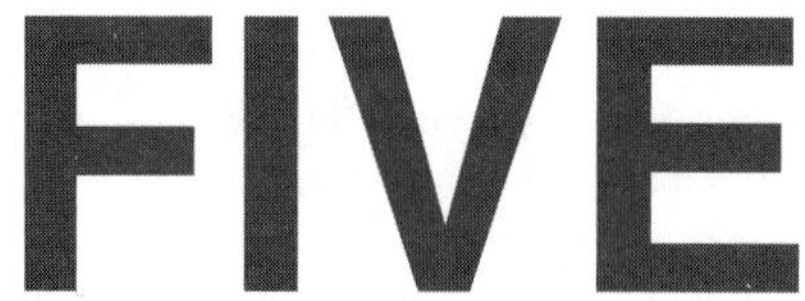

FIVE

Individuals: *De-psychologising Disability Studies*

****

Introduction

Why is disability understood as a problem that resides in the individual? What is 'the individual' and what kinds of individuals are valued by contemporary society? How have the social and human sciences contributed to common-sense understandings of what it means to be an individual? When we think of the 'disabled person' what frames of reference do we draw on to judge that personhood? What dominant 'other' is the disabled individual expected to judge themselves against? This chapter addresses these questions by considering the individual to be a problematic phenomenon, cherished and reified by capitalist societies of the Global North, which must be challenged by disability studies. We will consider how theories from psychology have helped to form what we know as 'the individual'.

The makings of the individual: psychology's subject

? *Thinking point: Consider these three quotations:*

> *It annoys me when able-bodied people hold forth about how we should be as independent as possible. Of course we should but I'd like to hear some talk about the able-bodied being a bit more independent too – how many of them cut their own hair for goodness sake? (Elsa, in Campling, 1981: 85)*
>
> *Whether it is the 'species typical body' (in science), the 'normative citizen' (in political theory), the 'reasonable man' (in law), all these signifiers point to a fabrication that reaches into the very soul that sweeps us into life. (Campbell, 2009: 7)*

> *The 'self-made man' is a fitting metaphor for the right, and 'good things happen to good people' a fitting motto. (Bratlinger, 2001: 4)*

What do these statements say about the kind of individual valued by contemporary society?

In this chapter, we follow Oliver (1990, 1996) when he suggests that *individualisation* is at the very centre of disablement. As Michalko (2002) argues, the problem of disability is firmly tied to the constitution of idealised individuals and their monstrous alternatives. A crucial element of individualisation is the process of *psychologisation*. This is not the same as psychology. There are, of course, psychological practices with dodgy histories in their treatment of disabled people (though the same can be said of any human and social sciences of disabling societies).[1] And, as we shall we see in Chapter 6, critical psychologies can be exploited for the purposes of disability studies. Psychologisation is a process that is testimony to certain aporias – contradictory assumptions approaches, prejudices and abuses – that emerged from the mapping of the individual by social and human sciences, institutions and nation states (Hardt and Negri, 2000). This chapter deconstructs 'the individual' and the associated elements of autonomy, ability and normality, troubling this very modern sovereign self (Davis, 2006b: xvii).

Let us start with a study. In 2007, the *Medical Hypotheses* journal published a paper by two Italian medics, Drs Mafrica and Fodale (2007). In the article entitled 'Down subjects and Oriental population share several specific attitudes and characteristics' [sic], the authors propose to provide:

> … in light of modern knowledge about the heredity of features, a reflection on those aspects and attitudes which highlight a very particular twinning between a Down person and Asiatic peoples [sic]. (Mafrica and Fodale, 2007: 438)

In their analysis, they list a number of 'similarities' between people with the label of Down syndrome and Asiatic people, including the 'shared typical habitus of squatting down when tired during waiting periods' (found in 'the Vietnamese, the Thai, the Cambodian, the Chinese, while they are waiting at a bus stop', 2007: 438); sitting 'crossed legged while eating, writing, watching TV' (2007: 439); oriental faces (fine, straight hair, fissures of eyes are oblique, short, flat nose); flat knape of neck; short limbs and alterations to the cardiovascular, respiratory, gastroentric and immunitary systems and 'tendencies of both groups to carry out recreative-rehabilitative activities (such as embroidery, wicker-working ceramics, book-binding, etc.)' (2007: 439). They conclude:

> these observations might highlight very interesting aspects connected to the super numeracy chromosome 21 in Down's syndrome, whereas they are natural features of the Asians … perhaps we could even clear Langdon [Down, the originator of Down syndrome] of all blame from the accusation of being a 'racist' for having first observed a sort of twinning which could be looked at in more depth in the light of modern knowledge on the heredity of features and on genic expression and inactivation. (2007: 439)

Thinking point: Thinking back to Chapter 4, which of the four sociological approaches would you assign to the study by Mafrica and Fodale (2007)?

This bizarre study, published in an established medical journal, highlights the individualism that dominates studies of disability. Human nature is explained in terms of the dispositional characteristics of particular individuals. So acceptable is this functionalist account, that accusations of racism and disablism can seemingly be surmounted in the name of 'good science'. Human nature is located in the individual raced/disabled body, receptive to study and observation, and generalisable, in this case, to whole sections of the Asiatic world and people with a specific label of intellectual disabilities. This study might be seen less as a strange outlier of the literature and more as a cultural vent of the individualisation of disability and the makings of non/disabled individuals.

The origin of the individual has been documented in many histories of social science and philosophical expositions of the Renaissance, imperialism, modernity, capitalism and patriarchy (Fox Keller, 1962). Davis (1995, 2002) and Finlay and Langdridge (2007) explain Cartesian dualism that followed the work of neoclassical scholars such as the seventeenth-century philosopher René Descartes, which saw human subjectivity as separate and fundamentally different from the objective world of matter and bodies. The mind was celebrated, individual human freedom upheld, each contrasted with the unruly depths of the body and the natural world. Western culture soaked up the mind–body dualism and unknowingly reproduced it. This, Finlay and Landbridge (2007: 75) argued, was particularly the case in social scientific disciplines such as psychology, in which 'the psychological and social complexity' of the individual and its body become lost.

Thinking point: 'Modernism is typically traced to the period in which culture moved from the so-called Dark Ages of medievalism (characterised by an unquestioning adherence to totalitarian royal or religious decree) to the Enlightenment (promising the bounded and sacred sanctuary of the mind, autonomous capacities and the beginnings of systematic human science)' Gergen, 2001: 803–804). The drawing of a boundary between nature and culture is distinctive to modernity (Tremain, 2000). The individual we have come to cherish is a 'post-Cartesian entrenchment of the notion that the self-possessive inviolability of the bounded body grounds the autonomous subject' (Shildrick, 2007a: 225). What is the modern individual's relationship with (a) religion, (b) the monarchy, and (c) science?

The 'individual' has a long socio-political history and etymology. It is tied to the Enlightenment rise of the *reasoned* individual and *his* democracy, over the sovereignty of church and monarchy. The 'individual' is also the creation of capitalism, a convenient signifier of an alienating symbolic order, which masks the inequities of social and political life. And individuals populate consumerist and marketised forms of education, work and leisure. Those able to benefit from this meritocracy flourish while the less able tend to flounder. In dominant ideas of everyday life, the 'individual' remains the key site of understanding for the aetiology of disablism. As Spivak (1985: 344) coins it, 'individualism in an age of imperialism relates to the making of human beings – the constitution and interpellation of the subject not only as an individual but as individualist'. Foucault provides a telling critique of this Cartesian subject, of which Biesta (1998: 5) explains:

> Foucault puts into question the very idea that there exists such a thing as a 'natural subject' that only needs to be interpreted. He stresses that the individual 'is not a pre-given entity which is seized on by the exercise of power,' it is itself 'the product of a relation of power exercised over bodies, multiplicities, movements, desires, forces' ... This at least can be learned from Foucault's *genealogical* writings, where he develops the thesis that the objects of the objectifying social sciences and the subjects of the subjectifying social sciences are the 'instrument-effects' of specific historical forms of power, namely disciplinary power ... and pastoral power.

In key texts such as *Discipline and Punish* (1977), *History of Sexuality* (1978), *The Birth of the Clinic* (1973a), *Madness and Civilisation* (1973b), Foucault variously describes a change in the ways in which citizens of societies are ordered, administered and disciplined by the institutions and human sciences of modern society. The Foucauldian accounts of Ball (1990), Allan (1999) and Armstrong (2002), for example, document the modernist move from the 'brute' sovereign powers of Church and monarchy to the 'humane' self-disciplining powers of citizenship, democracy and mass education. The individual becomes the hub around which is organised the maintenance of discipline, citizenship, rights and responsibilities demanded of democratic governments and its institutions of school, prison, welfare institution and workplace. Discourses of these institutions and their professionals served the disciplining of the individual. Human and social sciences informed their knowledge about the individual. But these sciences did not simply provide understandings of the individual: they made the individual in their own image.

We will return to Foucault later in Chapter 7. For now, let us consider how the human and social sciences helped to understand/create this individual of modern times. Clearly, the wide expanse of social science is too much to take on in this text, so let us turn briefly to the discipline of psychology, with a particular focus on its morphology during the twentieth century. The historiography of psychology is full of heretical characters and dramatic fractures. The account provided below attempts to pick up on a few of these fractures, to deconstruct 'psychology's individual', to contest the 'error-laden notion of the individual as whole, complete, perfect and self-sustaining' (Davis, 2006c: 236).

Average individuals

Psychology's history is one intertwined with biomedical approaches to the mind and body (Jung, 2002), the restoration of normality (Oliver, 1996), a jostling for position among the natural sciences (Kuhn, 1968), a key consultative role in various forms of state administrative rule (Rose, 1979) and a core discipline for the developing welfare services (Bogdan and Taylor, 1982). Key to the formation of the psychological individual was the discovery of the norm (Figure 5.1).

Davis (1995) provides a thoughtful account of the interlinking of 'norming', statistical analysis, eugenics and evolutionary social Darwinist theories of Karl Pearson

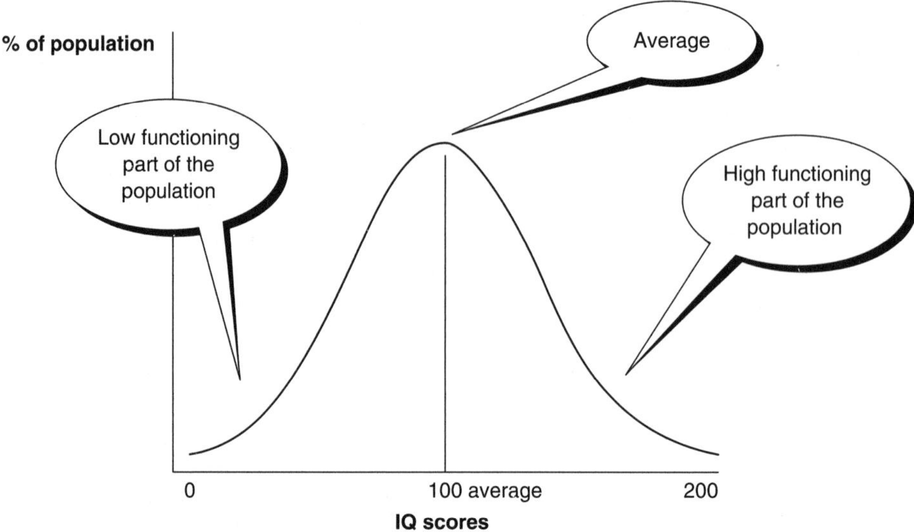

Figure 5.1 Norming the population

and Francis Galton in late nineteenth- and early twentieth-century thought. In these practices we can find the roots of normalcy. Davis (1995) argues that the 'normal individual' (and its counterpart the 'feebleminded, parasitic and morally questionable') is part of the history of modernist progress, industrialisation and the ideological consolidation of the power of the bourgeois. 'An able body', he argues, 'is the body of a citizen'. By contrast, 'deformed, deafened, amputated, obese, female, perverse, crippled, maimed and blinded bodies do not make up the body politic' (Davis, 1995: 71–72). The statistical average becomes equated with 'average man' – 'L'homme moyen' of the statistician Quetelet, who was working in the nineteenth century – typifying the expected and cherished norms of the ruling classes of a given time. For Davis, the attitudes of middle-class society can be characterised as a sensibility of individualism: the drama of individual attainment, exploration and achievement over the wild savagery of nature. The achievements of average man casts average man as heroic character. While it is possible to trace various civilisations rejecting disabled bodies and minds long before the twentieth century,[2] the sensibility of the average individual, Davis argues, seeped into early twentieth-century pseudoscientific theories of humanity and the population, to the extent that the norm and average became confused and fused as the same entity. As a result, psychological understandings of human development came to view the norm-as-average-as-natural.

Measuring the norm has served psychology well over the years, permitting psychologists to play an increasingly influential role in the social administration, assessment and classification of the population in the institutions of schools, prisons, work, welfare, social and health sectors. This, according to Rose (1985), has allowed psychologists to develop an industry around the individual, namely the *psy-complex*. Capitalist societies have administratively separated individuals on the basis of nativist-norming notions, such as ability and intelligence. We know, for example, that the entire category of borderline mental retardation was dropped in 1973 from the American Association on Mental Deficiency's *Manual of Terminology* – due to a shift in the use of IQ scores – ensuring

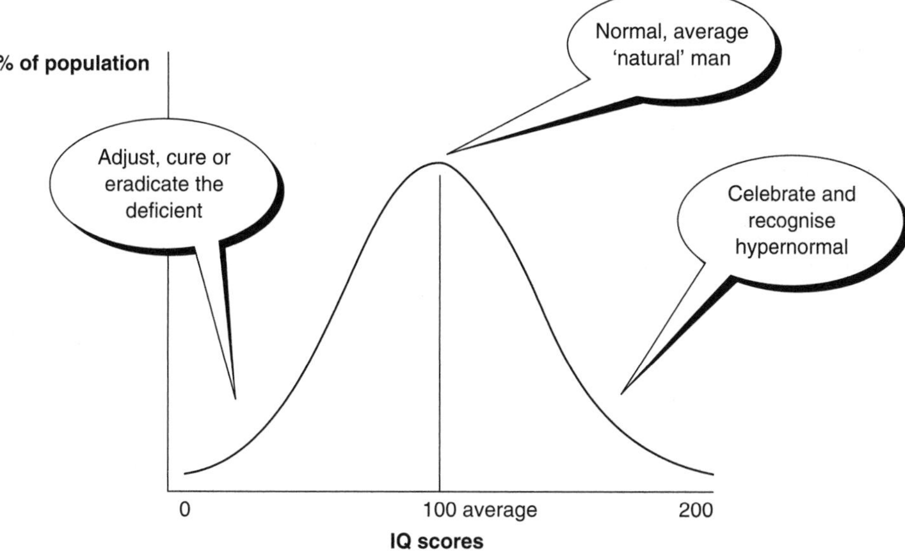

Figure 5.2 Treating the norm

that 'thousands were cured' overnight (see Ferguson et al., 1992).[3] For Michalko (2002: 30), the dominance of norming ideas around disabled individuals dismisses the metaphysical question of 'why me'? as superfluous:

> What shall we do now you are disabled?
> We shall cure you.
> How shall you live when our cure fails and you are now permanently disabled?
> You shall adjust.

Thinking point: What model of disability (Chapter 1) and sociological theory (Chapter 4) is Michalko describing?

Post-war, North American social psychological ideals of the individual implicitly and explicitly mirrored the values of those theorists who proffered them (Wright Mills, 1970). Social problems were understood as those events and occasions that deviated from the middle-class, small-town backgrounds of their bourgeois authors. Problems were found when certain individuals failed to fall in line with the stale principles of the American middle classes. Problems were marked by deviant individuals who threatened the consensual and valued idea(l)s of social theorist and their theories. The individual is closely tied to the social fabric of the status quo: a model and marker of societal progress and civilisation. Individuals who step out of such an ideal are dealt with accordingly. Groome (2007: 3) comments that in a more 'naïve time', disruptive individuals were simply exiled: 'by joining the French foreign legion or practising Zen or going on jungle safaris'. However, by the time of the late twentieth century, 'with the invention of modern designer drugs such as Prozac', these same individuals were now expected 'to be calm': drugged and compliant (Figure 5.2).

Self-contained individualism

In a landmark text, Henriques et al. (1984), Venn (1984) asks how does psychology understand its subject? Venn traces his answer back to modernist and Renaissance roots. The core conception of psychology's subject, the ***unitary rational subject***, is the sovereign self of modern individualism. As part of the modernist project, psychology became the science of the individual subject. This science, Venn argues, functions as a discourse that participates positively in the construction of the social world and the instrumental rationality of the individual (Venn, 1984: 122). Psychology is a science that speaks of the individual. Psychology has long held implicit assumptions (that are then made explicit) *about* the individual, and conversely, what is *required* to be an individual. The accepted individual, to whom many of us are expected to mirror, is adult, male, middle-class, heterosexual, rule-abiding, sane, non-disabled and European.[4] The converse – the Other – is the unacceptable: child, female, working-class, homosexual, criminal, insane, disabled, and resolutely non-European. Venn suggests that in order to promote the desired individual what is required is an obsessional focus on the abject Other, normalising and disciplining this section of the population as part of the quest for the model citizen and rational self.

The work of the American psychologist Edward Sampson has critically evaluated the individual that was created through this unholy alliance of cultural hegemony and psychological knowledge. Sampson (1977) describes our cultural ethos as the era of the ***self-contained individual***. This idealised form of personhood refers to a private, egocentric, self-sufficient, independent, agentic, cultural paragon who has little need for others, is antithetical to the notion of interdependence and mutuality, is inherently masculine and suitably (com)pliant to educational, workplace and industrial management. This ideal becomes psychology's big 'discovery' and the preferred ontological destiny for all persons. Psychology holds this aloft as an ideal to be achieved:

> By ignoring the cultural and historical conditions that present this as an ideal, it [psychology] fails to provide an adequate assessment of alternatives or the implications that derive from its ideal. For example, does self-contained individualism offer a reasonable way of dealing with the massive problems that confront a complex and interdependent world? (Sampson, 1977: 774)

The individual of post/industrial societies is a 'normal' one who will contribute to the making of society. An individual is ready, able and (preferably) willing: as a body-of-functions (Michalko, 2002: 156). A strange paradox emerges for disabled people. While they are cast as the dependent other, when they do attempt to gain a foothold on the ladder of individualism then they are expected to demonstrate extra-special, hyper-individual forms of being in order to maintain their place. As disability activist Martin Levine puts it, 'If someone else whispers a lot during the play people might ignore it or get angry. If we whisper it is because we are retarded [sic]. It's like we have to be more normal than normal people (in Freidman-Lambert, 1984: 15). Parents with the label of intellectual disabilities, for example, have to reach gold standards of parenting capabilities that are not expected of other non-disabled parents (Booth and Booth, 1994, 1998). Disabled people have to out-perform non-disabled people in their level of self-contained individualism. To show they *really* are able (not disabled) and

	Type 1 Self-contained individualism	Type 2 Ensembled individualism
Self/other boundary	Firm – 'peculiar' and 'eccentric' version of self; ideas planted early in history of western society and developed by capitalism (Morris, 1972)	Fluid – 'majority world' versions of self; captured in Maori (New Zealand/Aotearoa) and Chewong (Malaysian) cultures and beliefs such as Islamic thought (Harré, 1984)
Control	Personal – based on egocentric models of psychology; related to personal achievement of atomistic individuals; qualities of character	Field – based on socio-centric models; related to relational actions of communities of individuals; community cohesion
Conceptions of person/self	Excluding – an ontology of exclusion; internally directed subjectivism found in Shakespeare's time and characteristic of contemporaneous views of the person; atomistic strangers; independent and separated	Including – an ontology of inclusion; self-defined in relation to others; to be found in non-western, majority world contexts, 'I am who I am through my relations with other'; 'I am completed through these relations'; interdependent and connected

Figure 5.3 Self-contained and ensembled individualism: adapted version of Sampson's two indigenous psychologies of individualism (Sampson, 1988: 16)

individuals (not dependents). And if disabled people fail, then a host of professionals lie in wait to aid and (re)habilitate their journey towards self-containment.

Thinking point: To what extent can it be argued that physiotherapy, occupational therapy, psychology and social work seek to produce self-contained clients?

Such a vision of humanity threatens to individualise social life and fails to place people in their social contexts (see Figure 5.3). Type 1 is the preferred type of individual of modern psychology and the Global North. Sampson (1985) explains self-contained individualism through reference to popular psychological theories that helped develop the culturally dominant idea (and psychology's idea) that order and coherence are achieved by means of personal control and mastery. Erickson's (1959) 'ego identity' presents the self as a coherent whole, a desired unity of 'myself', an equilibrium structure designed to sustain the person in a generally stable and orderly state, rather than an undesirable, diffused, chaotic state. Langdon (2009) – no relation to Dr Down – notes that Erickson's last stage of the development of self is 'autonomous man'. The work of another psychologist, Greenwald (1980), is attacked by Sampson for its emphasis on the individual's ego as 'self as a totalitarian state': a person completely in control of themselves. For Sampson (1985: 1204), 'to centre order within the persona is a peculiarly Western worldview' that the individual will be the main architect of order and coherence. We associate a singular individual with control and connect manyness with chaos. In a later paper, Sampson (1993) suggests that psychology's conception of human nature is primarily a white, male and western 'United Statesian' character. Individuals who differ in their 'human nature' (or nationality) come off a poor second. The individual is self-contained in ways best suited to rich nations.

Cognitivism

Thus far, our brief exposition of psychology's individual reveals a deep problem for disabled people. As one informant in Shuttleworth's (2000: 266) study put it, 'we fly in the face of society's emphasis on being in control of one's self'. The problem, however, is not simply disabled people's. For Lash (2001: 109), individualism creates the interiority of the human subject. Nowhere is this more evident than in the epistemology of ***cognitivism***.

From the 1950s onwards, cognitivism provided psychology with what it had been waiting for: a form of scientific and empirical psychology that assumed rational processes of thought, within individual subjects, who were responsive to scientific study, analysis and treatment. The individual-as-cognitively-(dis)abled was rapidly embraced by psychology to categorise short- and long-term memory, assess problem solving, and measure levels of mental processing and conscious decision-making. Here was the all-singing-all-dancing rational thinker, primed and ready for investigation. Cognitivism gave a scientific language to the civilised notion of the *homunculus* – 'little man' in Latin – that is assumed to reside in each and every individual, giving them 'intelligence', 'awareness' and 'abilities' (Thomas and Loxley, 2001: 65). Applied to human beings, cognitivism, and its epistemological ally positivism, enlivens cognition but rarely touches feelings and often renders anonymous the very people it studies (Turner, 2008: 232–233).[5] When one holds that the primary ingredients of the mind are cognitive, this opens some doors but shuts others (Gergen, 2001: 808). Cognitivism has early historical origins in the proliferation of reason and rationality in the eighteenth and nineteenth centuries. As Davis (1995: 3) observes, when modernity's madhouses replaced the leper colonies, they switched the confinement of defects of the *body* to the confinement of defects of the *mind*. Here was an embracing of an age of reason and, by extension, madness. Cognitivism can be viewed as a hyper-reasoned, conscious and reasonable conceptualisation of the individual against which all individuals are universally marked and judged. It is a symptom of the modernist Cartesian distinction of the inner world of the mind and the external world of the social.

Thinking point: Visit the website www.giqtest.com and complete the online intelligence test. After completion, answer the following questions: (1) Do you feel that the test gave a fair measure of your intelligence? (2) Do you think the questions are valid measures of intelligence? (3) Does the test measure forms of intelligence such as emotional intelligence or empathy? (4) What are the limitations of intelligence testing?

The methodologies and ontologies of cognitive research have little time for the conjecture, subjectivity and partisanship of non-cognitivist approaches such as phenomenology and interpretivism, described in Chapter 4. Cognitivism was fit for purpose for psychology's quest for status as a functionalist science. In reality, cognitivism played handmaiden to social values (Shield, 1992: 102).[6] Cognitivism celebrates and measures the occidental logocentric subject so valued by contemporary Global North societies and allows for the sorting of people in terms of their cognitive worth. Deficit thinking is there to be found and eradicated. We should note that this subject is not just valued by cognitive psychologists. Psychoanalytic discourse has been used to advocate for preferred versions of the self – the ego – as the conscious regulatory manager and purveyor of adult consciousness (Parker, 1997). This, Davis (1995: 39) argues, means that psychoanalysis can be dismissed for promulgating the normal through the development of eugenics of the mind (which we will explore in Chapters 6 and 8).[7]

Solitary souls

Cognitivism's self-contained subject required a place in which it could be manipulated, controlled and measured. The experimental laboratory provided such a space (Gergen, 2001). Cognitivism embraces what Wright Mills (1970: 61–65) defines as 'abstracted empiricism', a pronounced tendency to study phenomena only within the curiously self-imposed limitations of an arbitrary epistemology.

? *Thinking point: A university lecturer was teaching a second-year undergraduate class on research methods in psychology. During the first session she asked the class, 'How would you find out how your friend was feeling?' After at least three minutes of silence, a student cautiously raised her hand to answer: 'I would send her a questionnaire.' The lecturer acknowledged that as a valid psychological measure. A short time later another member of the class raised her hand to suggest: 'Could you just ... eh, ring and ask how she was feeling?' What does this anecdote reveal about the status of science in psychological research?*

Psychologists from the 1950s onwards eagerly develop forms of experimentation that aimed to understand the individual. The individual became an ever more ***atomistic, solitary and isolated*** soul, a subject of scientific study that contrasted hugely with the unruly individual outside the laboratory in the 'real world' (Harré, 1984; Parker and Shotter, 1990). Studies such as the Asch paradigm (1951), Milgram's obedience studies and Zimbardo's prison experiment found that normally well-minded and reasonable individuals appeared to become suddenly afflicted by the irrational, infectious and destructive qualities of the social group (see Gabriel, 1985).

? *Thinking point: Type in 'Zimbardo-Stanford Prison experiment' on Google. Find and watch the video. What image of the individual is portrayed by this study?*

As Allport (1947) observed, it seemed as if Le Bon's (1896) conceptualisation of the 'horror of the crowd' infected the majority of social psychologists' understandings of the individual's relationship with others: the mindless entity of the group inflicted anarchy on the normally mild-mannered, self-contained world of the individual. Relationality was considered to be a risk to the atomistic being rather than a condition of being human. Studied in isolation, any problems of the individual (whether physical, sensory or cognitive) were invariably interpreted in isolationist ways: a problem *within* that individual. The social geographer, Sibley (2003: 397), refers to this as 'psychotic individualism: the drawing of strong subject boundaries around particular individual human entities devoid of any recourse to social or cultural formations'. Strange things happen when the complexity of the individual is lost.[8] In their beautifully written account of the experiences of institutionalised adults with the label of learning difficulties, Potts and Fido (1991: 139), conclude:

> Side by side with this painful awareness we have also become sensitive to their humour, resilience and determination. Far from accepting their lot in life, they recognise its injustices and have eagerly grasped the opportunity to give their views.

Similarly, in the conclusion of Ryan and Thomas (1987: 125), they state, 'the desire of mentally handicapped people themselves for a more normal life as part of society ... [is] a desire that is insufficiently heard but nonetheless there to be listened to'. Such conclusions might seem so obvious: of course people (with intellectual disabilities) know what they want from life! However, the omnipresence of atomistic views might explain why social researchers have found it hard to listen to the accounts of 'deficient individuals', because these individuals have been rendered asocial solitary beings.

Developmentalism

Thinking point: Visit the website www.teachernet.gov.uk/teachingand learning/EYFS/learning_development_requirements/early_learning_goals. Outline the key early learning goals for 'under 5s' identified by the British government. What kinds of assumptions do these goals hold about the development of the (normal) child?

A further under-girding assumption of psychology's individual is that of ***developmentalism***. The child is measured to ensure 'normal' development. When 'abnormal' or 'pathological' development is observed, they are classified and corrected. Walkerdine (1993) describes developmental psychology as one of the 'grand meta-narratives of science'; a story where the central character is the individual child but the story is grand, totalising and the story of children's development is made testable. The 'developing child' is not a description of a 'real' entity, but a powerful discursive prescription (Walkerdine, 1993: 454) written on to by a host of expectations such as 'meeting targets', 'age-appropriate behaviour' and marks of deficiency including 'educational subnormality', 'special educational needs' and 'below average intelligence' (see Goodley and Runswick-Cole, 2010). Following Burman (2008), children are understood through the application of developmentalist theories which promise universal progress of emotionality (self-containment), intelligence (cognitivism), independence (mastery) and rationality (reason) that meets an end point of normality (average man) or higher (high functioning man). Woollet and Marshall (1997) argue that while psychologies promoted their stage theories of universal development, in actuality these ideas were based on limited samples of people (normally white, middle-class and American subjects) for which independence, achievement and academic attainment were seen as *the* central tasks of development for *all* children and

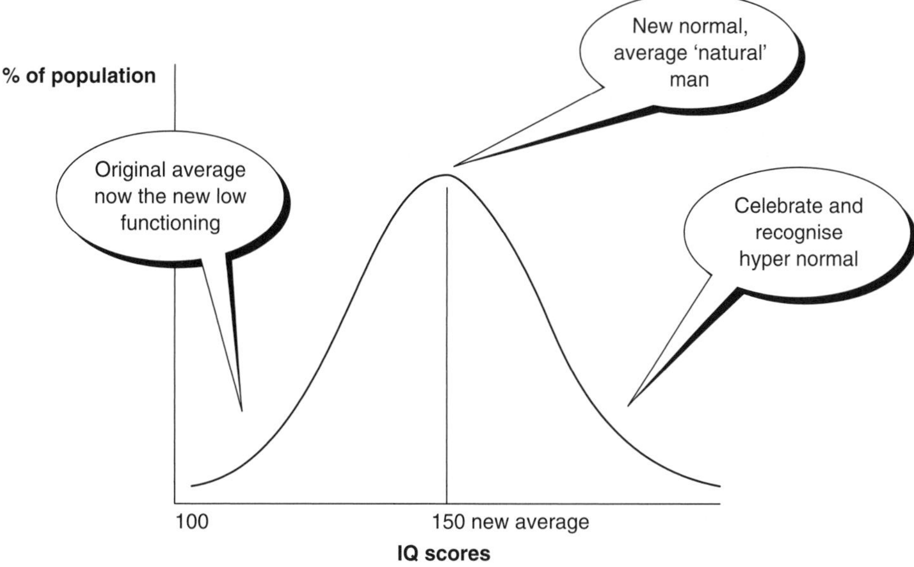

Figure 5.4 Re-norming the population: new averages of Global North countries

adolescence. Indeed, such is the seductive nature of developmentalism, Harwood and Humphrey (2008) observe that in Global North societies, the new average achievement of children expected by parents, schools and teachers is not 'average man' but 'gifted and talented man' (Figure 5.4).

Normalisation

Key to the makings of the developing individual is the process of ***normalisation***. A normalised individual is a confessional individual who is all too ready and willing to share their innermost thoughts and worries, not just with professional counsellors and therapists, but also in a public context that demands it. An individual wants to be normal (Parker et al., 1995). Whether psychoanalytic, humanist, complementary, new age or behaviourist, psychosurgery, therapy or self-help book, today's individual is tied to the Global North humanist myth of fullness and bliss, of abstract individualism, 'an ultimate self untied at last from dependency, a man in space' (Haraway, 1991: 151). This myth promotes psychological interventions to cure mental illness, improve education, reduce crime, stamp out prejudice and create fulfilling lives (Gergen, 2001: 804). Disabled people have been subjected to a number of questionable interventions in the name of these aims. When psychologists draw unproblematically on long-established indexes (personality traits, attitude types, social cognitions) of people's inner worlds (emotions and cognitions), they deem some individuals more rational and worthy of social position and wealth than others (Gergen, 2001: 805). A popular signifier of psychology is therapy. For disabled people, therapy equates with oppression. Reeve's (2004) critique of counselling in the lives of disabled people notes a tendency for loss models to dominate the therapeutic context – both therapy room and training literature – with the associated aim of 'adjustment' quickly following behind. She observes that when disabled people do seek counseling, this is automatically assumed to be because they are seeking to deal with the loss of wholeness that accompanies being impaired. They want to be normalised. As we shall see in Chapter 6 and 8, psychoanalysis (as part of a process of psychologisation) has entered popular culture, influencing how non/disabled people make sense of themselves and others. It is therefore important that we tackle the psychoanalytic register as a key site of the constitution of the individual. In particular, a key area of analysis relates to the ways in which psychoanalytic discourse demands its subjects to occupy a peculiarly western or occidental space of sameness and oneness: the healthy self-conscious individual (Venn, 2001).

Psychologisation

As Goodley and Lawthom have argued (Goodley and Lawthom, 2005a, 2005c; Lawthom and Goodley, 2005), developed in the edited collection *Psychology and Disability* (Goodley and Lawthom, 2005b), the components of the individual describe above capture the practices of ***psychologisation***: a view of the individual as a unitary-isolated cognitively-able-rational-developed-innately-normed-consensual being. Psychologisation reduces social problems to the level of the individual (Wright Mills, 1970: 69) and therefore has the potential to be:

- individualistic – the scientific study of mind and behaviour;
- bourgeois – ideas of the majority (and ruling) are exercised over the minority (www.fireflysun.com);
- apolitical – changing individuals rather than society (Masson, 1989);
- professional-led – experts over the lay;
- pseudo-scientific – an emphasis on science and a poor version of it at that;
- normalising – concerned with individuals adjusting to their impairment;
- oppressive – disabled people are mere subjects of psychology's individualising practices.

Psychologisation and its product – preferred individual – maintain the disabling status quo. This has huge implications for the 'disabled individual'.

Disability and the dominant alterity

A key site of the oppression of disabled people pertains to those moments when they are judged to fail to match up to the ideal individual; when they are categorised as embodying the failing individual. Mintz (2002: 162) suggests that social discourses about disability are not about disability at all. Rather they relate to the need to guarantee the privileged status of the non-disabled individual, 'a need that, in turn, emerges from fears about the fragility and unpredictability of embodied identities'. Similarly,

Marks (1999a) observes that disabled people constitute a huge problem for non-disabled society precisely because they disrupt the normative individual. The person that dribbles, she comments, disrupts a culture that emphasises bodily control and associated cultural norms around manners, convention and bodily comportment. An individual whose speech is difficult to understand is assumed to have a problem because they challenge a colonising stance of certainty about how people should speak. People who do not walk are understood as tragic because they do not embody the idealised mobility of the autonomous walker (Oliver, 1993a). People with learning difficulties, who fail to meet developmentalist stages, are discarded from mainstream educational systems because of their lack of fit with educational prerogatives. Individuals who depend on – or require connections with – others to live are not individuals at all. They are burdens. The disabled individual queers and crips the normative pitch of the autonomous citizen.

Alterity

The non-disabled alterity – the Other to disabled people – may be experienced as a threatening place. In recent years, there have been sustained analyses of otherness and the standards against which individuals are expected to judge themselves. So, what is alterity for disabled people? (Table 5.1.)

Thinking point: To what extent do you match up to the Other described in Table 5.1?

Table 5.1 Alterity of disablism

The big Other...	... is constituted through...
Cognitively, socially and emotionally able and competent Biologically and psychologically stable, genetically sound and ontologically responsible	Disabling society (Oliver, 1990, 1996) or ableist society (Campbell, 2008a, 2008b, 2009) Societies governed by bio and thanatopolitics (Rose, 2001); technology (Lash, 2001); new eugenics and Human Genome Project (Davis, 2002)
Normal: sane, autonomous, self-sufficient, reasonable, law-abiding and economically viable	Mentalism and sanism (Chamberlin, 1990; Lewis, 2006); normalcy (Davis, 1995); normate culture (Garland-Thomson, 1996; Michalko, 2002); normative mobility (Shuttleworth, 2002); normalising society (Tremain, 2005a); neurotic society (Marks, 1999a; Olkin and Pledger, 2003); meritocracy (Fukushima, 2009); entrepreneurial society (Masschelein and Simons, 2005)
White, heterosexual, male, adult, living in towns, global citizen of WENA	Heteronormativity (Sherry, 2004); occidentalism (Venn, 2001); colonialism (Fanon, 1993); self-contained individualism (Sampson, 1977, 1985, 1988, 1993); patriarchy, malestream and phallocentric society (Hare Mustin and Marecek, 1992); compulsory heterosexuality, masculinity and ablebodiedness (e.g. Rich, 1980; Connell, 2002; McRuer, 2006)

We will revisit many of the concepts outlined in Table 5.1 throughout this book. Suffice to say, just as 'alterity for the black man is the white man' (Fanon, 1993: 97); alterity for the disabled person is the non-disabled. Clearly, disabled people constitute a heterogeneous group within which there will be multifarious dealings with the world. Disabled men will have fundamentally different engagements with patriarchy from disabled women. Disabled high flyers demonstrate successfully meeting the standards of the Other (Shah, 2005). Moreover, these standards give rise to human diversity and different kinds of individuals. And, alterity can be actively fashioned for the benefit of the individual. Yet all of these forms of the non-disabled Other generate versions of the individual against which we all judge ourselves. Alterity illuminates powerful regimes of truth. One of these, *ableist society*, developed in particular by Campbell (2008a, 2008b, 2009), feeds on the psychologised individual described above. Campbell suggests that disability studies scholars need to shift their gaze from what she ironically terms the 'monstrous other' (disabled people) to the 'extraordinary other' (the abled). She argues that we should concentrate on the production, operation and maintenance of ableist-normativity (2008a: 1). In order to make a self ('the disabled individual') we require the Other ('abled individuals'). Ableist processes create a corporeal standard, which presumes able-bodiedness, inaugurates the norm and purifies the ableist ideal:

> Internalised ableism means that to emulate the norm, the disabled individual is required to embrace, indeed to assume, an 'identity' other than one's own. I am not implying that people have only one true or real essence. Indeed, identity formation is in a constant state of fluidity, multiplicity and (re)formation [but] … the desire to emulate the Other (the norm) establishes and maintains a wide gap between those who are loathed and that which is desired. (Campbell, 2009: 21)

As Fanon (1993: 97) reflects on the White Other:

> I begin to suffer from not being a white man to the degree that the white man imposes discrimination on me, makes me a colonised native, robs me of all my worth, all individuality, tells me that I am a parasite on the world.

The alterity knows disabled people in deficient ways. Disabled people are their impairment. *They* are broken individuals. *They* lack development. *They* cannot do. *They* do not have the abilities to lead an independent life. The dominant Other threatens to create epistemic invalidation: to make disabled people not know themselves (for further discussion, see Wendell, 1996; and Marks, 1999b).[9] When disabled fail to fit the alterity of the ideal individual, they are assigned the position of monstrous other. When the alterity gets hold of disabled people, it is all too ready to try to bring them back into the norm (re/habilitate, educate) or banish them (cure, segregate) from its ghostly centre. Alterity is staffed by individuals whose jobs are to correct monstrous others. Both Gallagher (1976) and MacMillan (1977) remind us that many professionals owe their jobs, many school districts their educational funding and many psychologists their capacity to work, to the labelling of children and the birth of special and inclusive forms of education. But too often is these contexts, the dominant Other negates the monstrous other.

Kennedy (1996: 123) tells of a paediatrician who, on examining a child with 'hypnotonic spastic quadriplegia' (sic), found vaginal injuries, anal scars and a sexually transmitted disease. He reported: 'These symptoms could be due to an obscure syndrome.' Goodwin (1982) recalls the case of a paediatrician belatedly and reluctantly reporting three boys who were having sexual intercourse with their sister, who had the label of learning difficulties. His 'excuse' was 'isn't it better to save three normal boys than one retarded girl? [sic]'. Professional wisdom becomes bound up in the ideals of alterity. The case of a counsellor's comments to a mother whose disabled son had been sexually abused was: 'At least it didn't happen to one of your non-disabled children.'

Dominant alterity struggles with any deviation from the norm-as-average, so new labels emerge each and every week to cope.[10] Alterity supports the demarcation of lives to be saved and lives to be sacrificed. As soon as the 'the disabled' act, their embodiment becomes conceptualised through a symbolic order that cherishes 'autonomy' and dispels difference (Michalko, 2002). A welcoming hand is offered to enter the non-disabled realm, through the restoration of the 'individual', via therapy, rehabilitation and counselling. The alterity separates disruptive individuals from productive individuals (Baker, 2002). It could be argued that the abuse, rejection and marginalisation of disabled people are symptoms of the ableist Other. Precisely because this framework demands logocentric self-contained individuals, and these valued members are conceptualised in direct opposition to disabled people, then disabled people become the ciphers of the failures of ableist society: 'disabled people lack the oneness, sameness and logocentric autonomy, not I!'

Working with/in alterity

While disabled people undoubtedly suffer the psychologisation of alterity, the individual remains a key site of everyday life, oppression and perhaps resistance for *everyone*. The fashioning of our selves takes place in relation to that which we are not: other people. Moreover, as Venn (2001) notes, the multiple objects of otherness allow us to cobble together an ontological sense of who we are. Hence, (disabled) people will find objects within the Other through which to fashion themselves as individuals. Indeed, the disabled people's movement has built a strong case around human rights and human capital, in which they demand to be part of a wider, more inclusive realm of independent living. Although the disabled individual sits uneasily with the narrow construction of the individual in contemporary society, so too do many other members of society, who are judged against equally pernicious standards of worth associated with the fully functioning individual of contemporary society. Indeed, we are *all* engaged in the constitution of ourselves every minute of every day, through our relationship with others. Our task, then, is to uncover new, hybridised forms of otherness that destabilise the individual of psychologisation. We will remain mindful, though, of the pernicious nature of the idealised individual, and its often-damaging impact on the development of psyches (Chapter 6), discourse (Chapter 7), culture (Chapter 8), education (Chapter 9) and forms of activism and community (Chapter 10).

Conclusions

As Garland-Thomson (2002: 20) puts it, disability challenges the cherished cultural belief in the individual and undermines our fantasies of stable, enduring identities. The truth of this individual is that it is a simulacrum, an idealised fantasy of modernity that has never existed (Hardt and Negri, 2000: 151). Biesta (1998: 13) suggests that what is required is a new attitude to the individual – a new style of political judgement and political imagination. An interdependent view of the individual suggests that health and illness are aspects of larger systems and are not located entirely within the single person (Sampson, 1977: 775).

> It is through the effort to recapture the self and to rescrutinise the self … that men [sic] will be able to create the ideal conditions of existence for a human world. … Why not the quite simple attempt to touch the other, to feel the other, to explain the other to myself. (Fanon, 1993: 231)

It is necessary to take seriously the psychologisation of everyday life: to recognise that the individual valued by contemporary society is a complex phenomenon made by long histories of oppression and domination of medicalisation, colonisation, patriarchy and heteronormativity. Shepherd (1966: 61–65) argues:

> Are any of us independent? Are we not all interdependent? … The norm is the man with a house, family, garden, job and a car at the gate. … [W]e have grown up with a great belief in the virtue of endless activity. … [T]he belief that it is better to do something active badly, rather that something more contemplative well, is almost universally accepted in Europe, if not in Asia.

Disability studies may find more answers for emancipation through these interdependent relationships.

Further reading

Campbell (2008a). Snappy overview of ableism.

Michalko (2002). Situates the tragedy of disability in the court of the non-disabled.

Parker, I. (2007). An amusing dismissal of all things 'psychologising'.

Rose (2001). A damning assessment of psychologisation.

Sampson (1977). Deconstructs the individual.

Notes

1 Barnes (2004: 30) defines disability studies as a reaction and challenge to the kind of orthodox thinking about disability hitherto generated in large part by scholars working in the established disciplines of medicine, sociology and psychology.

2 See, for example, Stratford's (1991) account of ancient Greece and the rejection of 'deformed children' and Barnes' (1998) analysis of ancient histories of disablement.

3 For Manion and Bersani (1987: 237), the statistical mode subsumed under the clinical system defines 'normalcy' relative to a frequency distribution of randomly selected individuals. Conversely, 'abnormalcy' is defined according to the extent to which an individual varies from the average of the population on particular traits, such as intelligence and adaptive behaviour. The norming of abnormalcy, therefore, is fundamentally limited and narrow in terms of the variables that are measured.

4 Weiss (1999: 164), following Rosi Braidotti (1994), suggests that in actuality the big subject is reasonable man: 'man-white-western-male-adult-reasonable-heterosexual-living-in-towns-speaking-a-standard-language'.

5 Recently, in the UK, Cognitive Behavioural Therapy has been rolled out as the 'preferred approach' in the public health services (Moloney and Kelly, 2004). This has led to huge debate in the UK around the dangers of CBT swamping the eclecticism of therapy and, more specifically, in relation to the accusations that CBT promotes individualising and conservative forms of counselling provision (House and Loewenthal, 2008).

6 Piagetian ideas of high-level cognitive functioning privileges mathematical and problem-solving types of intelligence over relational and human qualities.

7 Groome (2007: 1) offers a damning assessment of Freudian psychoanalysis's role in the constitution of the contained individual: 'By normal we understand not someone who knows what s/he wants and follows a process of accumulating wealth and health countering death and insanity, but that peculiar modern normality discovered by Freud in a society of consumption where the ego, in its claim to "good sense" and "life", becomes auto-destructive of its health, wealth and others.'

8 See C. Wright Mills (1970: 11 and 50) for a discussion of privacy as a key component of modern individualism: 'if we accept the Greek's definition of the idiot as an altogether private man, then we must conclude that many citizens are indeed idiots.'

9 'Man is human only to the extent to which he tries to impose his existence on another man in order to be recognised by him. As long as he has not been effectively recognised by the other, that other will remain the theme of his actions' (Fanon, 1993: 216–217).

10 At the time of writing, I had collected together a number of labels that parents, students, disabled activists and professionals had shared with me, including 'nearmentia', 'not-right syndrome' and, my personal favourite, 'low-self-esteemism.'

SIX

Psychology: *Critical Psychological Disability Studies*

****

Introduction

What is the psychological impact of living with impairment in a disabling society? How do disabled people deal with demanding publics? Why does normate society react to disabled people in the ways that it does? Could these reactions be understood as deep, unresolved, unconscious conflicts on the part of non-disabled people? Are disabled people feared and loathed as a consequence of non-disabled people's psychological baggage? Impairment conjures up feelings of lack, tragedy, vulnerability and fascination, and disablism clearly has a psychological element to it. Disabled people often complain at becoming the repositories of other's ontological anxieties (Marks, 1999a: 188). This chapter seeks to understand the psychology of these reactions and relationships.

Theorising the psychological

Disabled people's organisations have responded to the psychological impact of living in a disabling society through politicisation (Campbell and Oliver, 1996), the provision of peer counselling (Priestley, 1999) and the promotion of disability acts as powerful forms of catharsis (Hevey, 1992). The self-advocacy movement of people with the label of intellectual disabilities has established safe spaces for the sharing of aspirations (Goodley, 2000), mad pride has subverted normative understandings of sanity (Chamberlin, 1990) and 'queer crips' have celebrated their transgression (McRuer, 2003). Accordingly, disability studies have addressed the psychology of disablism. Fanon (1993: 12–13) describes this as a process of socio-diagnosis: of waging war on levels of both the socio-economic and the psychological. Disablism, like racism, can seriously threaten the ontological lives of disabled people.

Thinking point: 'For Lash (2001:107), ontology is the focal point of contemporary society. 'We are obsessed with life and the organic ... experiencing things, through being in the life-world with them, can open

up knowledge of things-in-themselves. To know things-in-themselves is to know them not epistemologically, but in their ontological structures. This sort of knowledge of deeper, ontological structures is also central to Freud, where the thing-in-itself was the unconscious; and for Marx, where it's social class (Klasse-an-sich). *Thus in forms of life, knowledge takes place in the life-world, through the subject understood as life (the body, class interest, the unconscious, the will to power). Through being no longer above things, but in the world with things, we come to grips not with epistemology and appearances, but with deeper ontological structure'. To what extent can it be argued that disablism threatens to create 'ontological anxiety' on the part of the disabled people?*

We must be careful not to reduce ontology to the individual (as we saw in the last chapter) and appeal instead to a relational ontology. Un/conscious selves and subjectivities are manufactured through our interactions with others. While sociological disability studies reject individualisation, it is possible to hit upon a strong psychological thread of disability studies thinking. In Britain, for example, Oliver et al. (1988), was one of the first disability studies texts to work with a clear politicised understanding of disability while representing the personal accounts of living with an acquired impairment. Thomas (1982) emphasised personal characterisations of disability over medical and administrative diagnoses. Similarly, Swain et al. (1993) included a number of biographical responses to disablement. And, perhaps most notably, the collection by Morris (1996) offered clear expositions of the subjective experiences of impairment and disability. Recent work by disabled feminists has familiarised disability studies with psychological ideas. As feminists, they view the socio-political as present in the interstices and intimacies of day-to-day private life, as they do in public domains (Thomas, 2002: 49). The significance of the personal is highlighted by Stramondo (2009), who observes that a recurring anxiety alluded to by those advocating for assisted suicide is the question of whether or not 'you would want someone to wipe your ass'. Intimate relationships are crucial because 'if we are seen in ways that make us feel we exist, that confirm us, then we are free to go on looking, and our sense of self is enlarged as we internalise the other and their sense of us (Hollway, 2007: 128).

Psychology has a troubling and troubled status in disability studies. When disability and psychology cross they tend to do so in terms of rehabilitation, treatment, therapy and cure. While there have been recent attempts to colonise psychology with disability studies (Goodley and Lawthom, 2005a, 2005b, 2005c), psychology has the potential to individualise material, political and cultural foci. Disabled people remain un(der)represented on psychology courses (Olkin, 2003), and, as indicated in the accounts of Levinson and Parritt (2005) and Stannett (2005), disabled psychologists remain excluded from the profession and psychologised as a problem. Any reference in this chapter to the psychological must remain politicised.

We will explore how non/disabled selves are constituted in relation to others, in a society that disables, against a backdrop of disabled people's resistance to their social exclusion. Relationality acknowledges that we all need others to develop an un/conscious sense of our selves. Alterity, according to Sampson (1988: 5), is at the heart of questions about subjectivity. We expect others are going to react to what we do (Wright Mills, 1970: 36). Through our relationships with other people and institutions of society,

Global North psychologies are characterised by a strict demarcation of those regions of 'the self' and 'the other'. The maintenance of these sharp boundaries is seen as central to well-being. As we saw in the last chapter, such an individualised view of the subject and their relationships with others holds particular dangers for disabled people. This is especially the case when others' boundary maintenance leads to the further othering of disabled people. A key element of this boundary work resides in the demarcation of distinct subjectivities of disabled (flawed, tragic) and abled (perfect, heroic). We need to understand the psychologies of 'able society' as much – or perhaps more – than the psychologies of disabled people.

Thinking point: 'It is axiomatic to assert that disability affects social interactions' (Olkin, 2009: 27). But in what ways can disability studies turn to the self, the subjective and the psychological, without depoliticising, individualising or psychologising disability studies? How can we develop a psychology of disability?

The disability studies response

In Goodley and Lawthom (2010), we identified disability studies literature that we felt maintained a politicised perspective while attending to a psychological realm of analysis (see Table 6.1). All the positions represented in Table 6.1 render the emotional and the intimate legitimate subjects of social scientific analysis (Thomas, 2004). Each contemplates the person's interiority and their relationship with the exteriority of others. Or, as Ghai (2006: 26) puts it, they attend to alterity: how the disabled self is made in the image of others. These developments have addressed what Finkelstein and French (1993) describe as the need for a psychology of disability, 'which focuses on the psychological anxieties and distresses caused by the social relations of disability' (Reeve, 2008: 53). Each, to varying extents, shifts attention from the psychology of impairment to a psychology of dis/ability and disablism.

Table 6.1 Psychology in disability studies

Psychoemotional disablism (e.g. Thomas, 1999; Reeve, 2008) – the psychological consequences and origins of direct and indirect forms of discrimination which might be manifested in terms of low self-esteem and psychological distress.
Distributed competence (e.g. Booth and Booth, 1994, 1998; Goodley, 2000; Tobbell and Lawthom, 2005) – the extent to which psychological competence is enabled or stifled through the networks of support one has in one's life. Intelligence and capacity are understood in terms of the quality of relational networks of support rather than the disposition of an individual.
The corporeal and carnal (e.g. Hughes, 1999, 2002a, 2004; Paterson and Hughes, 1999; Hughes and Paterson, 2000) – the embodied experience of disability and impairment that contribute to the psychological status of the individual, dependent not only on essentialist characteristics of the embodied being but also on the body's social and relational engagement with its environment.
Metaphorical (e.g. Davis, 1995; Mitchell and Snyder, 1997, 2006) – the manufacture of the disabled self in dominant forms of cultural production, where disability is used as a metaphor for psychological, social and cultural discourses of 'lack', 'tragedy' and 'flawed'.

(Continued)

Table 6.1 *(Continued)*

Internalised oppression (e.g. UPIAS, 1976; Oliver, 1996) – the psychological consequences of the material exclusion of disabled people from mainstream life, including false consciousness.
Relational/interactional (e.g. French, 1993; Wendell, 1996; Traustadóttir, 2004a, 2004b, 2006a; Tregaskis, 2004; Shakespeare, 2006a) – the dynamic interplay of biology, psychology and the environment.
Discursive (e.g. Corker and French, 1998; Corker, 1999; 2001; Corker and Shakespeare, 2002; Rapley, 2004; Tremain, 2005a) – the constitution of self, body and social world through the practices and discourses of societal institutions and cultural narratives.
Social psychoanalytic (e.g. Marks, 1999a, 1999b) – the dynamic relational and inseparable nature of the psychological and social life in the constitution of disabled and non-disabled subjectivities. The constitution of the self in relation to others.
Queer and postcolonial (e.g. Ghai, 2006; Sherry, 2007) – the blurring of self/other; nature/society; private/public; psychological/material through an analysis of heteronormative, occidental and patriarchal societies in which the psychology of disability is both oppositional to normative society but viewed as positively disruptive.
Existential/phenomenological – emotions are directly related to how close our expectations, hopes and desires come to being met (Shuttleworth, 2000; Michalko, 2002; Titchkosky, 2003). These issues manifest themselves in specific interventions with non-disabled people in relation to unspoken evaluations and judgements to be found in the body language and facial expressions of individuals and physical interactions between people (Shuttleworth, 2000: 269).

The critical psychology response

Outside disability studies, advances in ***critical psychology*** have recast psychology in ways amenable to disability politics. Critical psychologists contest the modernist view that psychology is a progressive science. For Fox and Prilleltensky (1997), psychology has hindered social justice, to the detriment of all communities and to oppressed groups in particular. Critical psychologists confront psychological practices that sustain oppression and seek, instead, to promote an ethical and politicised psychology that works alongside activists, users and survivors of psychology. The 1970s 'crisis in social psychology' saw a paradigm shift in thinking about how psychology should go about its business. For Parker (1989), a key site of contestation appeared through interpretivists, radical humanists and Marxists, writers who challenged the dominating forces of positivism (see Chapter 4). While there are strong traditions of qualitative research to be found in psychology (e.g. Nicholson, 1928; Allport, 1947), the crisis marked a sustained rejection of psychological functionalism: a mistaken view of isolated beings in socio-political vacuums – the roots of psychologisation.[1] Overall, the crisis pushed psychologists towards meaning-oriented persuasions, often with political affiliations. Again, feminists were well represented (e.g. Henriques et al., 1984; Burman, 1990; Ussher, 1991; Hare Mustin and Marecek, 1992) and critical writings came out in a number of journals.

Thinking point: Visit one or more of the following online journals: Theory and Psychology, Journal of Theoretical and Philosophical Psychology, New Ideas in Psychology, Feminism and Psychology, Feminism and Psychology, International Journal of Critical Psychology, Community, Work and Family. *Identify two papers that, while not mentioning disability, you think might aid the development of disability studies.*

Table 6.2 Critical psychology

Discursive and social constructionist psychology – deconstructs and destabilises the discursive construction of psychological phenomena such as personality, emotions, cognitions, attitudes, bodies and psychological disorders. Enacts this deconstruction through a range of discursive approaches ranging from the microscopic conversations of everyday life through to the truth claims promoted by the human and social sciences (e.g. Henriques et al., 1984; Potter and Wetherell, 1987; Burman, 1990, 2008; Parker and Shotter, 1990; Parker, 1992; Burman and Parker, 1993a; Curt, 1994; Cromby and Nightingale, 1999).
Social psychoanalytic – emphasises the dynamic relational and inseparable nature of un/conscious psychological and social life to look at how subjectivity emerges in the social domain. Understands anxiety and strategies developed to defend against the difficult feelings that anxiety provokes, playing an important part in the construction of individual, social and cultural and institutional lives (e.g. Bocock, 1976; Frosh, 1987; Hollway and Jefferson, 2000).
Narrative psychology – understands subjectivities as the stories people tell about their lives. These stories combine personal idiosyncrasies and novel experiences with wider cultural and political narratives that help the shaping of the storying of a sense of self (for wide overview, see Goodley et al., 2004).
Feminist psychologies – draws on the subjectivities of wo/men with explicit reference to patriarchal systems of domination and explores the role of malestream psychology in such practices as gender differentiation, the medicalisation of women's distress and constitution of pathologising therapeutic practices (e.g. Burman, 1990, 1998; Wilkinson and Kitzinger, 1995; K. Davis, 1997a).
Queer and postcolonial psychology – understands dominant forms of subjectivity as reflecting occidental and heteronormative ideals and poses alternative hybridised and queer subjectivities and subjugated/outlawed ontologies (e.g. Kitzinger, 1987; Bhavnani and Phoenix, 1994; Venn, 2001; www.queeryingpsychology.org.uk/).
Phenomenological psychology – explores the embodied, sensual, lived-in experiences of embodied subjectivities through a host of approaches which permit people to reflect upon their own life worlds and how these are intertwined with the embodied experiences of others (for overview, see Langdridge, 2007).
Sociological social psychology – situates an analysis of the psyche in the social, political and cultural life of any given individual. This contrasts with psychological social psychology which internalises and individualises social psychological phenomena through reference to concepts such as attitude, social cognition and personality trait (e.g. Sapsford 1998; Hollway, 2007).
Community psychology – understands subjectivity as a direct reflection of culture, politics and history but blends this position with an active commitment to social transformation and an agenda for change in order to promote well-being. Enacts forms of community activism, research and practice in communities alongside people in their own environments (e.g. Kagan, 2002; Kagan and Burton, 2002; Lawthom and Goodley, 2005).

Critical psychology shares much with disability studies. Each are reactions to hegemonic constructions of elitist subjectivities, the medicalisation of distress and the segregation of some from the mainstream. Each oppose the diagnosis, assessment and treatment of isolated individuals and seek to change cultural and environmental forms of alienation and marginalisation. Similarly, each has produced epistemologies that invite criticality on the part of activists, theorists and practitioners. They share a commitment to forming communities of practice that are engaged with social change. Critical psychologists have deconstructed and reconstructed, revised and rejected psychology (Fox and Prilleltensky, 1997; Parker, 2007). Some key responses are represented in Table 6.2.

Recent disability studies writings have unambiguously drawn on some of the critical psychology resources introduced in Table 6.2. For example, in education and childhood (Billington, 2000, 2002; Todd, 2005), intellectual disabilities (Goodley and

Table 6.3 Two psychologies of disability (adapted version of Olkin and Pledger, 2003: 301)

Paradigm 1 – Traditional	Paradigm 2 – New
Is based on a medical model of disability	Is based on a social model or the new paradigm of disability
Is pathology oriented	Shifts to a systemic and societal perspective
Views differences due to disability [impairment] as deficits or developmental aberrations	Takes a lifespan approach
Is usually cross-sectional	Uses concept of 'response' to disability as a fluid process
Sees people with disabilities [impairments] and their families as at high risk for difficulties	Promotes health and resilience
Focuses predominantly on intrapsychic,	Values disability history and culture as well as interpersonal relationships
personal characteristics or intrapersonal variables	
Research on disabled people – which is more likely to be inpatient or treatment settings	Research with disabled people – incorporates those being researched into the research process
Uses concept of 'adjustment' or 'adaptation' to disability	Sees the major problems of disability as social, political, economic, legal
Uses norms based on non-disabled/able-bodied individuals for comparison	Is grounded in the belief that those with impairments have been denied their civil rights
Is about, but rarely by, disabled people	Is usually not just about, but by, disabled people
Perpetuates a 'we–they' model	Seeks remedies in public policy, legislation and systemic programmatic changes

Source: Copyright 2003 by the American Psychological Association. Reproduced with permission.

Rapley, 2002; Rapley, 2004), reappraising the psychologist's role (Olkin, 2001, 2002, 2003, 2009; Olkin Source: corrlight 2003 by the American Psychological Association. Reproduced with permission. and Pledger, 2003; Roach, 2004; Levinson and Parrit, 2005; McKenzie, 2009) and ontological accounts of disablism (Blackmore, 2006; Blackmore et al., 2006; Chinn, 2006; Hodgkins and Bailey, 2006; Reeve, 2008). However, the resources described in Table 6.2 have failed to radically engage with disability studies, perhaps because of disability studies scholars' distrust of psychology. Similarly, these resources have developed on the periphery of psychology, often as counter-discourses to the science of psychology, as transformative alliances with feminism, queer theory and postcolonialism that aim to solicit more politicised versions of the psyche, subjectivity and relationality.

In this chapter we will see that their outlawed status makes them attractive propositions for the use of disability studies scholars. Fusing concepts from Tables 6.1 and 6.2 might permit us to cultivate a new psychology of disability (paradigm 2) in contrast with a traditional (rehabilitative and curative) psychology of disability (paradigm 1) (Table 6.3).

Thinking point: List the titles of those professions, disciplines and institutions which would fit neatly under either paradigm 1 and/or paradigm 2.

For the remainder of the chapter we will look at the possibilities of merging critical psychology and disability studies.

The psychoemotional subject

> You get that all the time. People stare, people comment, or people … I would rather people said to me, 'What's wrong?' rather than just stare. Then you can hear them as soon as you walk past [whisper sounds]. (Jemma, mother of a disabled child reported in McLaughlin et al., 2008: 96)

> When people comment on my impaired experience I am shocked, amused and angered all at once. (Hewitt, 2004: 13)

> White civilisation and European culture have forced an existential deviation on the negro [sic]. (Fanon, 1993: 16)

Recent work by writers such as Thomas (1999, 2001b, 2002, 2007) and Reeve (2002, 2004, 2005, 2006, 2007, 2008) have cleared a theoretical space for thinking creatively about the psychological. Both are sceptical about psychologisation but share an interest in what Reeve (2008: 1) describes as the 'barriers in here' that are often ignored by radical structuralist sociologists who are more focused on the 'barriers out there'. The psychoemotional register examines what 'disabled people can be' rather than what 'disabled people can do' and explores in/direct forms of psychoemotional disablism (Reeve, 2008: 1; see also Thomas, 2007: 72). Direct forms can be found in discriminatory interactions, acts of invalidation, patronising responses of others and hate crimes such as the destruction of group symbols and hate literature (Sherry, 2000). Recent crime statistics from Britain suggest that 25% of disabled people report being victimised (Roulstone and Balderston, 2009). Indirect forms may be due to the side-effects of structural disablism or unintended actions, words or deeds. The psychoemotional refers to the impact of these ingredients of disablism on the ontological security or confidence of disabled people (Thomas, 1999). A key psychic reaction to such hostility is internalised oppression: the re-injuring of self through internalising discriminatory values (Marks, 1999a), lowering self-worth and lessening a sense of intrinsic value (Thomas, 2007).

Reeve's work (2004, 2005, 2008) demonstrates how psychoemotional dimensions of disablism compound structural aspects. Our relationships with others demarcate us as social beings. For disabled people, however, scripts of everyday engagement are often ignored (by non-disabled others) in favour of 'othering' responses such as avoidance, fear, help or curiosity. The invalidating gaze of society impacts upon emotional well-being and feelings of worth (Reeve, 2002). Discourses around euthanasia, medical intervention, genetic counselling and bioethics signal clear indicators of disabled people's (lack of) worth. Psychoemotional disablism operates at un/conscious levels and it is to this that we will now turn.

Homo sacer

In Goodley and McLaughlin (2008) a question was asked: how and why are children excluded from childcare settings such as playgroups when, according to the anti-discriminatory legislation, they should be included? The study drew on a number of interviews with parents (see McLaughlin et al., 2008 for details of the research). Two extracts are reproduced below:

> I changed her playgroup because the playgroup she was at, they were quite precious over her, even though it was mixed ability, they did take special needs kids, they were kind of shooing all the other kids away from her… (Elizabeth)
>
> My Duncan is … how do you put it? Wild. I used to go along to this nursery with him when he was a little boy. It was held in my local library. There was a woman taking the register, a sort of committee and a list of rules as long as your arm. It was very cliquey. During coffee break, I was told by one of the other mothers that during coffee break 'we like the children to sit quietly at the table over there'. Then during singsong time, all the kids were expected to sit cross-legged on the floor. Totally not Duncan's place! (Cheryl)

Thinking point: Read the two extracts presented above and answer the following questions: (1) What do they say about the community membership of disabled children and their families? (2) How would you define / characterise the actions of the mothers?

Both extracts capture the subtleties of psychoemotional disablism as parents struggle to get their children included. Reeve's work (2007, 2008) provides an explanation, in which she draws on the work of Agamben, specifically his notion of *homo sacer* ('the sacred man'). This refers to a figure of Roman human law where the person is banned from the city or *polis* and is excluded from all civil rights. S/he is defined in law as an exile: so the law both excludes but also denies. Reeve (2007: 1–2) argues, quoting Agamben (1998: 28), that:

> 'He who has been banned is not, in fact, simply set outside the law and made indifferent to it but rather *abandoned* by it, that is, exposed and threatened on the threshold in which life and law, outside and inside, become indistinguishable.' (Italics in original)

This zone of indistinction represents a state of exception in which *homo sacer* is bare life, *zoē*, stripped of political rights and located outside the *polis* (city). In other words, *homo sacer* has biological life, but that life has no political significance. Reeve (2008) describes *homo sacer* – zones of indistinction, as in *but* outside the state – where the individual has no political life and can only obtain it through access to the *polis*. They are abject without citizenship. Reeve suggests that this concept resonates with the experiences of disabled people in the contemporary climate of anti-discrimination disability legislation. She gives the example of a wheelchair user being forced to use the goods lift to access a shop. Here the shop owners conform to the requirements of the 1995 British Disability Discrimination Act (they make the place physically accessible), but subject the wheelchair user to the indignities of accessing the shop via the 'back door' (they are not full members of the social context).

Similarly, in the accounts of parents presented above, while the parents' children are 'legislatively included' in the playgroups (thus conforming to recent legislation such as the Special Educational Needs and Disability Act, 2001), they are stripped of full status by the reactions of other parents who prevent connection between non/disabled children. According to Reeve (2007: 4), 'disabled people find themselves dependent on the goodwill of the service providers because, like *homo sacer*, they cannot rely on the law to fully protect them by ensuring that adjustments made to the environment restore independence *and* dignity and self-esteem to disabled people'. The indignities of *homo sacer* are psychologically draining. As Perreault (2004: 104) observes about accessing restaurants as a wheelchair user:

> Now, you might need to decide if you want to insist on a comfortable table in a good location instead of being relegated to a spot near the kitchen door. Sometimes, when all you want is a pleasant night out, such things aren't worth the battle. We have to choose our battles.

Reeve's analysis magnifies the subtle complexities of psychoemotional disablism through which disabled people are placed outside the *polis* in a 'psychic state of exception' (Reeve, 2008: 85).

Emotional labour and demanding publics

> A lifetime with psychic armour as sure as skin ... where thousands of daily encounters are layered with danger, disgust or distress. (Lurie, 2004: 85)

A further feature of psychoemotional disablism relates to the kinds of performances expected of disabled people. A theoretical route for making sense of these encounters is provided by Williams' (2003) discussion of *emotional labour*, a term coined by Hochschild (1983). This concept seeks to account for the assault on the self that occurs in response to demanding publics. Emotions are corporeal thoughts, embodied processes, imbricated with social values and frequently involved in preserving social bonds, social rules and displays of behaviour (Williams, 2003: 519–520). Hochschild's (1983) concept of emotional labour refers to those times when the self has to act in ways that fit the expectations of others. Disabled people learn to respond to the expectations of non-disabled culture – the demanding public – in ways that range from acting as the passive disabled bystander, the grateful recipient of others' support, the non-problematic receiver of others' disabling attitudes. Maintaining this emotional labour can be psychologically testing. Williams (2003) discusses the notion of 'corpsing', where the social actor fails to maintain the management of their emotional labour and the illusion of stability. They freeze. Corpsing can occur when publics demand too much. Following Fanon (1993: 33), these demands may reside in 'the stigmata of a dereliction' in non-disabled people's relationships with disabled others. Here are a few examples that I have collected:

> 'Your child's the naughty boy in my child's class, isn't he?' (A parent's question to the mother of a child with the label of ADHD)

'I never think of you as disabled.' (A common 'positive' comment from friends of the disabled writer Michalko, 2002)

'At least he's not *too* disabled.' (A health visitor's comments to the mother of a newborn baby)

'Did you read on the web that 52% of the American public would prefer to be dead than disabled?' (Bar chat on a November night)

'You are just so brave, I don't know how you cope.' (A mother's comment to another mother of a disabled child in the playground)

'I don't know how you can work with those people. ... It must be so rewarding to work with those people.' (Contradictory comments from a friend to a key worker for people with learning difficulties)

'I've had coins dropped in my lap by strangers in the street.' (Hewitt, 2004)

'Don't worry about paying love, we don't charge for retards.' (Comment from a fairground assistant to the mother of a disabled child, from Goodley and Runswick-Cole, 2010)

'The other mothers asked that I did not bring my Autistic sons on the school trip because they were worried that my boys might attack their children.' (Anonymous story handed to me after a seminar, April 2009)

? *Thinking point: What models (Chapter 1), theories (Chapter 4) and notions of the individual (Chapter 5) are being drawn upon in these accounts?*

When the public demands so much emotional labour from disabled people, then it is hardly surprising that the latter would corpse. People deal with corpsing in different ways. Some are productive (embracing disability activism, challenging the public, joking about it, kicking the cat), others potentially destructive (avoiding social settings where such questions may arise, internalising these comments as indicators of psychological flaws, feeling powerless). Williams' (2003) analysis presumes that the (non-disabled) public is already demanding. This rings true for many disabled people. Non-disabled people appear, at times, to expect responses to the most inappropriate of questions, assume that it is perfectly acceptable to share their own concerns about impairment with disabled people, demand quick responses to hurtful and thoughtless commentaries. Williams (2003) refers to these as 'strong scripts' of individuals in culturally powerful positions who feel authorised to make such demands. This might explain why disabled people find it easier to identify themselves as disabled to themselves (and other disabled people) than they do to other (non-disabled) people (Wendell, 1996).

Clearly, the emotional lives of disabled people risk being policed by these publics. Olkin (2002) describes the experience of affect regulation, that is the prescription of certain affects/emotions (such as cheerfulness and gratefulness) alongside the prohibition of other affects (including anger and resentment). When disabled people display the latter they are often dismissed by the demanding publics as arrogant, unreasonable and ungrateful. Just as black people are expected to be, in the words of Fanon (1993: 34), 'good niggers' [sic], disabled people are supposed to be 'good crips', 'eternal victims of an essence, of an appearance, for which they are not responsible' (Fanon, 1993: 34). The psychoemotional subject of disablism is one subjected to everyday, mundane and relentless examples of cultural and relational violence.

The social psychoanalytic subject

> The concept of normative order may be fetishized. (Wright Mills, 1970: 36)

Thinking point: What do you understand by the term psychoanalysis?

Psychoanalytic therapy has been denounced for its normalising aims (e.g. Masson, 1989). Interestingly, psychoanalysis is, in some respects, the 'repressed other of psychology' (Burman, 1994), at least in Anglo-American varieties. Sustained attempts by 'scientific psychology', including cognitive psychology, to shut away psychoanalysis might make it appealing. For our purposes, the psychoanalytic emphasis on subjectivity as a complex psychic, relational and socio-cultural artefact affords opportunities for theorising the psychology of disablism. Previous uses of psychoanalysis in disability studies have tended to emphasise the ways in which disabled subjectivities are constructed as tragic and secondary handicaps of living with impairment (e.g. Sinason, 1992). Yet, psychoanalysis does not automatically imply a reactionary turn to the inner troubles of the psyche (see the contributions to Goodley et al., 2011). A *social* psychoanalytic perspective scrutinises the ways in which social-cultural knowledge and practices impact upon the un/conscious (Mitchell, 1974; Frosh, 1987; Parker, 1997). Subjectivities are fashioned in and through socio-cultural arrangements (Marks, 1999b, 2002). Social psychoanalysis takes seriously disabled people's experiences of living with and challenging oppression: creating subjectivities that have the potential to refute disablism.

Social psychoanalytic encounters with subjectivity interrogate the relational and emotional aspects of exclusion and resistance: those private, hidden, personal elements of disability/impairment. We know that disability evokes fascination, fear, anxiety, hatred, paternalism and curiosity. The aim, however, is not to individualise explanations for these un/conscious responses but 'to choose action with respect to the real source of conflict – that is, towards social structures' (Fanon, 1993: 100). As Goodley and Lawthom (2010) have argued, a turn to social psychoanalysis must embrace theories that do not put the problems of disablism back on to disabled people but magnify processes of disablism that are produced in the relationships between people. This means taking seriously the role of ideology in relation to practices of oppression, repression, internalisation and individualisation. By attending to psychoanalytic metaphors that are emblematic of contemporary psychological life, we can provide useful adjuncts to social theories that have politicised disability.

Thinking point: Marks (1999a) proposes a view of psychoanalysis to be serviced by disability studies. She recognises that psychoanalysis might be misused, for example, to interpret social oppression theories of disabled

people as manic forms of denial, loss and difficulty. However, while these conservative views abound, she argues that disability studies and psychoanalysis both:

- *demand change to (psychic/environmental) structure rather than just attitudes;*
- *reject medicalisation in favour of more relational encounters;*
- *reject unitary, rational, fixed and stable conceptions of the individual and consider categories such as in/sane and dis/abled as cultural continua that raise questions about human worth;*
- *consider psychology in terms of a continuum rather than fixed categories (e.g. in/sane, dis/abled) and raise questions about which ends of the continuum we value;*
- *recognise difference as a key emotional hurdle;*
- *place primary focus on the development of selves in relation to others (alterity).*

To these, we could also add that both invite:

- *critical understandings of the conflict between independence and dependency, where the latter may unconsciously remain as an ideal location that jars with the demands of the former expected by society;*
- *views of the body as constituted through relationship with the environment;*
- *an exploration of simultaneous moments of identification and rejection;*
- *analyses of the constitution of 'child', 'adult', 'woman', 'mother' and 'father';*
- *an understanding of the family as a microcosm of, and early encounter with, culture;*
- *theories of oppression as a product of the unconscious desires, wishes and conflicts of non-disabled people and disablist culture to which disabled people are subjected to (transference).*

To what extent do you agree with these connections?

With these aims in mind, let us now turn to three areas of social psychoanalytic analysis.

Splitting

> We have been split into good and bad selves, split from each other, and split from greater society literally through environmental impediments and symbolically through feelings of invalidity. (Gerrschick, 2000: 46, cited in Olkin, 2008: 8)

This first social psychoanalytic thread considers the ways in which disabled people are subjected to cultural forms of division. The psychic apparatus described by Freud includes the unco-ordinated instinctual drives of the 'id' (this is the unconscious and where we can find our polymorphous drives of love and hate), the organising 'ego' (what we might understand as our conscious sense of self) and the moralising 'super-ego' (which we learn through identifications with our caregivers and internalising moral and social codes). The id, ego and super-ego are played out in the relationships between the self and other (people and culture). Marks (1999b: 613) explains a number of common reactions of non-disabled people to disability. These include psychological investments of non-disabled professionals in keeping their disabled clients dependent; unconscious reasons why individuals and communities scapegoat disabled people and the fantasies and fears around disability. She employs psychoanalytic concepts – *ego defence mechanisms* – to make sense of these processes (see Marks, 1999a). In our early years, these mechanisms are used, often unconsciously, in the development and maintenance of the ego, as the child becomes increasingly independent of the primary caregiver and, crucially, in adulthood as a means of dealing with un/conscious conflicts, desires and expectations of others. In early childhood, these mechanisms are to be found in the process of *splitting* good (e.g. present mother) and bad (e.g. absent m/other) feelings, in order to make sense of (and at times rationalise) the developing sense of self (ego). These ambivalent experiences of good/bad are made in relation to, and are *projected* on to the m/other. Projection can be described 'in the degree to which I find in myself something unheard-of, something reprehensible, only one solution remains for me: to get rid of it; to ascribe its origin to someone else' (Fanon, 1993: 191). The 'good' mother is where our pleasures are gratified, our nurture met, our psychoemotional needs addressed. The 'bad' mother is the barrier to these pleasures and is quickly associated with feelings of pain, frustration and anger. Caught up in the constant turmoil of independent/autonomous and dependent/nurtured selves, we turn to internalising (introjecting) the good whenever we can. And when bad is also internalised (as is often the case when we try in vain to keep only the good), this is felt as threatening. To deal with threat, we project out the bad, externalising the threat (Fanon, 1993). The internalised oppression of disabled people can be understood in terms of *introjection*: where societal norms of dependency and bodily imperfection are internalised, only to sit ambivalently, often shamefully, with one's psychical position in a disabling world (Marks, 1999a: 21). On a more positive note, disability pride may be viewed as the introjection of more enabling beliefs and identities from disability arts and disability politics. Common experiences of hostility or pitying stares, dismissive rejection, infantilisation, patronising attitudes, altruism, help and care on the part of non-disabled people, can be understood as a process of *splitting* (separating good (desired) and bad (not desired) areas of one's psyche), *introjection* (internalising those aspects of the good life (desired) that you want to keep dear to you) and *projection* (making sure you project out the bad (not desired) away from yourself on to others).

The root of much psychoemotional disablism might be understood, then, as a consequence of disabled people being literally hit with the projections or 'split off feelings which some non-disabled people cannot own' (Marks, 1999a: 23). In this sense, then, hate crime might, say, more about the general psychical organisation of *all* non-disabled people – in relation to disability *per se* – than simply the acts of a *few* extremists (see Sherry, 2000). Hate crime is the logical consequence of the animosity to be found in the psychical defence mechanisms of the wider community.

> The uncanny encounter with another, then, puts us face to face with our own vulnerability 'with and for others'. And, it is the fear and denial of our own vulnerability that causes us to hate and exploit the vulnerability of others. (K. Oliver, 2007: 349)

The consequence for disabled people of living in a hostile world can be profound, with the pain of rejection often being *repressed* in order to survive a barrage of rejected messages. For some, appropriate feelings of rage against inexcusable forms of disablism are inwardly directed, felt as inappropriate, leading to emotional invalidation and, at worse, self-harm (Marks, 1999b: 615). On a more enabling note, phenomenon such as challenging behaviour on the part of people with the label of learning disabilities might be understood as embodied reactions – *sublimated responses* – to the psychical experience of institutionalisation (Marks, 1999b). Davis (1995: 129–130) goes further to suggest that splitting is a cultural act, a residue of 'the splitting of our inner life and childhood images of noble princes, fairy godmothers, scary monsters and evil stepmothers' (and you can guess which roles are occupied by disabled people).

Splitting neatly covers over the frightening writing on the wall that we are no longer as nurtured as we once were. Disabled people become projection objects in the psychoanalytic splitting of good/bad, able/unable, whole/fragmented selves. This might explain why the helping and caring roles of non-disabled parents, friends, volunteers and professionals are depicted in such contradictory ways in disabling culture. These helpers are either devalued (they are 'only working with disabled people') or canonised ('How can you work with those people? You must have the patience of a saint'). Larson (1998: 866) suggests that as medical professionals 'lose the battle to save, rehabilitate and cure', their 'anger at the disease might spill over onto the bearer of the illness who represents medical failure'. The patient becomes the projection object for the professional in conflict. Splitting also might account for the deep ontological reasons associated with hierarchies of impairment.

? *Thinking point: Many commentators have drawn attention to the splits within communities of disabled people, between people with physical, sensory, cognitive impairments and labels of mental health. An aspect of retrieving a positive identity might include disassociating oneself with others ('I'm physically impaired, not stupid'; 'I am disabled, not mad'; 'I have learning difficulties, I'm not a wheelchair user'): 'separating the quads form the paras, those with power chairs from those with manuals and chairs, even walkers from canes' (Killacky, 2004: 60). Why might such splits occur between disabled people?*

Such splitting is understandable in a culture that values psychological mastery and bodily autonomy. Splitting is to be found in that common 'plucky-yet-mourning' paradox expected of disabled people. So strong is this paradox that disabled people who are not depressed are labelled as in denial. Equally, those who do show a fighting spirit are in danger of being understood as maladjusting to their impairments (Olkin, 2009). This combination of prescriptions ('mourn but be plucky') and prohibitions ('do not be angry') is a potent destructive force (Olkin, 2009: 34). It is clear, though, that the pain of disability does not reside in the disabled body. Instead, there is the potential for disabled people to hurt because non-disabled people refuse them entry into human communities.

Fear and loathing

> A vague notion of suffering and its potential deterrence drives much of the logic of elimination that rationalises selective abortion. (Garland-Thomson, 2002: 16)

Thomas (2007: 66) sets a challenge for psychoanalysis: 'to explain the often complex attraction to and repulsion from disabled people bound up with fear, guilt and many other emotions'. Clearly, discrimination is as much a reflection of unconscious fears and fantasies as it is indicator of ignorance, self-interest and indifference (Marks, 1999a). Shakespeare (2000) understands the fear of disabled people as (non-disabled) individuals' anxieties about death and physicality, which are projected on to disabled people.

Following Branson et al. (1988: 17), disabled people exist 'on the margins of society's consciousness, a living negativity, serving, by their very existence, as a "negative" segregated group to define the positive standards of 'normality' and acceptability'. Such fears are, obviously, more idealised than real. When parents account for the anxieties they felt imagining the birth of their disabled children, this demonstrates the emotional labour that goes into visualising disability even before it is materially present (McLaughlin and Goodley, 2008). It has been argued by Ghai (2006: 38) that fear operates at the level of the unconscious because 'if the non-disabled were fully conscious of the uncertainty of their own TAB (Temporarily Able Bodied) status, then their attitudes towards disability would be very different'. Fear, shame and loathing go hand in hand, to the extent that they are all symbolic acts of violence. Disabled children, for example, are in danger of introjecting others' feelings of fear into their own character armours, resulting in shame and alienation. This is particularly evident in light of the high numbers of disabled children who are sexually abused. Just as a psychotic belief in the white self can lead some to seek the expulsion of the black self (Fanon, 1993: 161), a psychotic belief in the non-disabled self may well lead to (sexual) violence against disabled people. And shame is not so much a psychologised state of mind of an individual but a socially based harm that oppressed groups are often subjected to in particular ways (Wilkerson, 2002: 44). In this sense, then, we must be wary of further pathologising the disability experience through individualising experiences of oppression, abuse, shame and marginalisation.

Thinking point: The resistance of disabled people to normalising society is evidenced in numerous accounts. Take, for example, the following:

In a current research project on the experiences of disabled children aged 5–16, a colleague and myself have worked with a number of families. One of these, a young man of 11, whom I'll call Kurt, wears a colostomy bag. Being born with no bladder meant that this had been a daily experience for him and was 'no big deal', though he had not told any of his close friends.

One day he plucked up the courage to tell a couple of pals about his bag. By the end of the day, his new name around the school was 'wee-wee boy'. This had made him very angry. He got his revenge against the main bully of the school, who had been using this new name, by emptying his colostomy bag in the boy's schoolbag, out of sight of the teacher in the maths lesson. (Interviewed by my colleague Katherine Runswick-Cole as part of an ongoing research project, www.rihsc.mmu.ac.uk/postblairproject).

In what ways is Kurt resisting 'social psychoanalytic disablism'?

Sadly, not all stories turn out as happily as Kurt's. The shame that disabled people are expected to bear can be seen as reflecting what Marks (1999a: 170) terms 'psychical investments in normalcy and fears about stupidity and monstrosity'. But these aspects of disability that generate the most anxiety are precisely those areas of human experience that everyone struggles with (Marks, 1999a).

Fantasy, confession and fetish

> The internalisation that I carried in such a cultural milieu [India] accustomed me to seeing my disability as a personal quest and tragedy to be borne alone. ... I learnt to cope with the limitations, imposed by my impairment. The recurring anxiety was placed in the realm of what Freud so aptly termed as the 'unconscious'. (Ghai, 2006: 14–15)

The normalising principles of psychologisation, described in the last chapter, are also evident in the ways in which psychoanalytic ideas have been folded into the everyday fabric of social and cultural life. As Parker (1997) has argued, all people are now expected to engage in pseudo-psychoanalytic confession and self-analysis. From chat show to self-help group, reality TV to the daily take up of counselling by more and more members of society, we live in a culture of therapy, where we demand to speak and know about ourselves and others.

Thinking point: Psychoanalytic culture invites non-disabled people to ask of disabled people:

'Why did you not have a test before you had your child?' (A stranger's question to the mother of a disabled child)
'What happened to you then?' (A stranger's question to a disabled woman in a supermarket)
'Well, are you going to do something funny, or what?' (Question asked of a disabled activist researcher with restricted growth)

Following Turner (1983), behind these personal anecdotes of the author 'lie deep fantasies about disability'. What kinds of fantasies could these include?

Fantasies are interspersed with stereotypes and images of eternal children, evil, depressed, deranged, bitter, dependent, God's children, ugly, asexual, tragic and burden, and evoked by terms such as crippled, deformed, mute, crazy, idiot and dumb

(Rauscher and McClintock, 1997). Indeed, in order to claim disability welfare support or obtain a diagnosis from a healthcare professional, disabled people and their families are expected to enact disabling fantasies. Marks (1999a), Tremain (2006a), Shildrick (2007a, 2007b) and Shildrick and Price (1999a, 1999b) use the example of applying for Disability Living Allowance in Britain, where claimants are expected not only to confess details of their own bodily inadequacies but, in many cases, to enact a fantasised version of their own impairments if they are to stand any chance of receiving the allowance. This fantasy produces the subject and object of impairment: the impaired applicant (see Chapter 7). This over-playing of deficiencies is captured in the words of a mother, whom I shall call Devina, interviewed by my colleague Katherine Runswick-Cole as part of an ongoing research project cited above:

> I did contact social services about two years ago when my daughter was very unwell and we didn't have a lot of support and I just felt like drowning. I knew what I'd have to say. I'd have to say I'm either going to hurt myself or my child and then they'd come thundering in to help, but I didn't feel emotionally strong enough at that point to fight with them.

The healthcare professional occupies the position of key other through which the (fantasised) disabled patient is recognised to exist. The professional gaze expects to see the disabled object as a grotesque sight (Ghai, 2006). That these social psychoanalytic processes are endemic to the helping professions might explain why many professionals find it seemingly impossible to limit the 'help' they offer. Disabled objects form the focus of that common professional pathology label: the 'need freak' (Dunst, 2008).

The fantasies of 'the disabled' are fuelled by fantasies of 'the normate'. As we saw in the last chapter, the normate individual required of contemporary culture clashes with the fantasy of the disabled child. Disabled children violate the model of the happy, playing, discovering child (Burman, 2008: 157). A consequence of this psychical work is the constitution of appalling children – from child killers to autistic children – who are no longer considered children. They function as others 'in order to restore our sense of ourselves and the world we want' (Burman, 2008: 159). In this sense, the child functions as a boundary object: defining the boundaries of what constitutes in/humanity. Disabled children function as the dumping ground for the projection of non-disabled society's fears of illness, frailty, incapacity and mortality (Shakespeare, 1997a).

A further element to the social psychoanalysis of disability relates to fetish. Broadly speaking, a fetish is that which we (mis)believe will sate our desires. In capitalist societies, the process of fetishisation describes the values that we inhere in objects or commodities that they do not intrinsically have. Fetishistic culture imbues objects with value (from sculpted pecs, to expensive wine, the latest iPhone, pathological children and uncivilised nations). The disabled body is also a fetishised object, on to which are conferred a whole host of (unconscious) values that sate a variety of desires. These might include desire of, or repulsion from, aspects of the disabled body, as demonstrated in Sable's (2004) account of the sexual relationships between disabled people and non-disabled fetishists.[2] Sable suggests that the active seeking of disabled bodies by potential sexual partners can be paradoxically empowering for disabled men (as their bodies are valued for their sexuality in their own right) and disempowering (as their bodies become *the* focus of sexual relationships).[3]

In broader terms, the fetishising of disabled bodies as vulnerable, dependent, broken, exotic, *uber*-different, reflect the wider societal fetishising practices of non-disabled people as they sate their own desires for wholeness and autonomy.[4] This can cause problems. The non-disabled helper can quickly turn 'from benevolent helper to Nurse Ratched' (Sable, 2004). We shall return to these practices in Chapter 8. Interestingly, a pop-psychology website on phobias lists a number of phobias specifically related to impaired body parts, including Apotemnophobia (fear of persons with amputations), scotomaphobia (fear of blindness in visual field), Psellismophobia (fear of stuttering) (www.phobialist.com).[5] Phobias are neuroses characterised by fear of an object in which the object is endowed with negative intensions (Fanon, 1993: 142). These contribute to a more general societal erotaphobia about the sexualities of disabled people (Stevens, 2008).

Thinking point: Lawson (1991: 64) has declared that 'disempowerment drives some of us crazy'. To what extent is this a dangerous admission?

A social psychoanalytic perspective would respond quickly to Lawson's admission, suggesting that society is pathological. The oppression of disabled people says more about the neurotic character of society than the neuroses of disabled people. Social psychoanalysis permits us to reject the psychologisation of disabled people through exposing and deconstructing taken-for-granted destructive disabling concepts. The dangers inherent within this framework are demonstrated when it identifies a defensive disabled self that is damaged, vulnerable and fragmented (e.g. Hollway and Jefferson, 2000). This is actually anti-psychoanalytic. For Freud, civilisation was necessarily neurotic, demanding a defence by the ego of instinctual drives of *eros* and *thanatos* as part of a wider conformity to societal norms (Bocock, 1976). Social psychoanalysis allows us to place the self in its social context: and ask questions about the damage done by society.

Conclusion

In this chapter we have developed a critical stance in relation to disability, self, psychology and the other. The critical psychologists Newman and Holzman (1993) argue that a sustained critical analysis of psychological life provides opportunities for mobilisation and social change:

> Psychologists should work alongside people to create a new social setting in which everybody is responsible for supporting emotional development in others, and where conflicts are used as growing points rather than disruptions in the proper activity of the establishment. (Newman and Holzman, 1993: 399)

This chapter raises the veil on the contribution of critical psychologies to our understandings of disablism.

Further reading

Frosh (1987). An introduction to key psychoanalytic theories from a politicised writer.

Goodley and McLaughlin (2008). Explores how disabled families negotiate the complex terrains and relationships of community life.

Marks (1999b). Reads psychoanalysis through the lens of the British social model.

Olkin and Pledger (2003). A rare disability studies encounter with psychology.

Reeve (2002). Accessible introduction to psychoemotional disablism.

Notes

1 Critical psychology does not reject all science. The work of the Radical Statistics Network (www.radstats.org.uk) and the scientific studies of capacity theories of disabled people and their families developed by Dunst and colleagues (www.researchtopractice.info/whatisebp.php) are just two examples of emancipatory work that has drawn on positivism.

2 Campbell (2009: 128) categories non-disabled people's desire of disabled bodies into ***Devotees***, who are attracted to people with a physical disability and their prostheses, ***Pretenders***, who simulate having impaired bodies through mimicry or the use of assistive devices like calipers, and ***transableists***, who have an overpowering desire to become physically or sensorially impaired.

3 As Sable (2004: 86) puts it: 'your whole psychosexual history [as a disabled person] will be threatened by the interest of fetishists because you have spent your whole life disidentifying with those parts of your body'. This rather negative reflection feeds into a common criticism of gay culture, which views it as inherently competitive and threatening for those gay male bodies that do not fit the scene queen model of body-beautiful.

4 Such deeply ingrained ideas require sifting through and challenging, 'below the rippling surface of the conscious', as Shepherd (1966: 58) argues in her contribution to Paul Hunt's *Stigma* (1966).

5 Fanon (1993: 141) describes 'the negro' [sic] as phobogenic object, a concept we can easily apply to disabled people.

SEVEN

Discourse: *Poststructuralist Disability Studies*

****

Introduction

Why is the talk of disability so pathological? How are common-sense ideas about impairment influenced by professionals and scientists? What possibilities are there for disrupting these ideas and offering more enabling alternatives? McRuer (2002) observes that disabled people are caught up in an 'epidemic of signification' where their bodies and minds are inscribed with a thousand words that threaten to leave them with deeply disablist 'epidermal schema'.[1] Schemas are relics of societal discourses, emanating from expert and lay knowledge, reproduced in institutions of family, school, prison, disability service and hospital. Our task in this chapter is to explore how discourses get into the bodies/minds of (non)disabled people in ways that might contribute to their disablism – with a particular focus on the institutional creation of impairment.

Poststructuralism and dis/ability

Discourses are regulated systems of statements, ideas and practices (McLaren, 2009: 72), providing ways of representing particular forms of knowledge, which we use to shape the subjective sense of who we and others are (Parker, 1989: 64; Marks, 1999a: 151). The study of discourse has brought an unruly onslaught of ideas to the social sciences (Erevelles, 2005: 421) and recent years have seen more discursive dealings with disability and impairment (Hughes and Paterson, 1997; Corker, 1998; Allan, 1999; Shakespeare, 2000; Corker and Shakespeare, 2002; Tremain, 2005b). A philosophical response to discourse is tendered by poststructuralism, which can be defined as the methodology of a given study (postmodernism) of a particular time (postmodernity). Lyotard (1979) described the postmodern condition as a time of incredulity towards modern grand narratives that (cl)aimed to be *overarching* (all-encompassing ideas such as science), *foundationalist* (built on claims of certainty) and *progressive* (proposing human emancipation). Lyotard questioned how we could continue to hold on to these grand narratives when they had found their inevitable enlightened 'logic' in the gas chambers of Auschwitz, the ruins of communism and the malpractices of science. Grand narratives serve some and fail many.

Poststructuralism replaces truth with discourse and scrutinises the latter. Consider the ways in which the world is textual: comprised of an infinite multitude of written or spoken words, signs, symbols, visual images, noise, cultural signs, sign language and Braille. Discourses are to be found at work in these texts (Parker, 1992), prescribing how the world can be known and how we can (perhaps should) live our lives. We use discourses to emote and reflect. Regulations and conventions are reproduced through discourse. Some discourses have more status than others. Discourses are ripe for analysis.

Thinking point: To what extent can it be argued that we live in a knowledge society? How has the making and distribution of knowledge changed over the last 30 years? What ideas are being peddled? Who gains and who loses?

Deconstruction

Thinking point:

There can be no understanding of able-bodied unless there is already an implicit distinction being made that to be able-bodied is not to be disabled. Yet because able-bodied carries with it the trace of the other – a trace which must be continually suppressed if able-bodied is to carry a delimited meaning – such closure is not possible ... the spectre of the other always already haunts the selfsame: it is the empty wheelchair that generates disease in the fully mobile. (Shildrick and Price, 1999b: 439)

Can disability only ever be understood in relation to ability?

For this chapter it might be more apt to use the sign 'dis/ability'. Why? Well, in order for a discourse to work it must make its case. It must counter the opposite and distinguish itself from its antithesis. In order to speak of *I* (able), I must distinguish it from an *other* (disabled). This simple relationship is the basis of poststructuralism. 'The signified (meaning) of a sign is understood only because of the relationship between two or more signifiers (words or symbols)' (Eagleton, 1983: 127). The sign 'disabled' gathers meaning through its contrast with the sign 'abled'.

Signifiers are assigned opposing poles so that one cannot exist without implying the existence of the other (Lindeman, 1997: 74). Interestingly, the *one* is not articulated while the *other* is. As Michalko (2002) observes: 'the sighted' are not named, they are just everywhere, while 'the blind' are pointed to, defined and inscribed. Poststructuralism demonstrates modernity's privileging of *one* (abled, sighted, independent) over the *other* (disabled, blind, dependent), in which the one is upheld as the transcendental signifier: the ideal sign around which all others can be anchored, 'Man, Freedom, Democracy, Independence, Authority, Order' (Eagleton, 1983: 131). The one becomes the pole around which to expound logocentricism (commitment to reason) and teleology (realising an end point). 'Man' constructs 'woman' as his opposite. Equally, 'man is what he is only by virtue of ceaselessly shutting out this other or opposite, defining himself in antithesis to it, and his whole identity is therefore caught up and put at risk in the very gesture by which he seeks to assert his unique, autonomous existence' (Eagleton, 1983: 132). Discourses of patriarchy retain their potency through advancing man over woman. Poststructuralism prises open these binary opposites – these dualisms – to ask how one has become empowered through comparison with, and denigration of, the other:

ONE	**OTHER**
Man	Woman
Reason	Passion
Normal	Abnormal
Mind	Body
Self	Others
Able	Disabled
Healthy	Diseased
White	Black
European	Oriental
Coloniser	Colonised
Global North	Global South
Science	Chaos

Binaries hunt in packs. Global North cultures celebrate their progression (teleology) and rational civilisation (logocentrism) through inscribing the other – the Global South – as oppositional: white/black, civilised/savage, reason/emotion and culture/nature (Burman, 2008: 170). The European self needs to confront its other to feel and maintain its own power (Hardt and Negri, 2000: 129). Children with Emotional Behavioural Disorders (EBD) – many of whom, incidentally, are black and working-class boys (so at the *other* end of the binary) – are understood as problematic through distinguishing them from morally absolute society (Danforth, 2008: 396). To these binaries we can add clever/stupid, mentally retarded/mentally accelerated, static/mobile, agile/lame, hearing/Deaf, sane/insane. Disability is 'the repudiation of ability' (Linton, 2006a: 171). Poststructuralism deconstructs these binaries through unveiling their hidden referents, against which one is upheld and the other found lacking, revealing that neither has a real basis in biology, nature or rationality (Hardt and Negri, 2000: 129).

There are many signifiers and associated signifieds. The signifier 'able-bodied' gives rise to a whole plethora of signifieds (competent, competitive, etc.). As soon as we analyse a sign we can see that the signifier is divided from many signifieds (Eagleton, 1983; Erevelles, 2005). Moreover, there are numerous signifiers that congregate around 'able', such as 'healthy', 'independent' and 'capable'. We are subjected to a shifting constellation of signifiers and signifieds. We are drenched in language. This leads Garland-Thomson (2002: 5) to define disability as a sign system differentiating bodies and minds. In postmodern societies the production of signs has grown exponentially so there are a myriad of signifiers. Furthermore, there are no longer simple correspondences between a signifier and a signified. Postmodernism is the logic by which global capital operates (Hardt and Negri, 2000: 151). Every difference is viewed as an opportunity. We have moved from a 'Fordist' (mass production and manufacturing) to a 'Toyotist' society (production responding to the market) (Hardt and Negri, 2000: 289). Dis/abling culture is part of this Toyotist economy, in which it seems that new disability signifiers/labels are produced on an almost daily basis (as we shall see in Chapter 9). Poststructuralism deconstructs the binary, privileges the other (e.g. woman, black, passion, irrational, disable) and opens up the in-betweenness of binaries. There might, then, be spaces for resistance – creating a new epidemic – a resignification of disability.

Biopower

?

Thinking point:

Subjectivity is a constant social process of generation … the material practices set out for the subject in the context of the institution (be they kneeling down to pray or changing hundreds of diapers) are the production processes of subjectivity … the institutions provide, above all, a discrete place (the home, the chapel, the classroom, the shop floor) where the production of subjectivity is enacted. (Hardt and Negri, 2000: 190)

Consider the institutions of school, family and workplace. How do we learn to act in ways that are in keeping with these institutions?

Discourses are used to make sense of who we (think) we are and are re/produced in social institutions. The work of Foucault is key here (Siebers, 2006; Harwood and Humphrey, 2008), whose methodology of *problematisation* poses two questions: How did something become constructed (e.g. the self)? How did something become a problem (e.g. the disabled self)? The answer to these questions is to be found in Foucault's notion of *biopower* and the (post)modern makings of the self. Techniques of post/modern biopower – statistics, demographics, assessment, education, measurement and surveillance – expand as knowledge from the human and social sciences grow and institutions of society become more pronounced. These techniques generate discourses of the self that people have come to know and constrain themselves by. Today, knowledge of oneself has become *the* fundamental principle of modern living. The self is at the centre of everything we value. Knowing oneself is *the object* of the quest for concern for self. We occupy ourselves with our selves. 'Self-help', 'self-actualisation', 'personal growth', 'bettering ourselves', 'therapy', 'empowerment' are the buzzwords and end goals of a discourse of individualism.

?

Thinking point: Reality TV, Oprah-esque confessional shows, Twittering and Facebooking are just some of the examples of what might be termed a 'culture of self-absorption'. To what extent do these contexts allow for various presentations of self?

We can view psychologisation (Chapter 5) as the construction of the self through the available discourses of cognitivism, self-containment and developmentalism. We come to understand ourselves through these discourses because they are re/produced in the institutional regimes of family, school, healthcare and welfare setting, prison and workplace (Foucault, 1973a, 1973b, 1983). Underpinning these goals is the big lie of modern civilisation: your self is free. For Foucault, *you are free only to govern yourself*, and discourse and practices of institutions aid in this 'freedom'. The ever-growing discourses of psychology, psychiatry, liberal education and the judicial systems produce specific techniques of *biopower* (Finkelstein, 1997: 160). For Foucault (1977), the modern prisoner is no longer chained to the wall of the medieval cell, banished out of sight and out of mind, s/he is gazed upon by professionals of the prison, rehabilitated and educated to fit corporeal standards. The hope is to become a responsible and law-abiding individual. Similarly, in schools, the spectacle of corporal punishment has been replaced by caring institutions and disciplining apparatus (curriculum and pedagogy) that govern and sift learners (Ball, 1990). Techniques of biopower are found in the employment of scientific categories (e.g. psychometric tests), explicit calculations (IQ scores) that objectify the body of the student (high or low IQ) to render them pliable (normal or SEN Child). Foucault (1973a, 1973b) views power as circulating – discourse working through us – persuading us to act in ways in keeping with institutional norms.

Psychology, medicine, social policy and education all come to occupy leading roles in the biopower of the self or, what Hardt and Negri (2000) call affective (that is, emotional) labour. Rose (2001) suggests this also works at the level of the state, particularly where political authorities have taken on the task of 'the management of life', in the name of the well-being of the population. These *biopolitics* have given birth to technologies, experts and apparatuses for the care and administration of life for each and all, from town planning to health services to schools. What is created is a specific form of biopolitics – *thanatopolitics* – the management of the body politic, the elimination of foreign bodies and the purification of the population (Rose, 2001: 2). There is, he argues, little clear distinction between preventive medicine and eugenics, between the pursuit of health and the elimination of illness, between consent and compulsion (2001: 4). Caught up in this biopolitical maelstrom, are specific manifestations. One of these, *biopolitics as risk politics*, describes the growing identification, treatment and administration of those individuals, groups or localities where risk is seen to be high in terms of their health, well-being and productivity. Here mothers carrying genetic defects are expected to do the responsible thing (terminate) and pastoral support of their bodies is offered through micro-technologies of pre-natal intervention, risk profiling and surveillance of high/low risk mothers-to-be (2001: 9). Genetic testing and antenatal consultations offered by GPs and other health professionals to mothers 'acts as an intensifier of ethicality. It mobilises affects of shame and guilt and reminds all of obligations to others'. This is the politics of life and how life should be lived. The biologically risky may be eradicated as part of the etho-political obsession with able somatic citizenship.

> Each session of genetic counselling, each act of amniocentesis, each prescription of an anti-depressant is predicated on the possibility, at least, of such a judgement about the relative and comparative 'quality of life' of differently composed human beings. ... We have become the kinds of people who think of our present and our future in terms of the quality of our individual biological lives. … We have entered the age of vital politics, or biological ethics and genetic responsibility. (Rose, 2001: 21–22)

We come to know others and ourselves through the discourses of biopolitics. The question is: to what extent do we fashion and resist these discourses in the construction of who we are?

Thinking point: Two couples are expecting their first baby. One couple decides not to have amniocentesis to test the relative 'health' of their child while the other couple choose to take the tests. What kinds of knowledge are the couples drawing on to inform their decisions? Where is this knowledge available (e.g. professional consultation, new parent classes, Internet site)? To what extent is this knowledge 'expert' or 'mass' knowledge?

The conundrum faced by these parents could be viewed not simply as a moral dilemma but an engagement with various powerful discourses of thanatopolitics about ab/normality and dis/ability.

Discourse analysis

We can approach the deconstruction and biopower of disability discourse through two approaches. The first considers the ***talk of discourse***. Talk is never a neutral medium through which to describe inner states, but is the medium through which these states are enacted. We need talk to think and feel. We require discourse to be. Talk not only allows us to be reflexive about actions and events; talk plays a constitutive part in these actions and events. For Potter and Wetherell (1987), utterances state and do things; talk is performative and follows particular rules and conventions, but talk is also sloppy (though sophisticated) in terms of its meaning-making (there is always an arbitrariness to the sign as concepts shift and change as they are used). We might like to think we hold stable attitudes or boast unwavering personalities. However, if we listen carefully to how we speak about our attitudes and personalities, we will find inconsistency and variability. Psychological concepts are relocated outside the head, in the workings of discourse, in the in/formal, spoken interactions of everyday conversation (see also Edwards, 1995, 1999; Edwards et al., 1995: Potter, 1996; Potter and Wetherell, 1995). Reasoning and emotions can only be performed through language.

> It is an illusion for me to believe that I can ever be fully present to you in what I say or write, because to use signs at all entails that my meaning is always somehow dispersed, divided and never quite at one with itself. Not only meaning, indeed, but *me*: since language is something I am made out of, rather than merely a convenient tool I use, the whole idea that I am a stable, unified entity must also be a fiction. (Eagleton, 1983: 130, italics in original)

The stability of interior states (such as intelligence, attitude, personality, disposition, attribution, social perception, cognition, emotion, ability, competence) is shown to be inherently complex and contradictory as soon as we start to talk (Potter, 2005). The self is less an interior phenomenon and more a phenomenon constituted through discourses of the external world (Sampson, 1985: 1207). As we shall see below, it is possible to identify how talk between powerful selves (researchers) and disabled others (participants with the label of intellectual disabilities) threaten to re-create impaired selves through these encounters. This approach to discourse analysis allows us to deconstruct the dis abling effects of talk by exposing its contradictions and inconsistencies.

The second approach attends to the ***power of discourse*** (Burman, 1990, 1994, 1995, 2008; Parker and Shotter, 1990; Parker, 1992, 2003; Burman and Parker, 1993a, 1993b; Parker and the Discourse Network, 1999). Discourses fold around people to give the effects of consciousness (Parker, 1997: 7), reproducing and transforming the material world (Nikander, 1995: 11). We use concepts such as 'intellectually disabled' as if they were 'real naturally occurring entities' because they are objects created by 'natural' biopolitical discourses that have come to be known as 'truth'. A discourse coheres around a set of shared meanings. Following Parker (1992), these discourses are sets of statements that construct objects ('the intellectually disabled'), make reference to subjects ('intellectually disabled children'), boast disciplinary histories (educational psychology, paediatrics), support institutions (schools, clinics) and reproduce power relations (adult/child, psychologist/client), with ideological effects (special or inclusive education).

Thinking point: In ordinary thinking, people use a 'common sense', which they do not themselves invent but which has a history. Common sense is a form of ideology. What 'common sense' ideas exist in relation to disabled people?

Reading across Foucault's work (e.g. 1973a, 1973b, 1977) identifies two broad methodologies for dealing with discourse: (1) *archaeology* which is interested in epistemology and the natural and human sciences (for example, how has psychology come to understand us?); and (2) *genealogy,* which is concerned with technologies of the self and the practices of human nature (for example, how have we come to know ourselves?). Disability is no longer considered as a signifier of abnormality but as a discourse of cultural diagnosis (Mitchell and Snyder, 2006: 12). How is the (impaired) self constructed through discourse? How is discourse used to create the other (impaired) as oppositional to the one (able)? Why is something considered to be 'real', 'truthful' or 'natural' (impairment) and what are its socio-historical, cultural and politics origins (disablism). This approach allows us to expose the biopolitical origins and effects of discourse.

Discourses of impairment

Thinking point: In this section we will adopt the two approaches outlined above to address two questions: (1) How is common knowledge of the nature of impairment reproduced through the talk of people? (2) To what extent is 'impairment' a biomedical or psychology concept? How would you answer these questions?

The talk of impairment

Intellectual disabilities have been subjected to critique by poststructuralist disability studies (e.g. Goodley, 2001; Chinn, 2006; Hickey-Moody, 2006, 2009; Roets et al.,

2007, 2008; Goodley and Roets, 2008; Yates et al., 2008; McKenzie, 2009). These writers challenge social and scientific beliefs that intellectual disability is a real impairment that renders people so-labelled as intrinsically incompetent, deficient and lacking. But, to what extent can we argue that this 'incompetence' of people with intellectual disabilities is constructed through the interactions of people so-labelled and others? What, if any, are the micro-social ingredients of the discursive construction of intellectual disabilities? And, how has social science research contributed to this widely-held belief that intellectual disability equates with incompetence? We will now turn to a piece by Goodley and Rapley (2002) which draws on the work of Rapley (see Rapley and Antaki, 1996; Rapley and Ridgway, 1998; Goodley and Rapley, 2001; Rapley, 2004), to explore how the assumption of incompetence is reproduced through the talk of researchers and people with the label of intellectual disabilities. In tune with Potter and Wetherell (1987), Rapley's approach treats language not as a *medium* for 'telementation'– the transmission of thoughts between minds – but rather as *the site* where social objects such as 'thoughts', 'minds' and 'intellectual (dis)abilities' are produced in talk in the conduct of social action. Without the *prior* existence of language, 'psychological' things such as 'intellectual (dis)abilities' can, quite literally, not sensibly be talked of. This approach examines *naturally occurring interaction* to understand the ways in which versions of the world, and our cultures' common knowledge of (the nature of) disability, are re/produced in and through interactional practices.

Thinking point: Research has shown that people with intellectual disabilities tend to give contradictory responses when asked questions by professionals? Thinking back to Chapter 4, how would functionalist, interpretivist, radical humanist and radical structuralist perspectives interpret this finding?

'Acquiescence bias' - the official version

In 'standard' research accounts of the competence of people described as 'intellectually disabled', the notion that people are unreliable reporters of their own subjectivity is firmly entrenched. The message is clear: the utterances of people with 'intellectual disabilities' are – in principle – not to be trusted as veridical reports of their actions, beliefs or feeling states. This version of what 'being intellectually disabled' means is routinely reproduced across research literature of psychology and sociology and is perhaps best summarised in the title of the first substantive paper on this supposed phenomenon 'When in doubt, say yes: acquiescence in interviews with mentally retarded persons' (Sigelman et al., 1981a). In the years since this publication, a series of other studies have served to reify the notion of 'acquiescence bias', and to translate what was always potentially readable as a sensible conversational strategy for powerless people confronted with authority, into an essential(ised), and implicitly also discreditable, component of the 'intellectually disabled' identity. Sigelman et al.'s work has legitimated the belief that one can 'validly' gain access to the views of people with 'intellectual disabilities' only with extreme difficulty. If there is a dispute between a person so-labelled and a carer or professional, the voice to suspect is that of the person with an 'intellectual disability', whose in-built 'acquiescence bias' fatally prejudices accurate reporting. But what is the foundation of the concept of acquiescence?

The Sigelman et al. studies (1980, 1981a, 1981b, 1982) involved formal interviews with people with 'intellectual disabilities' resident in long-stay institutional care in the USA. Sigelman et al. (1980) noticed that about half of a sample of 151 children and adults would answer 'yes' to both, mutually contradictory, questions about their happiness and loneliness in a formal interview schedule. Sigelman et al. (1981a) re-interviewed some of these people and, in the second interview, incorporated paired 'factual' questions about where the person lived (one accurate, the other not) and asked another five questions to which 'no' was the correct answer. These latter questions included the enquiries: 'are you Chinese?' (none of the sample were) and 'do you know how to fly an airplane?' (a little unlikely, perhaps, if one has lived all one's life in an institution). Based on this deceptive and rather bizarre methodology, Sigelman et al. report that 'the rate of acquiescence is staggering' (1981a: 56). Further papers in the series (Sigelman et al., 1981b, 1982) come to the same conclusion, put this way in Sigelman et al. (1981b: 57): 'because mentally retarded persons asked yes or no questions tend to acquiesce (say 'yes'), their answers are likely to be invalid'. Having thus reified 'acquiescence' as a naturalised aspect of 'mentally retarded persons', Sigelman et al. offer neither a clear specification of the notion, nor any analysis of the possible social circumstances in which such 'acquiescence' may occur. The possibility that the 'acquiescence' of their interviewees was merely an expression of politeness, for example, seems to have escaped Sigelman et al. It is simply something that 'mentally retarded persons' do.

Acquiescence, constructed as a dispositional submissiveness, an incapacity inherent in the 'fact' of 'being intellectually disabled', is in practice an extraordinarily over-inclusive and, simultaneously, pragmatically under-theorised notion. The unavoidable and unwitting submissiveness to authority implied by the notion may, in fact, be demonstrated to be *produced* by the very research practices that supposedly 'discover' 'it'. An appreciation of the active production of acquiescence is, however, entirely unavailable from a reading of the existing literature. This production *is* visible if the tools of discursive analysis are brought into play. If the fine detail of actual interactions between psychologists and people described as 'intellectually disabled' are examined, both the artefactual nature of 'acquiescence' and the interactional resilience of people with 'intellectual disabilities' come sharply into focus.

Producing and resisting acquiescence

If we look at actual interview practices using 'real' questions, to which 'real answers' are sought, the supposed phenomenon of 'acquiescence bias' assumes a rather different cast. It is, of course, a definitional feature of interviews that the normal, egalitarian distribution of question and answer turns at talk is suspended. This imbalance can produce what some might like to call 'acquiescence', particularly in those situations where, as here, the interviewer has a schedule to complete which specifies exactly the range of possible 'right' answers. In extract 1 (taken from Rapley and Antaki, 1996), not only can the interviewer (a researcher interested in the quality of life of his interviewees) only accept 'never', 'sometimes' or 'always' (or their synonyms) as 'valid' answers, but s/he is obliged (perhaps influenced by the work of Sigelman et al.) to offer the interviewee all three possible answers prior to accepting one as 'belonging' to the respondent.

Extract 1: Code MT/MR/JW

I	d'you feel out of place (..) >out an'
	about in< social (.) situations
AN	n ⌈o:
I	⌊Anne? (.) never?
AN	no
I	sometimes?
AN	°no°
I	or usually
AN	sometimes I do:
I	yeah? (..) ok we'll put a two down for
	that one then(sniff)

? *Thinking point: Looking at the above extract how would you describe the style and manner of the interviewer and interviewee? What issues of power and turn-taking are highlighted?*

Anne's reply at line 3 ('no') would seem, on the face of it, to be clear and unambiguous. But, by line 9, her answer has changed from a claim 'never' to feel 'out of place in social situations' (line 5) to an acknowledgement that yes, sometimes she does. What better example could there be of the 'if in doubt, say "yes"' phenomenon? This is, evidently, acquiescence in action: Anne has offered clearly contradictory responses. But if this interaction is examined more closely, we can see that the production of contradiction is, entirely, the work of the interviewer. The interviewer refuses to accept a perfectly acceptably designed, thrice-repeated, answer that, 'no', Anne does not feel out of place in social situations. It is a combination of the *requirements of the interview schedule*, and the *assiuousness of the interviewer's pursuit* of them, that *produces* the change in Anne's response, not some hazily defined intellectual defect in Anne which renders her incapable of 'validly' responding. Quite to the contrary, it is the mark of the competent conversationalist that they modify their initial response. Interviewees, if they are competent conversationalists, will, in the face of the demands set up by the utterances of the interviewer, change their position (and thereby seem to be 'acquiescing' in the motivated sense) until such time as the trouble brought about by these factors has been either averted or resolved. What we see in Extract 1, then, is not the playing out of a natural defect essential to 'mental retardation', but rather a demonstration that 'mentally retarded persons' may have as sophisticated a grasp of the preference organisation of interaction as their supposedly non-impaired interlocutors. A turn to the details of talk allows us to capture not only the deficit-approaches of the interviewer (who may have internalised the dominant disablist discourse that interviewees with intellectual disabilities cannot be trusted), but also that people so-labelled are more than able within the form and content of talk to respond in sophisticated ways to others' questioning. The 'medico-psychology assumption of individualised incompetence' (McKenzie, 2009) is therefore deconstructed.

Biopower and impairment

A wheelchair user steps out of her chair to make her way through the metal detectors and security at London Heathrow's Terminal 5. 'If you can walk, why are you using a wheelchair in the first place?' demands a member of the security staff. (A personal anecdote, June 2009)

Have you met X? She works for People First in London; you know the organisation for people with intellectual disabilities. She is very articulate – do you think she really has got intellectual disabilities? (Another personal anecdote, January 1998)

I love Down's syndrome people, don't you? They're always so happy and smiley. (And another, *circa* 1996)

Thinking point: What kinds of assumptions around impairment are at play in the above anecdotes? How is this thing called 'impairment' being understood?

A further deconstruction of impairment is offered by the Foucauldian disability studies scholar Tremain (2000, 2001, 2002, 2005a, 2005b, 2006a, 2006b). Among the rich vein of her work is the deconstruction she offers of the British social model's binary distinction between impairment and disability:

> **IMPAIRMENT**: is the functional limitation within the individual caused by physical, mental or sensory impairment.
>
> **DISABILITY**: is the loss or limitation of opportunities to take part in the normal life of the community on an equal level with others due to physical and social barriers. (DPI, 1982)

Tremain (e.g. 2002, 2006a) argues that this conception of impairment as a naturalised phenomenon endangers the potential critical work of disability studies. Impairment *is* an element of disablism because impairment is discursively constructed in ways that deny access to the normal life of the community. She develops this argument through reference to the endeavours of biopower which attempt to deal with the problems of sanitation, birth rate, longetivity and race sought through understanding and making healthy bodies (Tremain, 2006a: 185).

From the eighteenth century onwards, nation states became increasingly more competent in managing populations through the power/knowledge of natural and human sciences (epidemiology, social policy, medicine and psychology), the makings of institutions (welfare institutions and government departments), the development of forms of professional/expert intervention (rehabilitation, special education). The individual became the subject of state intervention, democracy and knowledge (Tremain, 2006b). As Davis (2002: 106–108) has argued, the formation of the modern nation state required the standardisation, homogenisation and normalisation of bodies and bodily practices to produce an ideal national physical and ethical type (see also Chapter 5 of this book). In constituting the ideal, nation states also constitute the imperfect. These discursive practices not only identify the problems that require measurement and treatment, but, in so doing, create the objects (impairments) and subjects (impaired people) of biopower that hope to secure the well-being of the population. Hence, the objects of bio-medicine (un/healthy, ir/rational, dis/abled), far from being ontologically real or material, are constructions of biopower, professional expertise and normalcy

(Davis, 2002). As McKenzie (2009) argues, eugenics discourse distinguished between those who would be productive citizens and those who would be a drain. Scientific assessment of 'the feebleminded' permitted society to intervene through sterilisation and institutionalisation to reduce the 'breeding' opportunities of these 'unproductive' individuals. More broadly speaking, impairment was and is conceded to bio-medical discourses.

In recent years, we have witnessed a rise in the sheer volume of impairment objects (e.g. ADHD, SEN, Autism, EBD), where children are subjected to a battery of diagnostic tests that purport to describe these phenomena objectively. Promulgated by the biopower of psychology, medicine and education, these diagnoses actually construct the very objects they seek to describe (Tremain, 2006a: 186). And in making these objects we find the accompaniment of discipline: forms of government that are designed to produce a 'docile' body, one that can be subjected, transformed and improved (2006a: 187). From a Foucauldian perspective, then, there is no such thing as 'impairment' outside these discourses (2006a: 190). Any 'hard biological fact' that we might want to point to already has a long history of discursive moulding and institutional usage. The impaired body is an educated, parented, observed, tested, measured, treated, psychologised entity with a long history of being materialised through a multitude of disciplinary practices and institutional discourses. The impaired body shares all of this shaping – perhaps more so than the non-impaired body – due to its consistent engagement with a whole plethora of disabling practices and discourses of the psy-complex. The impaired object and subject are codified to make them more governable (Tremain, 2005a). These processes are intimately felt in healthcare and psychological settings, as these stories from parents of disabled children testify (Goodley and Tregaskis, 2006: 639):

> I think that because of the diagnosis our son had, you miss out on your general child care, because you are so focused on how to help. The professionals that we were talking to were helping us with the 'Down's Syndrome' rather than helping us with child care, you know, nothing like how much milk and sleep he should be having, how to change nappies. (Mags Harcastle)
>
> Some of the consultants referred to her as 'the child with Down's Syndrome', rather than 'Izzy, with Down's Syndrome' ... it was as if ... y'know, her condition was put first. (Josie O'Hanlon)

Thinking point: Thinking back to Chapter 6, how could these accounts be read in terms of psychoemotional disablism and emotional labour?

The marker of impairment looms over a child's life (Overboe, 2007a: 226) and these accounts resonate with Tremain's (2000: 296) position that the (impaired) body has no pre-given materiality, structure or meaning prior to its articulation in discourse: the impaired body is materialised through discourse. Yet, in order to be presented as a medically understood and scientific phenomenon, the diagnosis of impairment must camouflage its institutional origins and socially constructed nature through an appeal to the 'natural' quality of impairment (Tremain, 2000: 192). The category of naturalised impairment persists in order to legitimise the governmental practices (such as medicine and social policy) that generated it in the first place (Tremain, 2005a). Jettison the myth of impairment as a natural entity and you lose the status of medicine and its allied professions. Promote its natural origins and you uphold the truth of the natural sciences:

> Impairment has been disability all along. Disciplinary practices in which the subject is inducted and divided from others produce the illusion of impairment as their pre-discursive antecedent in order to multiply, divide and expand their regulatory effects. (Tremain, 2002: 42)

Hence, *discourses of naturalised impairment* are testimony to decades of medicalisation (Chapter 1) and psychologisation (Chapter 5), continue to this day (see Chapter 10). This is the essence of a Foucauldian analysis – to question what has been regarded as natural or inevitable: to scrutinise a range of widely endorsed social practices surrounding disability, including rehabilitation, community care, inclusion, special education and genetic testing (Tremain, 2005b) that serve the state (biopolitics). Work on the de-pathologisation of childhood (Timimi, 2002, 2005) and adulthood (Breggin, 1991) deconstruct the bio-medical construction of distress. The medicalisation of distress is linked to the power of pharmaceutical companies and their funding of governments' healthcare priorities and policies. The pharmaceutical industry booms even in times of recession (for example, $21 billion sales of psychotherapeutics in 2002, compared with $11 billion in 1998, Lewis, 2006: 346). The marketisation of everyday life demands quick-and-easy treatment of those who threaten the market's efficiency. Hence, the globally expanding discourses of childhood psychiatric illnesses and intellectual impairments fit the maintenance of the marketplace of schools. The global expanse of cognitive and behavioural therapies conceptualise distress as an irrational response of individuals.

This realisation that impairment and disability are two sides of the same socially constituted coin (Tremain, 2002) allows us to ask ever more demanding questions about the ways in which disabled people are discursively constituted in disablist society.

? *Thinking point: How did we know fidgety children before Attention Deficit Hyperactivity Disorder (Davis, 2006c: 236)? To what extent can deep, seemingly organic structures like the immune system be reconceived as historically specific terrains of a high technology culture and a subject of a clinical discourse (Haraway, 1991)? To what extent are the molecular origins of mental illness the discursive product of a veritable superpower [American Psychiatric Association] whose main ally are the hugely profitable and very influential pharmaceutical industries (Lewis, 2006)? Why are Emotional and Behavioral Disorders disproportionately applied to black and working-class boys (Danforth, 2008)? To what extent have psychological discourses individualised the problems of impairment/disability? How can we trust medical labels when they are as amorphous and loose as the social labels that are attached to illness (Greenop, 2009)?*

Simultaneously, the binary of dis/ability serves to reinforce normality within our society (Overboe, 2007a: 226). Biopolitics have much to say about how we should live in and with our bodies:

> My body will bear the marks of all these smoothing machines – perfect vision (contact lenses, lens implants), perfect skin (cosmetic operations), perfect organs (transplants, artificial pumps and filters), perfect birth (episiotomy), perfect genes (spliced and diced). But marked as it is, that's what makes it a smooth body, a smoothing body. Fast and clean. (Bogard, 2000: 270)

A biopolitical perspective on discourse views the body as functioning like a language as a dynamic and unruly network of misfiring and arbitrary adaptations (Mitchell and Snyder, 2006: 207–217): 'To participate in an ideological system of bodily norms that promotes some kinds of bodies while devaluing others is to ignore the malleability of bodies and their definitively mutant nature.' What we know of bodies has been hardened into a form in the long, baking process of history (McKenzie, 2009: 60).

Realism versus relativism: but what about biology?

Thinking point: To what extent is Down syndrome (1) a biological fact or (2) a biopolitical construction?

> Perhaps the challenge in developing a non-reductionist materialist ontology of the body and of impairment is to try to overcome the dualisms that beset our thinking, especially essentialism/constructionism; biology/society; nature/culture. (Thomas, 2001a: 60)

As we saw in Chapter 2, the argument that impairment is discursively constructed has been challenged (Shakespeare and Watson, 1997, 2001a, 2001b; Shakespeare, 2000, 2006a; Watson, 2002; Terzi, 2004; Siebers, 2006; Vehmas and Mäkelä, 2008a, 2008b). Many of the misgivings of these writers relates to the inadequacies of disability theory to take seriously the real, material and ontological realities of impairment. This has led Shakespeare (2006a) to argue that the predicament of certain impairments, particularly those that lead to pain, suffering and death, have been brushed aside by disability theorists who want to further a totalising theory of the social constitution of disability and impairment. To *cast doubt* on the *hard* existence of 'intellectual disabilities', he suggests, denies the reality of 'impairment' (Shakespeare, 2006a: 39). Protagonists such as Shakespeare, Watson, Vehmas and Mäkelä identify themselves as *realists* who philosophically accept the material realities of impairment. For them, a discursive turn ignores this materiality. Vehmas and Mäkelä (2008a) argue that impairments whose aetiologies are known as biological entities – such as extra chromosome 21 (Trisomy 21) implicated in Down syndrome – are *brute physical facts.* Vehmas and Mäkelä (2008a) suggest that objective entities exist independently of any perceiver and subjective entities are dependent on perceivers. Mountains are ontologically objective because they exist independently of any perceiver; mountains would stay in the world even if all the humans and other subjects with senses disappeared from the earth. Here, they argue:

> The statement 'It is better not to have an extra chromosome 21 than to have it' is about an ontologically objective entity, but makes a subjective judgment about it. On the other hand, the statement 'The fact that my child has an extra chromosome 21 causes me emotional distress' reports an epistemically objective fact in the sense that it is made true by the existence of an actual fact that is not dependent on any opinion of observers. (Vehmas and Mäkelä, 2008a: 46)

Critiques such as these are important because they ask: *When does discourse end and a brute material fact begin?* We can address this question by visiting an argument from discursive psychology. The papers of Edwards et al. (1995) and Parker (1999b) encapsulate the contrary positions of relativists and critical realists.

Edwards et al. (1995) take to task critics of discursive determinism. Faced with the typical response of realist critics banging on tables ('look this is real') and pleading for a recognition of the material outside discourse ('death is not discursive'), they respond:

> All the pointing to, demonstrations of, and descriptions of brute reality are inevitably semiotically mediated and communicated. ... The very act of producing a non-represented, unconstructed external world is inevitably representational. (Edwards et al., 1995: 27)

Even when you bang on tables or hit on rocks (or mountains) to defend brute facts, one should remember that:

> Rocks are cultural too, in that they are thus categorized, included in the definition of the natural world, classified into sedimentary and igneous, divided into grains of sand, pieces of gravel, pebbles, stones, rocks, boulders, mountains, domesticated in parks and ornamental gardens, protected in wildernesses, cut, bought, used and displayed as 'precious stones', and include as a sub-category 'girls' best friends'; not to mention coolant for vodka! (Edwards et al., 1995: 30)

Relativists argue that when realists appeal to brute facts they uphold the common sense view that a phenomenon (e.g. impairment) is the real (material) aberrancy (McRuer, 2002: 225) but, also, ignore the construction of the facts that they describe. To suggest Trisomy 21 is a brute, biological fact kicks away its deep historical construction. Following Koch (2008), Trisomy 21 is anything but 'an epistemically objective fact not dependent on any opinion of observers' (the argument of Vehmas and Mäkelä, 2008a) when we consider that the identification of this 'fact' is intimately tied to processes of social disavowal that result in, for example, nine out of ten foetuses being terminated in North America.[2] We need, therefore, to remain vigilant of the (bio)politics of impairment that underpin these systems. It is impossible to simply pull Down syndrome out of its political location. For Hickey-Moody (2009), Down syndrome is a phenomenon created through signification (a collection of signs that identify the features of Down syndrome) which give rise to particular forms of subjectivity (expectations of how to 'be' Down syndrome). In order to 'become Down syndrome', the labelled subject is socially coded by the related discourses in ways that limit – dis-able – their subjectivities.

Furthermore, all cultural members risk being wrapped up in this process of signification, in which particular individuals are dis-abled through discourse.

While it may be acceptable to argue for the socially constituted nature of rocks, Edwards et al.'s second example of death has been seen as particularly pernicious (Parker, 1999b):

> Look closer at the commonsense conception of Death and, like the table, it starts to disappear: resurrection, the afterlife, survival of the spirit, the non-simultaneous criteria of brain death, the point when life support might as well be switched off, cryogenic suspension, the precise (how precise?) moment of death. There is 'natural death', with its images of peace, fulfilment and old age ('a little life, rounded with a sleep'), and 'unnatural death' (Death death), connoting violence, pain, waste and loss. There is murder (and its degrees), manslaughter, capital punishment, killing in war, justifiable homicide, *crime passionel*, accident, suicide: as everyone knows, these are categories which are as constructed as can be. Whole professions (lawyers, assassins, weapons manufacturers, detectives, novelists, criminologists) are dedicated to the assignment of events to one or other category. ... Death is never simple. We have far too much interest in it for that. (Edwards et al., 1995: 36)

Far from viewing their arguments as un*realistic,* Edwards et al. argue that the destabilisation of brute facts is exactly the kind of project that should inform critical thinking: 'Relativism is the quintessentially academic position, where all truths are to-be-established' (1995: 37).

Thinking point: 'All truth is up for grabs.' What are the potentials and pitfalls of this viewpoint?

A relativist position keeps buoyant debates around prickly issues such as 'quality of life' (Rapley and Ridgway, 1998) which underpin many ethical debates such as the right to die, the right to terminate, the meaning of pain and illness in the lives of disabled and non-disabled people and, crucially, the extent to which labels of impairment and disability are fobbed off as examples of brute facts.

For Parker (1999b), there is a problem. He suggests that by remaining in academic and philosophical circles, Edwards et al. (1995) are in danger of domesticating relativism; of turning clearly important issues of life, death (and disability) into interesting academic debates. Parker is therefore sceptical of the end game of relativism. Once relativists have committed themselves to the idea that 'anything goes', he argues, then it is difficult for them to be able to respond to revisionist histories (such as denials of the Holocaust). His argument, then, is for a particular form of what might be termed critical realism, which accepts the constituting nature of language but is mindful of the role of ideology and the need to consistently collectively locate the discourses of which we speak. Hence, critical realism does not do away with the real. In contrast, it attends to *very real* institutional practices in which entities such as Down syndrome are portrayed as *very real* unproblematic biological phenomena (see also Parker et al., 1995). Referring to 'brute facts' seriously ignores these very real institutional constructions and creates an artificial divide (between the discursive and the material) that was never there in the first place. Instead, a critical realist position like that described by Parker, allows us to engage with what Butler (1993) terms the materialisation of bodies (and minds), evidenced in this oft-cited passage:

> To 'concede' the undeniability of 'sex' or its 'materiality' is always to concede some version of 'sex', some formation of 'materiality' … there is no reference to pure body which is not at the same time a further formation of that body … in so far as the extra-discursive is delimited, it is formed by the very discourse from which it seeks to free itself. … The forming, crafting, bearing, circulation, signification of that sexed body will be mobilised by the law. (Butler, 1999: 240–241)

To talk of the 'brute facts' of impaired or normal bodies evokes a biology that has already been constructed. Regulatory norms hail subjects to assume positions (Shilling, 2005: 50). The body is not some entity prior to signification: it has already been through a process of signification. It is a 'fact' with a history of signification. Paraphrasing Butler (1993: 235–236), the category of 'sex' is, from the start, normative … a regulatory ideal. 'Sex' not only functions as a norm, but is a regulatory practice that produces the bodies it governs. Sex is an ideal construct that is forcibly materialised through time. To point to the brute facts of the body is to reinsert a regulatory vision of that body. Bodies are materialised through performativity – the reiterative and citational practices by which discourse produces the effect that it names. What is left of 'sex' (biology) once it assumes its social character as gender (discursive) is very little: sex is replaced by social meaning, absorbed by gender and then reappears like a fiction, fantasy, retroactively installed at a prelinguistic site (Butler, 1993).[3]

As Aalten (1997) has argued, even as a material reality the body is never there: it always has a meaning brought about through the reiterative and citational workings of discourses that produce the effects they name. The body bears the marks of time and acts of production. This has led to a huge body of literature (no pun intended) that takes to task the simplistic distinction between body/society (Crossley, 1995; Shilling, 2005; Cregan, 2006; Turner, 2008;). Social scientific studies of pain, for example, have demonstrated its discursive complexity (Olkin, 2009). 'Unliveable pain' for one person might be an 'ordinary bodily experience' for another. At times, it seems that disability studies lacks the language – the discourse – to speak of the body in ways other than deficient:

> One research domain that is yet to be fully explored from the perspectives of disabled people is the kinaesthetic, sensory and cognitive experiences of people with an array of impairments. … [W]e are missing the constructs and theoretical material needed to articulate the ways in which impairment shapes disabled people's version of the world. Even as I write this I am struggling to find the words to adequately describe these phenomena. … The fact that impairment has almost always been studied from a deficit model means that we are deficient in language to describe it any other way than as a 'problem'. (Linton, 1998a: 530)

Thinking point: 'Over 20 years of writing in this area [sociology of the body] has demonstrated that the human body is socially conditioned to undertake "even the most basic of tasks including sitting, walking and running" (Turner, 2008: 12). The child is therefore a 'social construction'. Discuss.

Bodies that do not 'naturally' enact such activities described in the thinking point above will face related regimes of instruction. Indeed, to recall Reeve's work and her use of Agamben in Chapter 6, it would appear that realist disability scholars want to insert a version of the disabled body as *zoë* (natural/bare life) over *bios* (forms of life). But, to try to strip away the natural from the social, might ignore the political makings of these artifacts.[4] Rather than a reduced signification of the body, perhaps we need to increase it. Perhaps we need to think of impaired bodies in terms of what they can be rather than medicalised categories of what they are not (Hickey-Moody, 2009: 30). Discoursing impairment allows for possibilities for resistance as evidenced in the Canadian Down Syndrome Society's redefinition of Down syndrome as a normal, 'naturally occurring' condition of society rather than an affliction or suffering (see Koch, 2008). Perhaps, Shakespeare and Watson (2001a) capture the realist/relativist nature of disability well when they state that disability is the quintessential postmodern concept, because it is so complex, so variable, so contingent, so situated. It sits at the intersection of biology and society and of agency and structure. Disability cannot be reduced to a singular identity: it is multiplicity, a plurality (Shakespeare and Watson, 2001a).

Conclusion

For Barker and Campbell (2006: 321), as soon as we discursively interrogate impairment its meaning loses fixity, generality and ultimately collapses. But this is not to say that discourse leaves us with an empty phantom body. Nor does it mean the death of the human being. As Koch (2008: 20) puts it: the 'thingness' that is the physical is real but it is the social construction of that reality that makes for dis-ability.[5] This point links neatly to Davis's (2002: 26–27) call for dismodernism, which recognises that we all have difference in common; that identity is malleable not fixed; that technology is not separate but part of the body; that dependence, not individual independence, is the rule. We are all networked into a discursive society.

Further reading

Burman and Parker (1993a). Great introductory collection available to download for free from www.discourseunit.com.

Edwards, Ashmore and Potter (1995). A readable defence of discursive relativism.

Goodley and Rapley (2002). Discursive psychological analyses of intellectual disabilities.

Samuels (2002). An application of Judith Butler to disability studies.

Tremain (2005a). *The* text on Michel Foucault and disability studies.

Notes

1 Adapted from Fanon (1993: 112): 'racialised epidermal schema is one in which "I was battered down by tom-toms, cannibalism, intellectual deficiency, fetishism, racial defects, slave ships"'.
2 Deleuze and Guattari (1987) develop further a cultural and political analysis of these brutal facts – such as the marking of the body through diagnosis – by suggesting that such truths threaten to codify, block, stratify and repress the becomings of human life (see Goodley and Roets, 2008).
3 See Samuel's (2002) use of Butler and the constitution of the impaired/disabled body.
4 This point is taken up by Fanon (1993: 29), who proclaims: 'when someone strives and strains to prove to me that black men are as intelligent as white men, I say that intelligence has never saved anyone ... [intelligence has] also been employed to justify the extermination of men'.
5 Frank (2005: 972) argues that 'the relative standard of moral worth is neither relativist, situating moral worth solely within the conditions of one individual life, nor absolute, emanating from a space of no specific life. Dialogue is the space between those extremes.'

EIGHT

Culture: *Psychoanalytic Disability Studies*

****

Introduction

Mintz (2002) defines disability as a symbolic event situated in culture. It is possible to find a rich tradition of cultural disability studies in the work of the cultural modellists (Chapter 1) and radical humanists (Chapter 3). Specific examples from cultural studies, sociology, anthropology and radical psychiatry include interrogations of the intersections of patriarchy and disablist culture (Fine and Asch, 1988), the reliance of disabling understandings on popular literature and film (Garland-Thomson, 1997, 2005), culturally moulded components of intelligence (Langness and Levine, 1986a), long deep-seated histories of normalcy (Davis, 1995), strict modernist constructions of an abled or disabled body (Hughes, 2000, 2002a, 2002b), medicalised diagnoses of pathology that have been exploited to maintain cultural standards of childhood (Timimi, 2002, 2005) and the inevitably complex relationship of culture and identity formation (Watson et al., 2003). We take a different tack in this chapter compared to previous ones by focusing in on *one* theoretical resource – psychoanalysis – in order to expose the intricate relation of self, relationships and ideology played out in the makings of culture. Specifically, we explore the making of the human subject envisaged by the French psychoanalyst Jacques Lacan, through his imaginary and symbolic phases of development, as laying the foundations for a disabling culture. This theory also allows us to pick out possibilities for resistance and we conclude with some thoughts on the use of psychoanalytic metaphors for cultural disability studies.

Psychoanalytic culture

> When Freud ... rendered visible the predominant role of the unconscious in psychic processes, it became clear that our ego is not even a master in its own house. (Žižek, 2006: 1)

Bocock (1976) champions psychoanalytic theories as cultural statements about society. These ideas allow us to make sense of psychic factors because psychoanalytic discourses are everywhere (Parker, 1997, 1999a). Psychoanalytic concepts enrich our understandings of culture because culture is comprised of these concepts (Burman, 2008: 144). Mitchell (1974) suggests that psychoanalytic theories have explanatory rather than prescriptive value in making sense of inequities in society. Woodhill (1994: 219) blends an interest in semiotics, disability and psychoanalysis, advocating that a:

> social semiotics of disability is a powerful tool in the analysis of the situation and social construction of persons with disabilities. It shows us how signs of difference that are learned and used from an early age by people both within and without disabilities can create our conscious and unconscious images of what it means to be disabled, and how these representations can perpetuate oppression and helplessness. By uncovering and debunking, by appropriating and deploying the signs denoting disability, we can move towards emancipation of all.

This chapter works with ideas that provide 'a non-normative appreciation' of psychoanalytic theory (Shildrick, 2007b: 266) that take seriously *disabling culture*. We will examine how psychoanalysis provides a metaphorical resource for untying the complicated knot of psychic and cultural factors, which, if read politically, can expose the subtle, everyday, mundane conditions of disabling culture. It also provides an account of ideology that complements sociological (Chapter 4), critical psychological (Chapter 6) and poststructuralist disability studies (Chapter 7). But, be warned: always view psychoanalysis with healthy scepticism rather than deluded affiliation!

A Lacanian account

This chapter demonstrates how Lacanian ideas provide metaphors for untangling the emptiness of capitalistic endeavour (we desire things we lack); the lie of neoliberal autonomy (which we all fail to live up to); the unconscious nature of consumerism (we fetishise things to fill the void of living with what we lack); and the alienated differentiation of self and other (we fantasise that we are autonomous while others are not).

Thinking point: In what ways can the psychoanalytic concepts of 'fantasy', 'desire', 'denial', 'the unconscious' and 'identification' be used to make sense of disabling culture?

For Parker (1997: 186–187), Lacanian psychoanalysis offers an account of the development of the human being, his/her relationship to other people (alterity), their early entrance into the cultural world and the residues of conflict and desire that inflict on later adult life (and cultural production). What makes Lacanian thinking unique, in contrast to popular views of psychoanalysis, is the centrality given to language. If we adopt the position explored in Chapter 7, that discourse constitutes culture, than Lacanian theory can be used as cultural theory. There is much to Lacan that will be skimmed over in this brief account, but a number of key ideas will be introduced. At the root of these ideas is the alienation that occurs when we become our selves in relation to others in a culture that appears to offer much but gives very little.

Lacanian encounters in disability studies include Frank's (1994) engagements with medical sociology, Davis's (1995) analyses of normalcy, Michalko's (2002) explorations of 'disability-as-difference', Wilton's (2003) comparison of Lacan and Freud in relation to disabling geographies, Shildrick's (2004, 2007a, 2007b) rather non-plussed view of the merits of psychoanalytic ideas and Erevelles's (2005) very brief use of Lacan in relation to education. While these are helpful, they are somewhat speculative and underdeveloped. This chapter attempts to provide a closer reading of key Lacanian concepts.

Lacan was interested in the construction of human subjectivity in cultures that demand rational, conscious and accountable individuals (Chapter 5). His work has been linked to poststructuralist critiques of modernity (Chapter 7) and rejections of capitalist forms of psychologisation (Chapter 5). Although his work boasts some alliances with phenomenology (see Chapter 4), his work can also be seen as radical humanism (also Chapter 4), in the sense that the conscious, rational human subject of modern society is viewed with suspicion. The human subject for Lacan is not the same as the 'ego' nor the illusory 'unitary individual self' of psychologisation (Chapter 5). The subject is about human *being*.

Early infancy is characterised by dependency. In early childhood we start to realise ourselves as split from others. We rely on others in order to see ourselves. For the rest of our lives we remain fascinated with, and perturbed by, others and their views of us (Marks, 1999a: 173). Adulthood is typified by conflicts around idealised versions of whom we should be, and through our relationships with others, including little others (parent, lover, colleague, friend), big others (science, God, truth, masculinity) and demonised others who fail to fit idealised images (which in contemporary society are occupied with black, disabled, feminine, gay – in short the non-normative – *Other*). Our selves are dependent on the images and meanings that abound. In the final analysis we are always split from ourselves, the world and the others in it.

Lacanian psychoanalysis starts with a familiar context for the re/production of culture: the family. In terms of WENA cultures, the family is 'the miniature of the nation … the workshop in which one is trained' (Fanon, 1993: 142–149). There are two phases to childhood: the pre-linguistic ***mirror phase*** and the linguistic ***symbolic phase***. However, before these, following Parker (1993, 1997), is the pre-mirror phase. Up to six months of life, the body is fragmented, a collection of unco-ordinated body parts, reliant on/and fused with the primary caregiver (often the mother). As with Freud, Lacan says the baby has no sense of oneself as separate from the mother. The child is driven by a polymorphous perversity, in the sense that their drives are directed out to various parts of the body (physiology) and mind (psychical), where pleasures are gratified. Body parts are where our instincts are made. This state is understood as the ***real*** in Lacanian theory: there is nothing but need. At the heart of the child's psychic life is a fragmented body: the body is an assemblage of parts or pieces (arms, legs, surfaces), of turbulent movements (Lacan, 1977). The child is a 'hommelette': a psychical scrambled egg whose processes remain anarchical and chaotically integrated (Grosz, 1999: 268). Lacan suggests that from the very outset the child is mediated through cultural signs and symbols that aid the signifying of desire. Hence, the child's eyes are a site for desire (gazing and being gazed at), as much as their limbs (touching and being touched).

Thinking point: Infancy provides the original experience of narcissism. In attempting to make sense of these early psychic and physiological encounters,

the child's mental representations are equally chaotic: 'of castration, mutilation, dismemberment, dislocation, evisceration, devouring and bursting out of the body' (Parker, 1997: 217). There is nothing but bewilderment in the real for the child, who has no language to speak of the real (Michalko, 2002: 132). How does this Lacanian description fit with common-sense ideas of the 'world of the baby'?

Between the age of 6 months and 18 months, the child enters the imaginary world: the *mirror phase*. Through reflections in the mirror, the child becomes (narcissistically) captivated by its own fixed image (*imago*), which symbolically cuts him/her from the real 'dangerous plenitude and jouissance[1] of the maternal-infant dyad' (Shildrick, 2007a: 234). The real is now lost. Instead, in the reflection of the mirror, the child sees a unitary, whole self, which contrasts so markedly with the ***real***ity of its own fragmented, unco-ordinated 'body in pieces' (*corps morcelé*). The *imago* freezes the body image and conceals the infant's lack of co-ordination. It is salutary for the child because it gives them their first sense of a 'coherent identity', in which they see the first term, 'that is me' (J. Rose, 1986). However, this captivation with the illusory whole self is actually a misrecognition (*meconnaisance*): we misrecognise our selves as whole, perfect, unitary bodies. What we see is a *fantasy of wholeness* because the child is actually still chaotic (they are still in the real) (Grosz, 1999).

The child sees its self outside itself: in an order external to itself. They also misrecognise the wholeness of a crucial other, the 'second term'; the mirror image of the primary caregiver, often the mother, who supplies the child with the illusion of wholeness. And this view of oneself as separate is dependent on, of course, seeing others as separate (and those others seeing us as separate). 'I recognise myself, me, in the mirror, and where I recognise myself with an other sharing the qualities of similar beings' (Miller, 2008: 4). This existential wholeness is constituted in relationships with others (Frank, 2000: 153). Here, there is a Lacanian emphasis on the constitution of the subject *in relation to others* (alterity, as we saw, in Chapter 6). We produce an image of ourselves because we see others recognising us. This (mis)perceived wholeness is felt as threatening to the child (she notices that she is often in her mother's arms, her body is turbulent and dependent rather than whole), so she feels hostile (and directs these feelings out at the 'me' and, unavoidably, the 'other' – the mother). A recurring trope of psychoanalysis comes to play at this point; the child tries to resolve her anger and ambivalence through jubilantly *identifying* with both the image of their own *me* (the whole/unitary image in the mirror) and *the other* (the mother), each supplying the child with an imaginary sense of mastery: the Ideal-I (Lacan, 1977).

The child's *I* is made, recognising and desired by *others*, as the *I* recognises and desires those *others* too. The child starts the lifetime process of seeking (and often failing) to repress the realities of their fragmented bodies (the real) while embracing relationships with themselves and others (Shildrick, 2007a: 231). We are forever torn between the conscious desire to represent our selves as 'normal' (the *imago*) and being compelled to repress all the meanings of our actual 'fragmented other' to the realm of the unconscious (Erevelles, 2005: 426). Simultaneously, the child introjects that most important relationship of her young life, the most precious other, (the *imago* of) the loving mother. Such psychical work has a number of long-standing consequences, all of which are associated around desiring what we *lack*. First, the child/subject is now always in a place of *lack* because she will never achieve what she desires to be because she never matches up to the original whole, independent, masterful image of her 'I' portrayed in the mirror.[2] This is why the term *meconnaisance* is employed: the illusion of autonomy to which we entrust ourselves forms the armour of an alienating identity (Lacan, 1977). This is the vital lie required to become a subject (Wilton, 2003) and a lingering force in later relationships: 'desire is, therefore, among many things about the fantasy of finding images (*imago*) of the self in others' (Parker, 1993: 11). Second, for the rest of her life, the child will always lack that initial desire of the mother and, simultaneously, find the mother (and many others) lacking. We are also always in lack, as we seek out the fantasised original object (the mother), who desired us as we desired them: the 'objet-petit-a' (Parker, 1993: 11). We desire an idealised other to confer perfection on us, to see us as whole and total in their eyes, as special, unique and endearing. Consequently, we spend our lives trying to find different forms of wholeness (the *imago*) and *objet-petit-a* (the m/other who desired us), seeking the 'perfect job', 'perfect partner', 'perfect family', and so on (which are classically referred to as 'ego ideals' in psychoanalysis). Desire is insatiable; a hopeless attempt to find that which desired us (the original object) through *objet-petit-a*. In short, all our unconscious lives, the desire of the subject is the desire of the other (Lacan, 1977). As soon as I desire I am asking to be considered: 'I look for admiration in the eyes of the other – the other corroborates in me my search for self-validation' (Fanon, 1993: 218). This is, however, hopeless because the other we desire always lets us down.[3]

Thinking point: Consider the following statement. 'We are what we are because of how others see us.'

This account of 'I', the (m)other, lack and desire does not stop with the mirror. Clearly, a child develops in culture. The *symbolic* appears between 18 months and four years of life (Parker, 1997: 215). While the mirror phase starts the child's ascent into the imaginary, illusory world of 'I' and 'others', the symbolic comprises an alienating set of signs, in which we start to speak of others and ourselves as people or subject(s) (Parker, 1993: 1).[4] The symbolic is radical alterity – language – that is understood broadly and includes visual and tactile images as well as linguistic constructions (discourse, as described in Chapter 7). *The symbolic is culture*; where we learn to use signifiers (such as 'I', 'you' and 'them'); to speak of ourselves and others as separate entities, to talk of our desires, control and autonomy; of *ourselves in an order outside ourselves* (J. Rose, 1986). Hence, the *imago* that the child buys into is not simply a mirror image but an *imago* located in an order of signs *outside* the child (Rose, 1986). Here, as with the mirror, there is alienation, but this has been multiplied infinitely because of the sheer size and expanse of language.

Language, as we saw in Chapter 7, creates a variety of meanings in excess of what is intended or actually needed (Hare Mustin and Marecek, 1992). Signs are made up of signifiers (terms such as 'I') and signifieds (meanings such as 'I am separate from others'). For Lacan, the key aspect of the sign is the signifier. During the mirror phase, and from then on, the child's *I* (and its misrecognised autonomy) is made in a system of signifiers, in culture. However, signifiers are constantly shifting, in moving chains, so that 'I' is never stable. Following Eagelton (1983: 127–129), meaning is never *present* in the signifier; the meaning of a signifier is a matter of what it is *not* ('I' am not 'you') and each signifier is underscored by a host of other signifiers ('I' has to fend off 'you' 'them', 'mother', 'God', and so on). In the symbolic, then, we are always insecure of our 'I' – our ontology – and we find ourselves lacking.

Thinking point: Complete the following sentence 20 times. 'I am ... .' Look at the sentences you gave. In what ways do these sentences define your relationship with culture?

Ontological insecurity is the norm for Lacan because language is made up of huge chains of signifiers that promise ontological security but actually give nothing. Just as the image of the body in the mirror phase displayed the fiction of autonomy, the symbolic phase presents the self as similarly alienating. The self lacks any stable centre because it is caught up in an endless movement of signifier to signifier along a linguistic chain that constantly divides us (Erevelles, 2005: 426).[5] The 'I' is always insufficient: 'I' never matches up to the associated desire to be autonomous and independent. And, following Eagleton (1983: 128), every signifier, every 'I', is scored over or traced through with all other signifiers. As we saw in the last chapter, since the meaning of a sign is a matter of what it is not, its meaning is always in some sense absent from what it is. Just as sane can only be understood in relation to insane. And man to woman. Both sane and man never really stand up as strong, clear, understandable ontologies. Descartes' maxim of 'I think therefore I am' is rejigged by Lacan: 'I think where I am not, therefore I am where I do not think'. The 'I', initially alienated through the misrecognition of the whole self in the mirror phase, is now further alienated from itself,[6] and from others, through its location in the symbolic ordering of subjects (Lacan, 1977). When we speak, we lose ourselves in language, to the symbolic sea of signifiers that float around and through us. We are dislocated, empty and incomplete.

But what about our relationships with others in the symbolic? Lacan reminds us that when the child first speaks s/he learns of his/her loss in language. A call of 'Mama' speaks of a (m)other who is not there (as they always seemed to be in the real), whose absence has to be called back. Language therefore appears to close down the possibility of ever being at one with the (m)other. Hence, our first desire, which is spoken of in the symbolic, is of loss and lack. The symbolic is also lack in a bigger sense. The symbolic is disorientating. There are millions of 'I's to choose from. Caught up in this dislocation of culture, we are drawn to the impossibility of constituting an identity. Like the mirror phase, we are phenomenologically severed from the 'I' we now speak. As Rose (1986) reminds us, we also speak in ways that give us a sense of being *outside* language and the symbolic ('I am me' – outside culture). And, as with the original harrowing separation from the (m)other, the symbolic is dealt with like any other threatening concept: it is repressed into the unconscious:

> Language provides us with the means to articulate desires, but it simultaneously turns experience into something symbolically mediated and broken from that which it is supposed to be express, that which vanishes into the unconscious as a fantasy space constituted in the very same moment. (Parker, 1997: 167)

The unconscious is structured by the symbolic, and includes the underside of language, the network of signifiers, which the child must learn to repress in order to be able to speak (Parker, 1997). Hence, not only is the 'out there' of the symbolic (culture) alienating, but so too is the 'in there' (unconscious) of the symbolic. Because language belongs to the general population of 'others' of the symbolic – so *the unconscious is the discourse of the other*. The unconscious is made up of a string of signifiers influencing what we say, how we desire and how we understand ourselves and others (Parker, 1997). Where the imaginary phase for children was associated with a fascination with the *imago*, the symbolic phase commences the child's journey into different positions in language. The subject now speaks culture, but will also lose itself to the moral authorities of that culture.[7] There are too many truths out there to speak with authority.

Thinking point: Thinking back to the last chapter, in what ways can it be argued that we are drenched in language? Is there a possibility of 'drowning' in words?

A key part of the symbolic refers to the inclusion of the 'third term' of psychoanalysis: the father. After the 'I' and the (m)other, there is the father, or in Lacanian parlance the law of the father or the ***phallus***. Symptomatic of patriarchal and capitalist societies, phallocentric discourses govern and inform the symbolic, aiding the separation of mother–child dyad, the emergence of the self and centralising authority. The phallus normalises familial relationships of child, mother and father along the lines of the nuclear family. This authority of the phallus rules over 'la puissance' – the ideal of integrity and control (Cregan, 2006) – instilling morality through prohibition of the unruly real and promotion of the symbolic order. The phallus relates to codes of behaviour and social laws. The phallus is ideology. As Rose (1986) notes, the phallus dictates who can use language and imbues the symbolic with certainty. One key marker of the phallus on the symbolic is in relation to gender. Phallocentric cultures separate men and women in terms of what can be said and by whom.[8]

Thinking point: Spender (1982) argues that the patriarchal order of language is skewed in such a way that the 'proper human being' is a male one and female is 'a negative category'. In order to explore this assertion, work with a partner to identify words used to describe (a) a man who is sexually promiscuous and (b) a woman who is sexually promiscuous. What did you find? Which list was the longest – (a) or (b)? Did you find that there were more (negatively loaded) words/signifiers for (b) than for (a)? How do your findings relate to Spender's argument?

In phallocentric societies woman does not exist: she is either excluded by the symbolic or defined as exclusion (Rose, 1986). Men have power to use the symbolic, women do not. Thinking back to Chapter 7, the phallus upholds the grand narratives of patriarchy and capitalism. Resolving this involves an accent to the symbolic for boys pursuing masculinity (with a lifelong aim to gain the power of immersion within the symbolic, to find the phallus, to speak of 'I') and submission to the symbolic for girls embracing femininity (to be simply something to be desired by men). But for *all*, the phallus extends beyond sex/gender, acting as a master signifier – the One – that demands unconscious autonomy and slavery to the symbolic (Miller, 2008). Following Eagleton (1983), the phallocentric binary opposition of man/woman is reminiscent of patriarchal ideology, which requires the drawing of rigid boundaries to maintain the dominant and exclude the alternative. The phallus lays the foundations for other ideologies, including the heteronormative, occidental, capitalist and the able (Chapter 3). Wilton (2003) observes that we are *all* symbolically castrated in and through language. Our narcissistic fascination with ourselves (which is empty in the realities of the symbolic) is now precariously held together without the desire of the mother (which has been taken away) and the phallus that reminds us that we are nothing (that we will never be part of language).

Lac(k)an and disablist culture

> Disabled people's experience can only be understood in relation to alterity. The creation of the devalued 'Other' is a necessary precondition for the creation of the able-bodied rational subject who is the all-pervasive agency that sets the term of the dialogue. (Ghai, 2006: 79)
>
> The fear of the unwhole body, of the altered body, is kept at bay by the depictions of the whole, systematized body ... the disabled body is a direct imago of the repressed fragmented body. The disabled body causes a kind of hallucination of the mirror phase gone wrong. (Davis, 1995: 134)

Lacanian theory allows for a cultural disability studies reading because of its interest in the formulation of ideology in the imaginary and the symbolic elements of culture. As a description of patriarchy (Mitchell, 1974) and capitalism (Parker, 1997), we can see the emptiness of neoliberal autonomy (the mirror phase); the relentless nature of self-help consumerism (seeking *objet-petit-a*); the vacuous promise of male-stream truths such as science and capitalism (phallus) and the precariousness of humanity (real fragmented bodied) throughout a hapless culture (symbolic). Potentially, the primacy of language pulls an analysis of disability away from biological determinism towards cultural analysis, just as it did for feminist uses of Lacanian theory in the 1970s (see Feher-Gurewich, 2001). Lacan's analysis of empty signifiers can be used to great effect to explain the emptiness of culture in which 'ability' is held up as a phallocentric symbolic destiny (though one clearly unattainable *for us all*).

Thinking point: Consider the following statement. 'Disabled children are sources of fear *and* fascination*'. How does this observation contribute to our understandings of disablism?*

If the symbolic is empty for non-disabled people, then it is further emptied and lacking for disabled people, captured in common terms and couplets that indicate their exclusion from the symbolic, such as 'suffering from', 'afflicted by', 'persistent vegetative state', 'the mentality of an eight-year-old', 'useless limb', 'good and bad leg', 'mentally unstable', 'deranged' and 'abnormal' (Olkin, 2009: 17). Disabled people become ~~Other~~: the absolute other crossed through (Rose, 1986). As Campbell (2009: 17) has argued, the processes of ableism, like those of racism, induce an internalisation that devalues disabled people. We can, therefore, explain some of the ambivalent unconscious discourses around disability.

Life is *lack* for Lacanian theory and this can have major impacts on the lives of disabled people. All of us are born into the real with fragmented bodies that then lack the imaginary wholeness of the original *imago*. The cultural prerogative is to refute those who remind us of our own fragmentation (e.g. impaired bodies) and disability, by definition, implies 'lacking' or 'flaw' (Ghai, 2002: 51). Simultaneously, disability can also imply excess, requiring moderation (Davis, 2002). The emptiness of the symbolic is dealt with by projecting our feelings of alienation on to others. Caught up in mourning the original desire of the (m)other, we endeavour to find the absent other somewhere, anywhere, but quickly find these others lacking. While this demonstrates the shared vulnerability of all human beings, and therefore has links with attempts to combine disability studies and feminist ethics of care literature (Shakespeare, 2000; McLaughlin et al., 2008), the *other is in all of us* but its legacy is that we see the other outside ourselves:

> If it is impossible for an able-bodied man to meet the fantasy model of sex, a man with a disability faces an even more devastating task to live up to the ideal male model. (Tepper, 1999: 45)
>
> We all tire of independence and would like to be taken care of, but that wish conflicts with our own concept of ourselves as able to cope. (Bardach, 2007: 249)

Dominant cultural tropes of 'the disabled' as the other emerge in a variety of guises. Campbell (2008a: 5) argues that the cultural artefact of the unruly, uncivil, disabled body is a necessary symbolic construction for the reiteration of the 'truth' of the 'real/essential' human self who is endowed with masculinist attributes of certainty, mastery and autonomy. It is no surprise to find culture reacting to and constituting disabled people as lacking, monstrous and fragmented. The disabled body becomes *the* site for cultural projection. The 'non-disabled' points to 'the disabled' as if to say: 'You are in lack, not I'. This clearly is a way of dealing with the lack that every person finds (and at heart knows) himself or herself caught up in: of not matching the autonomous 'I' (the *imago* of the mirror) or demands of the big other (the impossibility of language of the symbolic).[9] But rather than recognise this in themselves, the non-disabled firmly locate the lack in disabled others and continue with their misrecognised fantasies of autonomy.

A disabled body becomes an *imago* of what we lack but, paradoxically, that in which we see ourselves. Disabling images of dependency and nurture remind us of life before the *meconnaisance* of 'I' in the mirror phase and the emptiness of the 'I' in the symbolic. Disability evokes the real (Davis, 1995). Disability is therefore not simply a site for violently discarding that which we are no longer; it is also where we find the fantasy of that which we were. Disabled people are therefore subjected to curiosity and dismissal; they are cared for and infantilised; ignored and stared at; nurtured and violently expelled; ignored and overly intervened with; shunned and touched; made grotesque and sexualised. They become the object of the concomitant defences of the repressed fragmented body (Davis, 1995: 130). This ambivalence resonates strongly with the concept of ***disavowal***, which is a key motif of psychoanalytic theory (Marks, 1999a, 1999b; Shildrick, 2007a, 2007b; Olkin, 2009), and a term used in two influential texts on the cultural representations of disabled people (Hevey, 1992; Shakespeare, 1997a).

Disavowal equates with staring at while staring through (Campbell, 2009): holding simultaneously two opposing views. Hence, while disability studies has drawn attention to the oppression of disabled people, we must remember that disabling culture also reacts to disabled people in contradictory ways: as appalling/appealing, fear/fascination, hate/love, genocide/paternalism. *We can understand a culture of disablism as a culture of disavowal.* Disabled people are cast as the starring roles of socio-cultural shows of disavowal. With roots in the fragmented pre-mirror real phase (that is mourned) and the autonomous body of the mirror and symbolic (which is idealised), cultural responses may be understood as that which Lacan (1977: 4) indicates as a retrospective condition of the subject who experiences the succession of phantasies that extend from a fragmented body-image (pre-mirror) to a form of its totality (found in the imaginary and symbolic) (Shildrick, 2007b: 264). *Disability-as-non-unitary is in all of us.* We all have corporeal (real) and ontological (mirror and symbolic) anxieties. As the body is the reflection of the image of subject, physical disability is not simply a disruption to the semiotic field of the observer (as argued by Davis, 2002). It is also a disruption to the observer's psychic field (Shildrick, 2007a: 224). As Olkin (2009: 6) puts it: 'there is a disavowal of disability. It just cannot be psychologically healthy or easy to have a part of oneself that is simultaneously so tangible and undeniable, yet so unacceptable': 'The black is not a man … the man who adores the negro [sic] is as 'sick' as the man who abominates him' (Fanon, 1993: 10). Non-disabled people are disturbed by disability because it reminds them of their own fragility (Michalko, 2002: 95). The social pain of disability, for Michalko, is not to be found in disabled people but in the non-disabled majority. And as disability threatens the boundaries of self, it requires us to look away but also to look at (Burman, 2008: 155–156). Disabled people represent a forbidden and desired other (Shildrick, 2007a: 236).

?

Thinking point: Contrast the accounts of two wheelchair users. First, Rhodri, in Reeve (2008), who complains about the unwillingness of people to open doors for him in the local shopping centre, which makes shopping difficult and unwelcoming. Second, Hewitt (2004), who amusingly recalls being carried up the escalator by two complete strangers, only to have to inform the helpers that he had never wanted to go up the escalator in the first place and could he be taken back down so he could meet his friend. In what ways do these contrasting accounts capture the following observation: 'Disgust, repulsion are often accompanied by, and mask, secret attraction:' (Davis, 1995: 12)

Disability invokes a double circulation of fear and fascination (Shildrick, 2007a: 236). Disabled paralympians occupy a position of 'super cripple' (Barnes, 1993), precisely because they achieve in the face of their apparent broken bodies. They are still real (cripple) though they embody the symbolic (super). Hence, the fetishised object[10] (super-cripple) is the product of disavowal. In contrast, the disabled person as 'tragic victim' (common to filmic representations of disability and impairment)[11] allows the illusory wholeness of the phallic male, the supposed integrity of the able-bodied, to be sustained because lack is localised in the body of an other (Wilton, 2003: 358):

> The complex and fragmented self employs projection to expel troubling psychical content out in the social world on the body of the other… these

> reactions in turn sustain the outward projection of one's own loss – *there* is the body that lacks, not here.

Following Rudberg (1997: 185), the non-disabled directs an intense gaze as well as a phallic index finger towards an object that is totally different from himself: an object who seems to close herself around her own great secret. This might explain disavowal in the growing tendency for the labelling of autism: *there* is to be found the fascinating real of disability (impairment, lacking sociability, hyper-individualism) not *here* in the rapidly individualising non-disabled world.[12] It allows us to make sense of the common stereotype of the Down syndrome child as happy-smiley caricature – as fetishised stand-in for the monstrous object of 'the disabled' – a disabled object we can 'ruffle the hair of' (but then turn away from). It might explain the recent complaints by parents to the BBC about a children's TV presenter who, only having one arm, was scar(r)-ing their children (www.news.bbc.co.uk/1/hi/magazine/7906507.stm). We do not need an *imago* that reminds us of our own fragmentation. And even when the disabled other speaks back – when *it* has the temerity to speak of its own autonomy – we still cannot allow *it* to name *its* own agency: so disabled people 'self-advocate' rather than speak for themselves. Their activism is fetishised.

The illusory ideal whole of the non-disabled white Western adult male – a reality of living in the symbolic under the phallus – is sustained by the localisation of lack in the disabled body: there is castration, not here. Attempts to get disabled people into the symbolic are found in rehabilitation. As Michalko (2002: 137) observes, treatments focused on getting blind children to 'pass' as sighted people; teaching techniques to stop blind children from enacting unsociable behaviour (such as head rocking, rolling eyes, hand flapping) all attempt to create a sighted imaginary for blind children. We are reminded of Fanon's observation: 'when Negroes [sic] are accepted they are no longer Negroes they are "one of us", that is civilised' (Fanon, 1993: 65). The fear of the unwhole body, of the altered body, is kept at bay by depictions of the whole, systematised body (Davis, 1995: 1134). Such oppressive strategies are forged upon a celebration of autonomous/non-disabled imaginary and symbolic orders, which attempt to erase the real of disability.

Richard Reiser (in the BBC Television series *Nobody's Normal*, episode 'Education, Education, Education', 2007), the director of Disability Equality in Education (DISEED), recalls his childhood as a disabled child sent to special school to become a 'collection of super-crips'. He recalls treatments that were set up to instil a lack of recognition of impairment. He was swimming before he was walking and never expected to identify himself as a disabled person. Consequently, he was shocked when he caught a sight of himself in a shop window: 'I did not recognise myself in the reflection. I can remember thinking: who is that child with the lop-sided gait?' He did not identify that this was he. He had been trained not to. He had been given different images to identify with. The experiences of parents of disabled children are magnified because of being doubly lost in the symbolic. When parents dream of wanting their children to learn to speak rather than use sign symbols such as Makaton, or seek to stop their children from flapping their hands or rocking their heads back and forth to behave more normally (McLaughlin et al., 2008), they are describing their fight with the symbolic which, in the end, promises much but delivers nothing. This is a conclusion reached by Rebecca Greenwood:

> You see, I can't keep chasing the normal. I mean I've done so much to try and make my son normal but I can't keep that up. … I need to accept him in the ways that he is and just enjoy them and him. I must stop pressurizing myself. (Rebecca Greenwood, quoted in Goodley, 2007b: 152)

Rebecca exposes the illusory nature of the albeit symbolic and reminds us that such an illusion of normative wholeness is predicated on the existence of the disabled Other (Ghai, 2002: 53).

Evaluating Lacan

This chapter has deliberately avoided using Lacanian ideas to make sense of the development of the disabled body, disabled psyche or disabled human subject. Indeed, for some, it is difficult to see how the disabled body/psyche can actually develop through real, mirror and symbolic phases, when some impaired disabled bodies *really* fail to fit the *imago* of wholeness and autonomy. 'Queer crip' Lurie writes:

> Eli [Lurie's lover] once wrote, 'me, looking at me in the mirror and liking what I see, is a minor miracle' … someone has to do a lot of convincing for us to be able to peek at the mirror. And we still have to do a lot of work ourselves. (Lurie, 2004: 84)

Shildrick (2004) is particularly scathing about the application of Lacan to the subjectivities and embodiment of disabled people:

> For both Freud and Lacan the acquisition and stabilisation of self-image is dependent on a certain corporeal introjection, not directly of the infant's own bodily boundaries and sensations, but of an ideal body image representing, as Liz Grosz puts it, 'a map of the body's surface and a reflection of the image of the other's body' (1994: 38). … The disabled body, then, could be read as both insufficient as an object of desire, and an unwelcome intimation of the *corps morcelé* that the emergent subject must disavow or abject. It is not that the disabled infant would fail to negotiate the mirror stage – for in the psychic register all self-identity is based on a mis-recognition. Rather, in its apparent lack of wholeness, the infant becomes other, its self-positioning as a subject of desire – like that of women – denied recognition. To escape the Lacanian impasse, perhaps it is necessary to look elsewhere.

This analysis of Lacan is in line with Fanon's (1993) reading of the mirror phase: where black people are constantly in conflict with their own *imago* because the *imago* does not mirror the black viewer. He is always denied recognition and has to seek recognition in the (white) other. Similarly, Gatens (1999) argues that Lacanian psychoanalysis constructs female bodies as lacking or castrated and male bodies as full and phallic. Shildrick and Price (1999: 6) suggest that the mirror phase leaves the disabled child as deeply ontologically anxious. Disabled people are denied entrance to both the non-disabled symbolic (they are not allowed to speak) and the misrecognised *imago* of the mirror (they are not allowed to appear). While, Michalko (2002) goes further, in reference to blindness, to suggest that the blind child remains in the real: the bewilderment of the original chaos of not seeing in a world understood as something to see (2002: 137). These interpretations might well ring true for disabled people in terms of struggling with the (mis)recognition of bodies that fail to fit the phallocentric prerogative of a whole body.

We do, however, need to be careful not to align disabled, female and black bodies with the fragmented and lacking, as if only people with such bodies struggle with the conventions of the symbolic. This would risk recreating what Gatens (1999) views as a tendency within psychoanalysis to produce monologues about fragmented bodies, including 'hysterical females', 'the unruly poor', 'uncivilised racialised bodies' and 'damaged disabled selves'. Such a tendency misunderstands the potential of psychoanalysis to critique culture and its impact on *all* bodies. Shildrick's refusal of psychoanalysis, presented above, is, we could argue, premature. First, she views the disabled body rather literally in terms of its materialist non-alignment with the mirror. In truth, non-alignment is a common experience for *all* bodies. Lacan is clear: all bodies refuse to match up to the original *imago*, never re-find the original desiring (m)other and, crucially, are castrated and rejected by the symbolic. *The tragedy is that non/disabled people do not recognise that we all share the experience of alienation and that different bodies, whether fe/male, queer/normative, black/white, all, to varying extents, are destined to fail to meet the demands of the symbolic.* Second, Shildrick also skims over the connections between gender and disability (and race and sexuality) by failing to highlight possibilities for affirmation that occur on *not entering* the symbolic (or at least being interpolated into a particular space within it). If we view psychoanalytic ideas as cultural resources, then they can provide useful metaphors for challenging the normative symbolic's tendency to place disability in a state of abjection (Erevelles, 2005).

Thinking point: If culture and language fail to recognise us, in what ways can this force us to create our own cultures? Answer this question with reference to either (1) Disability Arts or (2) Music of Black Origin.

As evidenced in some feminist responses to Lacan (e.g. Butler, 1990, 1993; Grosz, 1994), the Other of disability might well constitute a position from which to speak differently. Following Davis (1995), perhaps the disabled body, along with black, gay, south, female, trans, queer bodies, offers new sights for *jouissance*, because these bodies are 'not simply oppressed but can be heretical and even empowering as well' (Davis, 1995: 9). This feeds into the notion of jouissance of the intellectual left; of the unruly, radical and resistant body as a native ground of pleasure (1995: 5). Indeed, as Butler (1993) suggests, disavowed bodies provide opportunities for rearticulating symbolic legitimacy: to see how bodies are secured through identificatory, regulatory and governing schemas of the symbolic. And as Fanon (1993) has argued, rather than rejecting the *imago* of the Negro [sic], a different strategy is to make others aware of this *imago*. Michalko (2002: 166) captures this well when he argues:

> Disability possesses the inherent 'prestige' of the possibility to disrupt. The disruption of contemporary hegemonic ideas of reason over passion of mind is perhaps disability's greatest possibility.

This strategy involves finding 'cracks' in the symbolic nature of culture, developing alternative signifiers around, for example, disability politics and arts, which allow other routes for interpolation for disabled people. Lacanian discourse allows seeing the first misrecognition – the purported stability of self – as a myth and encourages us to disrupt this social mythology and reap the rewards (Finkelstein, 1997). It draws attention also to the myth of the 'natural/able body' and its converse. *There is no natural dis/abled body.* Increasingly, in this ocean of signifiers that threatens to engulf, we can make choices about those to use, mindful of the fact that even the big signifiers (e.g. phallus) may be omnipotent but offer us very little.

The truth is that none of us matches up to the phallus, that everyone is felt lacking, that the real can never be regained because we are so locked into language and the symbolic. The big lie of contemporary society is that it is only disabled people who are lacking. *To demand disabled people to meet the symbolic is clearly an act of cultural violence.* The 'nightmare' of the disabled body – deformed, maimed, mutilated and broken – is no more than a cultural recall of the unattainable position of the real, pre-symbolic, narcissistic of early childhood. To paraphrase Davis (1995: 142), the disabled/fragmented body, rather than the normal/autonomous body, is actually the one common to us all (in the real). The normal body is a phantasm constituted in the imaginary and symbolic: a mythical entity that will never be owned. Crucially, when bodies do break down, when they seem to offer us access to the real, when we think we can say, 'there is disabled, there is dependent, there is illness, there is a lacking body', the symbolic quickly enters the fray and signification takes over. The truth is that the natural or unnatural body is already materially dead as soon as we enter the symbolic (Burman, 2008: 261–274). Here we are reminded of the ideas of Tremain and Butler introduced in the last chapter.

Conclusions

Psychoanalysis might be at its most powerful when employed to make sense of organisational prejudice and discrimination against disabled people and the phantasised ideals of hyper-rationality and independence of contemporary culture (Goodley et al., 2011). This would allow for an analysis of the symbolic, personal, psychical and discursive cultural practices that surround the exclusion of disabled people. This analysis would enable the destiny described by Davis (1995: 157):

> Only when disability is made visible as a compulsory term in a hegemonic process, only when the binary is exposed and the continuum acknowledged ... only then will normalcy cease being a term of enforcement in a somatic judicial system.

Problems abound in relation to psychoanalysis. It is important to remain mindful that classic Freudian theory views politicised theories such as disability studies as illusory positions,[13] has heteronormative tendencies (Feher-Gurewich, 2001) and is inherently conservative.[14] At its most analytical, a psychoanalytic perspective refutes the compulsory nature of able-bodiedness and exposes the impossibilities of entrance into the able-bodied symbolic. As a response, we are reminded of McRuer's (2006) point that the able-bodied system is doomed to fail: because the ideal able-bodied identity can never, once and for all, be achieved. Everyone is virtually disabled, in the sense that able-bodied norms are intrinsically impossible to embody. Perhaps disabled bodies are the best placed to refute the symbolic and resituate cultural norms and expectations: because disabled/fragmented bodies are real to us all, offering possibilities for unruly *jouissance*, pleasure and resistance.

Further reading

Erevelles (2005). Permits thinking about the application of Lacan to inclusive education (next chapter).

Fanon (1993). A Lacanian piece and a classic in the field of critical race and postcolonial thinking.

Parker (1997). Overview of different psychoanalytic approaches and their impact on culture.

Wilton (2003). One of the few texts that brings together disability studies and psychoanalysis.

Notes

1 This refers to the sensuous love of mother and child, typified by the Freudian Oedipus complex that will reappear in adult life as sexual love. '*Jouissance* refers to the subject's experience of being for the Other an object to be enjoyed' (Feher-Gurewich, 2001: 3). A key aspect of much of psychoanalytic theory relates to the relational, social, cultural and historical factors that are at play in separating the child–mother dyad through psychosexual development. For Freud, this is tied to the Oedipus complex and, later, the necessary severing of incestuous child–mother relationships, described in Freud's *Totem and Taboo* (see, for an overview, Žižek, 1997).

2 'The normal body is created in the imaginary and the fragmented body is to be found in the real. But this fragmented body remains in all of us, at all times, for ever' (Davis, 1995: 140–142).

3 The child also, crucially, sees the mother as lacking – the primary object seeks love and togetherness from the child – hence the lack is felt in the self and the other.

4 Whereas the mirror phase gives us a sense of self in the imaginary, 'we have to enter language in order to be able to refer to ourselves as separate; we have to enter the symbolic … [and] the symbolic enters us' (Parker, 1993: 11).

5 As Fanon (1993) observes, the symbolic is empty for all, but perhaps less so for those who occupy the more powerful positions.

6 Alienation is defined by Miller (2008) as the dual process of identification and repression.

7 The world of symbols becomes disconnected from our affective and psychic lives. The result is an inability to represent (and thereby live) our emotional lives outside the economy of spectacle of the symbolic (K. Oliver, 2007).

8 Those readers with experience of psychoanalytic ideas may well pick up on the moral status conferred through entrance into the symbolic – which can also sometimes function

as the superego of Freudian theory – in which psychical inventions of the phallus attempt to deny the threat posed to the subject by the *jouissance* of the Other (Feher-Gurewich, 2001). Tremain takes this further (2000: 293), explaining that the sexual division of labour and the psychological construction of desire (especially the oedipal formation) are the foundations of a system of the production of human beings which vests men with rights in women that they do not have in themselves. Similar comments could be made about disabling society through reference to non-disabled professional industries and their reliance on (and ownership of) disabled people.

9 As articulated by Finkelstein (1997: 156), female bodies become fantasised as incomplete and lacking, in order to 'annul the fragmented condition of modernity' and contrast with 'the imposition of a coherent subjectivity' of non-female bodies.

10 As we saw in Chapter 5, we can understand fetish here as the symbolic meaning of an item/object that is more important than the item/object's reality.

11 See Barnes' (1993) account of cultural shorthand, including *tragic heroes* forced to overcome acquired impairments (e.g. *Born on the Fourth of July), super cripples* (e.g. *My Left Foot*) and *sinister characters* (e.g. many of the villains of the Bond movies).

12 Fanon (1993: 225) makes a similar point in relation to the disavowal of the black body:

> In the remotest depth of the European unconscious an inordinately black hollow has been made in which the most immoral impulses, the most shameful desires lie dormant. And as every man climbs up toward whiteness and light, the European has tried to repudiate this uncivilised self, which has attempted to defend itself. When European civilisation came into contact with the black world, with those savage peoples, everyone agreed: those Negroes [sic] were the principal evil.

13 'An illusion is the idealisation of the ego brought about by a fusion of the ego and the ego-ideal' (Chasseguet-Smirgel and Grunberger, 1986: 199).

14 Can we trust any theory that maintains 'biology is destiny' and aims only to change 'historical misery into common happiness? This is typified by Chasseguet-Smirgel and Grunberger (1986: 213): 'Psychoanalysis, ... maintains that human incompleteness and thus desire will never disappear ... humanity is destined to dream from here to eternity'.

NINE

Education: *Inclusive Disability Studies*

****

Introduction

To what extent are disabled children fully included in their schools? How do different approaches of special and inclusive education understand disabled children? How can teachers respond in enabling ways? Contemporaneously, more and more disabled children have entered their local mainstream schools. Disability studies and social justice meet at the crossroads of inclusive education. But this approach can only be understood in relation to its antithesis: special education. Mass public education was never designed with disabled learners in mind (Gerber, 1996: 156). Apple (1982) argues that compulsory schooling in the Global North is bound to the demands of capitalism but school curricula refer to far more than what is taught in schools. The 'hidden curricula' of schools are where the values, rituals and routines of wider society are acculturated within students. Corbett and Slee (2002: 134) urge inclusive educators to ask questions about the deep cultures of schools to find alternative curricula that are more in tune with needs of diverse learners. In this chapter we will explore the meaning of inclusive/special education but contextualise this in relation to the influence of marketisation. We will then turn to critical pedagogy as a possible resource for the promotion of inclusion.

Inclusive education

Thinking point: Inclusive education is understood by Lipsky and Gartner (1996: 151) 'as equitable opportunities for all learners to receive effective educational services, with supplementary aids and support, in age-appropriate classes in their neighbourhoods to prepare them for contributing lives as full members of society'. Identify a number of social barriers that might prevent disabled children experiencing inclusion.

For Booth (2002), inclusive education refers to the increasing participation of learners in the culture, curricula and communities of their neighbourhood centres of learning. For Booth, achievements of schools mean nothing if school communities fail to enhance the spirit of all teachers and pupils. Clough and Corbett (2000) sketch out an historical overview of educational responses to disability. The 1950s was typified by a psychomedical view of the disabled child requiring specialist intervention. These were the halcyon days for special educators and psychologists and their knowledge production around the disabled learner. The 1960s saw a sociological response that viewed special educational needs and learning disabilities as the direct product of exclusionary schooling. The 1970s was characterised by curricular approaches that met, or failed to meet, the learning needs of pupils. The 1980s saw attention turn to school improvement via comprehensive schooling and the systemic reorganisation of schools. The focus was on communities of schools rather than the achievements of individuals. The 1990s onwards has seen interventions from disability studies. At the heart of this critique is a call for inclusive education.

What is inclusion (and what about special)?

In order to understand inclusive education we need to briefly probe special education. The latter has been described by Armstrong (2002) as a 'wild profusion of entangled ideas', including charity, medicalisation and psychologisation. Special education places the disabled child in a specialist setting supported by specially trained professionals who intervene to improve the child. Proponents argue that this provides a more suitable context for the needs of disabled children to be met. But children who experience special education often have a narrow education, achieve low levels of academic attainment and leave schools only to enter other segregated arenas of work and education (Lipsky and Gartner, 1996). Special schools transplant the failings of mass education into the minds and bodies of disabled children. The special child is viewed through the lens of functionalism (Chapter 4); a learner who fails to fit in and learn (Thomas and Loxley, 2001: 5), marked by the processes of psychologisation (Chapter 5). Special schools collude in the failure of all schools to accommodate difference.

But special education does not just appear in segregated schools. It can refer to special procedures and systems, that are also to be found in mainstream schools. Special educators, according to Isaacs (1996: 41–42), succeed in 'promoting limited ontologies of personhood, exaggerated legitimations of the normal, based on an ever-growing and insidious idea that the failings of children can be explained in terms of a medical deficit-model of the disabled child'. Special education has therefore been described as a 'segregating, insulated, self-protecting, racially biased philosophy and array of practices, a product of … misguided scientific positivism, or merely as an ineffective, overblown problem to easily solvable school problems' (Gerber, 1996: 159).

Thinking point: How do you think special educators would defend these charges?

For Erevelles (2005), the first special education classes in North America included the urban poor, Native, Hispanic and African Americans. Black and working-class children have always been over-represented in special schools, leading Mercer (1973) to argue that measures of intelligence, social incompetence and maladaptive functioning say more about the racialised biases of professional assessment than they do of the deficits of 'mentally handicapped children'. Whether or not one accepts these criticisms, it is safe to say that the drive for special schools and the growing professionalism of special educators are intimately connected (Meekosha and Jakubowicz, 1996: 81). When the problems of educational achievement are understood as residing within the 'special child', then schools and teachers 'remain outside of this diagnostic glare' (Slee, 1996: 105). And, special schools breed 'unusual practices enacted by specialist teachers to instruct or manage the exotic and homogenised groups of special needs children' (Gerber, 1996: 157). According to Slee (2004: 47), special education remains bound to an 'inherent technicism, rooted in deficit-bound psycho-medical paradigms of individual pathological defects'. These assumptions continue to influence inclusive education (Ware, 2004b).

Practices of integration emerged in the 1960s in reaction to special education (Vislie, 2003). Integration promoted the right to education for disabled children in their local schools. In Britain, the Warnock Committee (1978) report, *Special Educational Needs*, was hugely influential in unsettling special school categories of impairment. Warnock proposed the use of 'Special Educational Needs' or 'SEN' as a catchall term for identifying those children who required extra support in mainstream schools.

Thinking point: Read the Warnock report online at the following website: www.sen.ttrb.ac.uk/viewArticle2.aspx?contentId=13852. In what ways has language around disability and education changed since this report was published?

For Rioux (1994b), integration was doomed to fail disabled children because it smuggled in unproblematic ideas of disability, meritocracy and self-reliance that ignored wider structural inequalities. She argued that integrated students still remained the focus of special educators even when they were in mainstream schools. According to Christensen (1996), the development of techniques such as the Individual Education Plan (IEP) – an artefact of special schools and widely used in schools in WENA and as an accompanying practice to the identification of SEN – allocate resources to a child based on the identification of individual requirements (often understood as learning problems and educational deficits).[1] Special Educational Needs Co-ordinators (SENCOs) in British schools (trained teachers with specialist interests in the support of disabled pupils) were established to provide professional support to those with this new label. But IEPs and SENCOs still addressed individual children rather than the school culture. Too often SENCOs were the sole agitators in schools and they, like their SEN children, were marginalised by the wider school culture (Booth, 2002).

Slee (1997: 411) observes that simply cleaning up exclusionary contexts do not make them more inclusionary spaces if the values of regular schooling remain. Following Tomlinson (1982) and Troyna and Vincent (1996), integration is a reformist agenda that is both exclusive (in, for example, only allowing the least disruptive to be included in schools) and inadequate (failing to address the structural inequalities within education). Differences are only incrementally accommodated in existing mainstream systems (Graham and Slee, 2008).

Thinking point: Evaluate the statement, adapted from Rioux (1994b), that: 'Programs such as affirmative action, which aim to promote the participation of minority groups in educational, work and welfare contexts, are flawed because they are based on the principles of accommodation rather than transformation.'

In the mid-1990s, a body of inclusive education literature emerged to challenge functionalist deficit 'within child' thinking of special education and the conservative compromises of integration (Tomlinson, 1982; Reiser and Mason, 1992; Clough and Barton, 1995; Christensen and Rizvi, 1996; Skrtic, 1995; Slee, 1996, 1997; Clough and Barton, 1998; Allan, 1999, 2004a, 2004b; Clough and Corbett, 2000; Barton, 2001, 2004b; Armstrong et al., 2002; Corbett and Slee, 2002; Ware, 2002, 2004a, 2004b: Allan and Slee, 2008; Graham and Slee, 2008). Armed with damning evidence on the failure of special schools, inclusive educators called for a change to the disabling ethos and philosophies of *all* mainstream schools.

Sociological theory was a key resource and a host of materialist, radical humanist and social constructionists theories were employed to critique existing educational arrangements and foster more inclusive alternatives (e.g. Skritc, 1995). Inclusive education sought to broaden the options available to a variety of learners, develop the skills and confidence of all teachers and develop a general political project that opened up the complex realities of educational settings (Slee, 1997: 410), while exposing the deleterious impact of sexist, disablist and racist education (Slee, 2004: 55). If we think back to Chapter 4, we can see that accommodation, assimilation and integration fit with a *consensus* model of society: disabled children are expected to fit into existing schooling arrangements. In contrast, inclusive education approaches seek changes in line with *conflict* approaches to sociology, demanding educators to rethink education and disability. As Slee (1997: 412) puts it:

> Are we talking about where children are placed and with what level of resource provision? Or, are we talking about the politics of value, about the purpose and content of curriculum, and about the range and conduct of pedagogy?

Inclusion is therefore a response to special education and integration in which children with SEN are understood as comprising a group constituted by a 'bureaucratic device for dealing with the complications arising from clashes between narrow waspish curricula and disabled students' (Slee, 1997: 412). Inclusive education:

- is a process by which a school attempts to respond to all pupils as individuals;
- records inclusion and exclusion as connected processes, schools developing more inclusive practices may need to consider both;
- emphasises overall school effectiveness;
- is of relevance to all phases and types of school, possibly including special schools, since within any educational provision teachers face groups of students with diverse needs and are required to respond to this diversity. (Vislie, 2003: 21)

Thinking point: Visit the following websites to explore different perspectives on inclusion:
www.edcm.org.uk/page.asp – The Every Disabled Child Matters *campaign in England.*

www.csie.org.uk/about – The Centre for Studies on Inclusive Education is an established centre that works with policy makers, professionals and parents to promote inclusion.
www.cafamily.org.uk/index.php?section=861 – Contact A Family provides support to parents of disabled children and is at the heart of these debates.
www.ibkinitiatives.com – This is a Sheffield-based organisation that provides support to parents and the research consultancy.

Enforcing inclusion

Inclusive education has become internationally enshrined in documents such as UNESCO's (1990) *World Declaration on the Education for All*, UNESCO's (1994) *Salamanca Statement and Framework for Action on Special Education Needs* and the United Nations (2007) *Convention on the Rights of Persons with Disabilities*. These initiatives aim to 'promote disabled people's human rights through access to the physical, social, educational, health, economic and cultural environment (UN, 2007: v, cited in Gabel and Danforth, 2008b). The *Salamanca Statement,* adopted by 92 governments and 25 international organisations in June 1994, set the policy agenda for inclusive education on a global scale (Vislie, 2003). Inclusive education, based on a growing international consensus of the rights of all children to a common education in their locality regardless of their background, attainment or disability, seeks to provide good quality education for learners and a community-based education for all (Vislie, 2003: 18). In Britain, *The Warnock Report* (1978), the Disability Discrimination Act 1995, the Special Educational Needs and Disability Act 2001 and the *Special Educational Needs: Code of Practice* (2001), made schools responsible for proactively meeting the needs of disabled learners.

Yet, a recent review of Britain and other countries in western Europe revealed that over the 1990s special educational provision had lost little ground and inclusive education had not grown as one might hope (Vislie, 2003). While more and more disabled students are entering post-compulsory education and universities, questions still remain about the extent to which they belong. The narrowness of curricula means exclusion for many non-normative children. This might explain why some observers, who were previously key proponents of inclusive education, have recently contributed their voice to the special educational backlash (Warnock, 2005; see also the response from Barton, 2005). In 1993, special education was a $30 billion a year industry in the USA (Peters and Chimedza, 2000: 265). Special schools become 'centres of excellence' that cling as much as they can to the retention of their special pupils. When it costs the Government £100,000 per year to house a child in a residential special school, it is perhaps unsurprising that these schools are keen not to let go of their pupils (Thomas and Loxley, 2001: 96). The continued presence of organisations such as Inclusion International suggests that much is still being done. This begs the question, why is inclusive education failing? To answer this we need to turn to wider systemic issues.

Neoliberal education

Thinking point: Read the following narrative:

The head teacher addressed the school staff meeting about the need for all pupils in the school to hit the targets set for them at the beginning of every year. A new piece of software was being trialled, one that was already being used in 'beacon schools' which allowed teachers to track the 'flight paths' of students on maths, science and literacy. A child's 'flight path' could be checked to see if it fitted the expected path for a child of their age, taking into account various statistical measures, such as free school meals and socio-economic background. The head explained that the school had to perform better in maths and English – particularly when a government inspection of the school was expected in the coming year. Later, the issue of inclusion was raised. The head teacher acknowledged that inclusion was important but 'not as important as the priority of the school, over the next two years, to raise maths and English standards'. A few weeks later the head teacher received a formal complaint from four parents about a 7 year-old boy named Danny. They claimed that their own children's learning in school was being interrupted by the disruptive behaviour of this pupil, who had the label of autism. Over the nine-month period that led up to the school's inspection, the head teacher received over 60 complaints from the same small number of parents. They threatened that unless Danny was excluded they would take their own children out of the school and 'go to the press' about the failure of the school to protect their children. (A story from a mainstream school, somewhere in Wales, anonymous, January 2009)

Now complete the following: 'Schools in twenty-first-century Wales are characterised by' … .

Neoliberalism refers to monetary and trade policies of a pro-corporate free market economy that has dominated WENA economic and cultural politics and global markets since the early 1980s (Richardson, 2005). The state is 'rolled back', unproductive welfare spending is reduced and public services and social provisions are increasingly taken over by, or aligned with the principles of, business. Public entitlements, such as welfare and education, have become dismantled through an alliance with market freedom and the essence of the Washington consensus, the driving force of global progression and the deregulation of the market. It is linked to a context of austerity; a change of economic context in which countries have to compete internationally and economic rationality overtakes social welfare reform (Rizvi and Lingard, 1996: 13). The individual consumer and family unit constitute key sites for private welfare. Neoliberal philosophies are enshrined in the aims of supranational organisations such as the World Bank, the World Health Organization (WHO) and Organisation for Economic Co-operation and Development (OECD). As Vislie (2003) observes, the OECD represents 30 of the richest incomes countries, all of which espouse the virtues of western democracy and the principles of the free market. When these same countries are behind OECD initiatives around inclusive education, questions are raised about the meaning of education that is sanctioned and the conditions that are placed on other, poorer countries, to enact such educational philosophies. Democracy has now been reduced to a metaphor of the 'free market' (Giroux, 2004: 35).

Neoliberal education, at its most seemingly benign, calls upon common standards, assessment and accountability of schools and teachers to pupils and parents. At its most damaging, these values are characterised by shrinking resources, schools are pulled into the competitive marketplace where productivity and accountability (to consumers and government assessment bodies) are paramount. We see, too, the application of increasingly more stringent academic criteria and higher standards of education, a narrowing of the curriculum and an increase in educational testing and assessment (Jung, 2002).[2] This 'McDonaldisation of education' (surveillance, testing, targeting, performativity and marketisation, according to Gabel and Danforth, 2008b) or 'human capital paradigm approach to education' (a focus on work-related competencies and skills, Peters et al., 2008) has led to a splintering of teachers unions and an erosion of morality. In the context of Neoliberalism, services are no longer regarded as a civic or human right but as commodities for consumers. The 'common good' equates with free competition, consumer power and profitability (Rizvi and Lingard, 1996: 14–15).

Schools are high-pressure places; subjected to league tables, children to endless SATS,[3] teachers to inspection. Curricula are nationalised, allowing comparison between schools, teachers and pupils, and focused on science, maths and literacy – key requirements of capitalist economies (McLaren, 2009). Neoliberal ideology risks submission to economic rationality (Bratlinger, 2004: 21).

Thinking point: For Barton (2004b: 64), market ideology means we view education 'through the lens of cost-effectiveness, efficiency, and value for money leading to more competition, selection and social divisions'. How do these values compare with the ones you hold about the meaning and aims of education?

Schools become increasingly governed and assessed through a culture of performativity. Key to this, as we saw in Chapters 5–8, is the self-producing, self-regulating autonomous individual learner (Richardson, 2005).[4] The grade-based system of schooling requires an homogeneous group of students to function effectively (Christensen, 1996: 65). In short, the market makes market agents – rational agentic and normal subjects of contemporary society who look after themselves and their own (Reindall, 1999; Richardson, 2005). Neoliberalism is sometimes referred to as new right thinking: an ideology that ignores social and cultural histories by focusing on an individualistic understanding of human behaviour (Munford, 1994: 273); a libertarian new right way of thinking that cherishes self-interest, self-contentment, selfishness and distrust (Ballard, 2004).[5] New right thinking combines the marketisation of Neoliberalism and the neo-conservatism of late capitalism, which values nation, family and duty (Thomas and Loxley, 2001: 91). 'Choice' allows schools to select desirable and reject troublesome customers (Tomlinson, 1996).

Neoliberal schools are stressful places. Teachers are held to greater accountability, more assessment and a loss of autonomy (Barton, 2004b). Teachers are implementers of the decisions of others – like policy makers – and are assessed in terms of how well they implement these decisions. In Britain, teachers teach the National Curriculum and are placed under immense pressure to stick to this curriculum every day of the school week. This has led to rigid timetabling, inflexible staffing and a lack of inventiveness in schools. Difficult, objectionable or unwanted children are at risk of being placed in segregated provision. Schools become more interested in managing themselves rather than their pupils. And the naming and shaming of low performing schools is, for Booth (2002: 79), a witch-hunt that 'rivals the excesses of the Chinese cultural revolution'. What this means for social justice is highly problematic, leading Wedell (2008: 128) to argue that in the current climate, schools that do successfully include do so 'in spite of the system'.

New norms, new eugenics

In neoliberal education, parents are consumers. In Global North countries, such as Britain, the wealthiest move house to locate themselves in desirable catchment areas: to ensure the 'best education' for their children. Inner-city schools suffer as a consequence and reflect the socio-economic deprivation of their communities. Many of these schools fall into 'special measures,' requiring state intervention and heightened monitoring. Leafy suburb and quaint village schools boast 'beacon school' status.[6] The gap widens between rich and poor.

Thinking point:
Activity – Option Every Child Matters *from the UK* (www.everychildmatters.gov.uk/aims) *is the current policy related to the well-being of children and young people from birth to age 19. The government's aim is for every child, whatever their background or their circumstances, to have the support they need to be healthy, stay safe, enjoy and achieve, make a positive contribution, achieve economic well-being.*

Activity – Option 2: No Child Left Behind *in the USA (www.ed.gov/about/landing.jhtml?src=gu) was created in 1980 by combining offices from several federal agencies 'to promote student achievement and preparation for global competitiveness by fostering educational excellence and ensuring equal access'.*

Question to address for each activity: What are the possible positive and negative applications of this agenda to the well-being of disabled children?

While we might applaud any educational initiative that aims, for example, to work poor families out of poverty, questions are raised about the kinds of children valued, and perhaps, made by these policy formations. Does a disabled child fit? All policy formations have within them contradictions that cause a problem for the neoliberal child, and this is particularly the case for the disabled child (see Malacrida and Duguay, 2009).

> Three children with labels of SEN (autism, ADHD) were not allowed to attend a residential school trip. After much discussion, and advice from an educational psychologist and the health and safety team of the local educational authority, the school management team decided that these three children were deemed a health and safety risk. Their parents were asked if they were prepared to attend the residential with their children. One parent refused, the other two parents were prepared to come along but explained that their children did not want them to attend. (A story from a mainstream school, somewhere in Scotland, anonymous, June 2008).

The problem for *Every Child Matters* and *No Child Left Behind* is their reliance on normative understandings of the child (Biesta, 1998). The (preferred) child, the child that is meaningfully included, is the neoliberal subject of a neoliberal capitalist society. While the majority world might view the child in terms of community contribution, economic capital and lineage (Ghai, 2006: 157), in minority world contexts like Britain, the neoliberal child is a vessel (though a knowing and autonomous one) for all of contemporary society's contradictions. The child is innocent/responsible, player/worker, achiever/learner. This criss-crossing of discourses raise questions about the values we place on (disabled) children and the futures we envisage for them. The marketisation of education creates a paradox: the development of new norms and the promotion of new forms of deviancy.

Neoliberal conceptions of education and the neoliberal child find their way into the subjectivities of children, parents and professionals. As Burman (2008: 50) notes, parents worry about 'whether our child is doing well enough, is developing at the right pace, is going through the milestones correctly'. This not only isolates each mother and treats her as the originator or responsible agent of the 'problem', but also sets her in competition with other mothers (Burman, 2008). Education and citizenship are closely related. Questions arise about the restricted image of the 'ideal citizen' that the norms of developmentalism embody (Baker, 2002: 688). Developmentalism is wedded to the structure of schooling and provides a restricted image of the ideal citizen/learner. This learner is what Young (1990, cited in Wilkerson, 2002) terms the *respectable* middle citizen (see also Chapter 5). In contrast, following Burman (2008), disabled children are deemed to be appalling (so to be excluded) and appealing (so to be an endless source of fascination) and this 'disavowal of children' lies at the heart of debates about the inclusion of disabled children (see Chapter 8). There is a cultural imperative to fit it, under the rubric of normality, to strive to be normal (Davis, 1995). Marks (1999a: 170–171) mischievously draws our attention to the psychoanalytic idea of 'normotic illness' developed by Bollas (1987). Individuals with this 'illness' are abnormally normal (sic): overly stable, secure, comfortable and socially extravert; ultra-rational, objective, lacking imagination and empathy. But normotic illness might be seen more correctly as the logical subjectivity of neoliberal education: hyper-normal rather than normal. This point is developed further by Harwood and Humphrey (2008), who suggest that a new norm is emerging in the Global North. Parents are no longer worrying about whether or not their child is normal – they are more interested and anxious about whether or not their children are 'exceptional' or 'gifted and talented'. This heightened sense of normality is not only exclusionary to those disabled and marginalised children it leaves behind; it also fans the flames of competition, assessment and testing around all children.

Thinking point: The eugenics movement of the early twentieth century sought to identify and segregate 'feeble-minded' people from wider society because of a perceived need to maintain the intellectual health of nations. To what extent can you identify contemporary forms of eugenics? To help with your answer, read Baker (2002).

Education increasingly defines the (hyper-)normal and its opposition the (hyper-) abnormal. There is an increase in the diagnostic rituals historically associated with special education (Vislie, 2003: 3). It has become more difficult to talk of students failing in education without calling on scholastic labels (Slee, 1996: 107). Following Fanon (1993: 111), a whole host of professional discourses have been woven out of disabled children – 'a thousand details, anecdotes and stories'. This has developed a language of new eugenics which:

> privileges certain kinds of whiteness over certain kinds of colour … certain kinds of ability over certain kinds of 'corporeallly anomalous body kinds' … in the absence of corporate punishment that might leave a mark on the skin, an array of internally corporeal medicalisations have emerged whose marks are more difficult to photograph and therefore to contest. (Smith, 2008: 665–681)

A new eugenics of sorting and differentiation has created a disability service industry which is powerfully iatrogenic, with billion-dollar outputs (Smith, 2008). New forms of 'fix it and get better' treatments are being devised all the time, with labels such as ADHD, EBD and Autism inducing a clinical mindset from which it is difficult to escape (Thomas and Loxley, 2001: 44–48). The growth of ADHD, for example, transforms pupil disruption into pupil dysfunction, negates the changing of school cultures and, instead, leads to the medicalisation of childhood.[7] Children with impairments and SEN become increasingly patrolled and monitored. ADHD is a culturally acceptable explanation for when a child does not fit into a socially desirable shape. Hence, ADHD is an ideal position to act as a cultural defence mechanism (Timimi, 2002). ADHD acts as an inference ticket to a quasimedical diagnosis, a sticky label to apply to a child to maintain the organisational systems of schools (Thomas and Loxley, 2001).

Autistic children are increasingly commonplace in schools. In 2005, the Autistic Society in England produced a number of 'alert' cards for autistic people to carry with them to present if their difference elicited interest from the police or other members of the public. These labels re-inscribe an 'outlaw ontology', re-inventing eugenics discourse in a new language that maintains an abliest normativity (Baker, 2002: 665). Slee (1996: 108) suggests that for teachers, these labels resist applying diagnostic probes to their own teaching, the curriculum they use and the organisation of the schools in which they work.

Inclusion for some?

For Slee (1996: 97), inclusive education, like special education and integration before it, has become nothing more than a bureaucratic means to the minimisation of difference in order to maintain the existing structural and cultural relations of schooling. Increasingly fierce competition among students for limited funding and enrolment restrictions in particular courses of study give weight to the argument that chronically disabled students unnecessarily drain or waste scarce educational resources (Jung, 2002: 184–185). Becoming visible as a disabled person in the neoliberal educational context puts one in a vulnerable position, as 'they' raise questions about 'fairplay' and 'educational quality' (Jung, 2002). Disabled people are in danger of being hit by a politically correct backlash – where 'inclusion' is seen as devaluing and ignoring the educational requirements of 'normal' (read unproblematic) children. Inclusion and quality education are seen as polar opposites: each potentially cancelling the other out:

> Within a school curriculum committed to the discourses and material practices of technical rationality and capitalist accumulation, disabled students are assigned little worth because they are not seen as economic assets in the community. … [A]t the level of systems change, a radical transformation would require that educational theorists begin to dismantle the normalising ideologies that serve as the cornerstone of even radical theories of difference and explore the implications of such changes on school reform. (Erevelles, 2005: 436)

As Goodley (2007a) argues, too often, when we think of involving students in educational practices, we assume students to be productive, skilled, accountable individuals who are ready and willing to lead developments within the classroom (see also Gabel, 2002). In short, our students are 'able'. Such a construction of the learner is hugely problematic for students with disabilities and/or special educational needs, who require the support of others. Indeed, for Masschelein and Simons (2005), inclusive education *fails* students because it maintains a particular vision of the ideal learner – the entrepreneurial pupil:

> Inclusion … is linked up with entrepreneurship … the willingness to live an entrepreneurial life and to put one's capital to work. An inclusive society, therefore, is not a society of equals in a principled way, but a society in which everyone has the qualities to meet their needs in an entrepreneurial way.
>
> (Masschelein and Simons, 2005: 127)

Fanon (1993: 118) was aware of the pernicious nature of the dominant entrepreneurial (white) Other, when he observed the tendency of white colleagues to appraise blackness alongside assumed qualities of whiteness: 'we have a black teacher – he is quite bright'; 'we have a black doctor – he is gentle'. In each of these statements is an un/conscious accentuation of values of the dominant alterity (Chapter 5), which can also be found in relation to the education of disabled people:

> He has Asperger's Syndrome – but he is really bright.
> She has an intellectual disability – but is really articulate.
> He is a disabled child – but he is good at maths.
> He has ADHD – but he is brilliant at rugby.
> She has Down syndrome – but is studying for her GCSEs.
>
> (Anonymous observations collected by the author)

As Fanon (1993: 170), puts it, 'Face to face with this man who is "different from himself" … the Other will become the mainstay of his preoccupations and his desires. … [A] negro [sic] is forever in combat with his own image.' So can schools only include those who match up to the able entrepreneurial Other?

Challenging (neoliberal) education: critical pedagogy

Barton (2004b: 74) argues that 'in this struggle, I do most passionately believe that a political analysis is now even more important and requires our most serious attention'. Fortunately, many people value social justice more than they do wealth, in their conception of the good society (Wong, 2002). Inclusion means much more than inclusion in the classroom (Ballard, 2004), attending, instead, to alternative, resistant and hidden curricula (Apple, 1982). This involves building up the confidence of all teachers whose own skills might feel devalued in light of the growing expertise of special education.

The approach of critical pedagogy has long been held up as the means to confront the cultural violence of neoliberal education. With its roots in the work of Paulo Freire and Augusto Boal, critical pedagogy emerged in the USA and Britain as a re-reading of *education as liberation*. Early writings were unashamedly Marxist and Gramscian in perspective (Giroux, 2009) and later contributions have embraced feminist and anti-racist ambitions too (hooks, 1989; Bell et al., 2000). Alliances between disability studies and critical pedagogy have been less well developed. However, as seen in Peters and Chimedza (2000), Gabel (2001, 2002), Goodley (2007b), Jarman (2008) and Ware (2009), inclusive education and critical pedagogy share the ambition of reshaping education, captured by Giroux (2003: 14):

> Educators and others require a politics of resistance that extends beyond the classroom as part of a broader struggle to challenge those forces of neo-liberalism that currently wage war against all collective structures capable of defending vital social institutions as a public good.

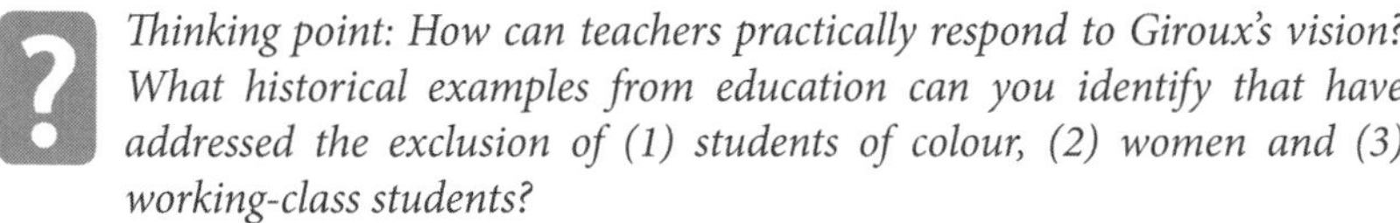

Thinking point: How can teachers practically respond to Giroux's vision? What historical examples from education can you identify that have addressed the exclusion of (1) students of colour, (2) women and (3) working-class students?

Inclusive spaces are found in critical pedagogy's emphasis on 'creating a new environment in which non-aggressive, receptive faculties of human beings, in harmony with the consciousness of freedom, are developed' (Giroux, 2009: 49).

Transforming the meaning of education

The essence of critical pedagogy is captured by the following key points (drawing on Apple, 1982; Lather, 1986; Isaacs, 1996; Bell et al., 2000; Peter and Chimedza, 2000; Gabel, 2001; Bratlinger, 2004; Giroux, 2004; Ware, 2004a; Lynn, 2006; Van Hove et al., 2008; Darder et al., 2009; McLaren, 2009) (see Table 9.1).

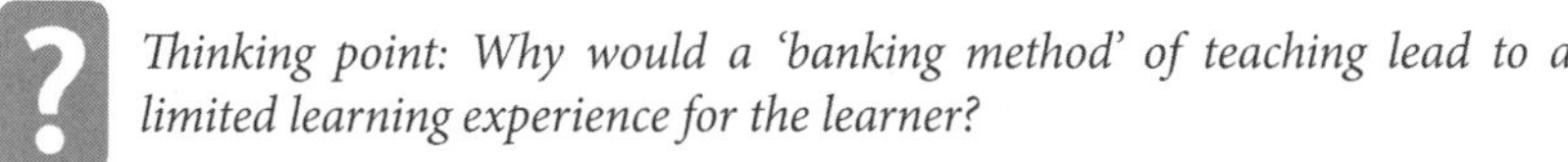

Thinking point: Why would a 'banking method' of teaching lead to a limited learning experience for the learner?

Critical pedagogy addresses Titchkosky's (2008) observation that the focus on assessing difficulties in children fails to ask why these difficulties were there in the first

Table 9.1 Critical pedagogy

- transforms the meaning of education, teaching, relationships and self-awareness;
- is a moral and political practice that informs how we see ourselves and our politics;
- is an organising act of collective education;
- argues that the authority-based *banking method* to neoliberal education (filling empty student vessels with knowledge) must be replaced with liberatory-based methods of *conscientizacao* (promoting critical, politicised and socially aware learners);
- is less to do with technique and methodology and more to do with cultural politics that offers a vision of civic life, ourselves, others and the future – praxiological rather than technicist – bringing critical theory to bear on real world struggles;
- resists the corporatisation of education, which attempts to reduce teachers to technicians or corporate pawns;
- views education as part of the community as well as the school;
- views education as social transformation and potentially subversive;
- challenges the privileging of reason and rationality and embraces alternative forms of knowledge;
- does not process received knowledge but transforms knowledge as part of a more expansive struggle for human rights and social justice;
- is animated by a sense of critique and possibility provoking students to deliberate, resist and cultivate a range of capacities;
- views the classroom as inherently ideological and contradictory;
- embraces the subaltern and resistant voices of learners but does not take a *laissez-faire* approach to the role of the educator;
- looks for incidences of student resistance which might take shape through disruptive and challenging behaviour and attitudes;
- contests the desirability of advancing the cause of minorities through the confines of a liberal, rights-based agenda;
- promotes tolerance, dialogue, alliance and works on a principle of recognition;
- is responsive to oppressive language and vocabularies of education and develops alternative critical forms of literacy

place. Schools are challenged when they perpetuate or reproduce the social relationships and attitudes needed to sustain the existing dominant culture (McLaren, 2009: 77). Rethinking education and its relationship with communities and society places well-being at the very centre of educational design. Rioux (1994b) draws on the work of Baker (1983) to describe a model of community and education in which:

- all individuals, in spite of difficulties, are respected as equals;
- it is accepted that participation might be different for some people but inclusion in social life is the goal for all;
- equality is an end not a means;
- it is not necessary to be equal in terms of ability or talent as one can still contribute to the community;
- the value of non-marketised and non-productive contributions is recognised;
- a redistribution of resources is required.

Underpinning this model, according to Thomas and Loxley (2001), should be key values of inclusive education: social justice, recognition and solidarity.

Critical pedagogy and inclusive education in practice: a narrative of possibility

Rizvi and Lingard (1996) argue that for teachers to commit to inclusion and for schools to enable the widest participation, this requires broadened curricula choice and radical changes to pedagogical practice. So what might these ideas look like in practice?

Change in school culture

A critical pedagogy of school culture places moral and political principles before administrative convenience. For Isaacs (1996: 43), the 'good life' is one of *freedom within the community*: interdependence in which one strives for individual needs alongside communitarian needs, where the community values, celebrates and responds energetically to diversity. Inclusive schools are humane environments (Thomas and Loxley, 2001). Diversity is the starting point for schools rather than an after-thought (Wedell, 2008). Education is resituated as an *enabling good* that recognises the diversity of backgrounds and life circumstances of the children it seeks to educate (Howe, 1996: 55). Fostering care, belonging and community are prerequisites for social justice. Schools should provide belonging even if the child cannot attain (Howe, 1996: 58). The first virtue of social institutions such as schools is that they appeal to the requirements of *justice* (Howe, 1996: 60).

The development of an 'alternative social model of education' (Apple, 1982: 173) places emphasis on acceptance, tolerance and creativity rather than simply a technology for raising the performance of individuals and the economy (Booth, in Clough and Corbett, 2000). The 'Stop the SATs' campaign in England, sponsored by a teacher's union, sits against neoliberal education. Bloggers argue that the SATs are nothing more than 'superfluous asinine torture for students' (www.freewebs.com/nosats). Educators must remain *insatiable in their desire for change* (Ware, 2002). Following Corbett and Slee (2002: 143), inclusion is engaged with *cultural synergies and the hidden curricula* of schools. For Booth (2002: 88), inclusion is transformational because:

> it involves seeing difference within education as an aspect of reality rather than a source of difficulty. It recognises the tyranny of views of normality as homogeneous and sees normality as constituted only by difference. It starts from an assumption of difference in groups of learners and involves a pedagogy of diversity.

Inclusive schools say: 'come in, we celebrate difference here. You can be yourself and not struggle to fit in' (Corbett and Slee, 2002: 143). This is a 'politics of difference' discourse that contrasts with the politics of sameness (Peters and Chimedza, 2000: 269).

Broadened curricula

When students follow narrow curricula they are in danger of being excluded from the outset. Wedell (2008) observes that 35 years of research in special and inclusive education has clearly shown that school curricula contribute hugely to the 'poor behaviour of pupils' because they do not engage with the whole range of students. Innovative curricula developments, which, for example, have included foci on citizenship, managing life situations and personal development, have demonstrated success by bringing pupils into the activities of the classroom. For Erevelles (2005: 432), not only would students be able to access different aspects of the curriculum, but also in an inclusive school the curriculum would be entrenched in a disability studies perspective. Recasting the curriculum in ways that are sensitive to the politics, history and theories of disability studies may engender forms of *critical literacy* in school. This, a key part of critical pedagogy, questions how we are shaped by the words we use and develops oppositional discourses so as to remake ourselves and our culture (Shor, 2009: 282). Hence, the notion of developing 'impairment literacy', would aim to challenge 'the tyranny of disabling environments and ablest embodied knowledge and practices' (Marks, 1999a: 133). Pedagogy must be an encounter with the disabled self (Gabel, 2001: 33). This promotes understandings of disability among the school community that view it not as a constituency (of special education) but as the product of a hostile environment and organisational pathology (Ware, 2009).

For Jarman (2008), disability studies should be an ethical component of all curricula, aiding teachers and pupils to articulate an 'ethics of disability' (critiquing normality and promoting interdependence), viewing disability as an alternative source of values and norms (inclusion rather than marketisation) and helping to promote alternative teacher–learner relationships.

Revisioning the relationship of teacher and learner

An inclusive school nurtures particular teacher–learner relationships. For Wedell (2008: 131), a child's learning problem becomes a teacher's teaching problem. Jarman (2008) suggests that a feminist ethics of care approach complements a disability studies perspective in that support, teaching, facilitation and guidance are refigured in terms of their emotionality, mutuality and interdependence (see also Kittay, 1999a, 1999b, 2002, 2006; McLaughlin et al., 2008). This is captured well by Fanon:

> We need to mutually recognise each other ... to educate man [sic] to be actional, preserving in all his relations his respect for the basic values that constitute a human world, is the prime task of him who, having taken thought, prepares to act. (Fanon, 1993: 222)

Wedell (2008) suggests that the issue for inclusion is not about treating everyone the same but in treating everyone equally. The label of SEN is considered primarily as the *means to access support* that increases the meaning of education for pupils rather than simply being a commodity that is exploited and used by an ever-growing panoply of professionals. But, in line with Apple's (1982) stance, teachers become more in tune with the kinds of relationships that already exist – and work – in the 'hidden curricula' of pupils – promoting an horizontal pedagogy:

> In school, 7 year-old Danny has EBD, ADHD and dyslexia. The educational psychologist has advised that Danny has 'wrap around support'. A support worker is with him all day, every day, even when he visits the washrooms. At the end of each day, it has been decided that Danny must wait in a separate room, until the other children have collected their coats and school bags. The school fears Danny might harm one of his classmates. When the other children have finally spilled out into the playground to their waiting parents and childminders, and they have left the playground, Danny is then allowed to leave the school. Each day, every day, Danny and Mum leave the school grounds alone. Meanwhile, to his classmates Danny is ...? Rosa says 'He is naughty, sometimes. He pulls my hair'. But he is also 'funny Danny, he makes us laugh. He is good at Football. He's good at sorting things out when my friends argue. Can he come to my birthday party, Dad?' (A personal anecdote)

Inclusive education might involve working alongside pupils as agents of their own learning, permitting more 'unruly' or 'Tom Sawyeresque' behaviour (like that of Danny) to be permitted while not violating the rights of other children (Mercogliano, 2009: 384). This contrasts with the vertical model of teaching – the technical/administrative style of pedagogy that is actually more in keeping with the style of management in corporate organisations (Apple, 1982: 34).

Critical pedagogies are also caring pedagogies. This may well involve elucidating those everyday happenings that constitute social justice: caring, reciprocity in the educational relationship, ordinariness, extraordinariness, intuition and personal shared understandings between the agents of pedagogy. It also involves accepting and facilitating 'becomings' rather than beings (Goodley, 2007a). Is Danny allowed 'to become' in the company of his peers like Rosa? Or is he always 'being': a difficult, deficient, SEN being? Inclusive schools require all their staff to be trained to support children with labels of SEN and disability. Education becomes linked to the everyday rather than simply being preparation for democratic citizenship (Peters and Chimedza, 2000). This would include inclusive education and disability studies being key elements of teaching training programmes (Ware, 2009). Moreover, the actual professional role of teachers and their teaching assistants might be recast in more embracing ways. As Ferri (2008) argues in relation to Italian education, the 1971 legislation specified the rights of disabled children to be educated in regular classes, making Italy a model of inclusive education, according to UNESCO and OECD. There is now 99% inclusion of disabled students. Key to this inclusion has been the role of the *sostegno*, a teaching position equivalent to the teacher dual certificate in the USA, who works for the class not the individual, modifying the curriculum where needed. They 'consider the classroom as a family or community and address whole class issues not just a specific population' (Terri, 2008: 48). This approach to teaching and learning is what Wedell (2008: 134) defines as 'co-production – treating everyone equally but not necessarily the same'. Teachers are involved in a process of continual self-critique (Gabel, 2001).

Conscientisation

Pupils and teachers undergo *conscientisation,* achieving a deeper awareness of the social realities which shape their lives and discover their own capacities to recreate them (Darder et al., 2009). This involves unveiling a world of oppression and then developing a pedagogy for liberation.

Thinking point: Educational institutions respond to the expertise and training of disabled people's organisations – (for example, Disability Equality in Education (DEE), www.diseed.org.uk) which promote disability equality training. In what ways can equality training promote an agenda of inclusive education?

Here, the cultural (Ware, 2009) and the social (Peters and Chimedza, 2000) origins of disablism would be understood and alternative inclusive practices shared and developed. Schools should proactively engage pupils with the *politics of disability*, particularly when disabled students – like black and working-class students before them – experience curricula that have been cut off from their past (Apple, 1982: 130). For praxis to be possible, not only must theory illuminate the lived experience of progressive social groups, it must also be illuminated by their struggles (Lather, 1986: 262). For Lavia (2007), postcolonial critical pedagogies create 'dialogic spaces' to unlearn learned helplessness, interrupt dominant arguments of imperialism, regain cultural confidence and resuscitate indigenous culture. These dialogues would open up and develop more responsive curricula and professional support of inclusion. Recent moves in the UK around Single Equality Schemes could be viewed as examples of schools having to provide proactive support to the inclusion of disabled students. However, the school culture's willingness to embrace diverse learners can only be encouraged through conscientisation around the politics of disability.

Recent research by Beckett (2009) on disability-aware non/fiction books for primary school children indicates that 'inclusive reading material is important because it reflects the increasing social diversity of their classrooms, promotes positive attitudes towards peers of all abilities and, in the case of disabled children, supports the development of a positive self-image'. Similar findings have been reported with regards to queer curricula content and its impact on homophobia (Atkinson and DePalma, 2008; see also www.nooutsiders.sunderland.ac.uk/). Education can also turn to the creative industries for guidance around inclusion, for example, the training and consultancy of disabled performing artists such as the Lawnmowers (www.thelawnmowers.co.uk), whose performance and workshop theatre act in educational settings to promote disability awareness. 'The members of the Company place themselves alongside the daily struggles faced by people with learning disabilities. All of our projects are working towards a future, just and equal society'. Conscientisation can enact a new ontology of disability (Peters and Chimedza, 2000: 249).

Thinking point: Complete the statement. 'The ideal school of the twenty-first century would promote the following philosophies and practices…'

Conclusions

> The political class can't face up to the scale of this crisis.
>
> The free market of capitalism, which has held sway across the world for more than two decades, is rapidly coming to an end ... the neoliberal order is transparently falling apart. (Milne, S., The *Guardian*, 18 September 2008: 37)

As Azzopardi (2000, 2003, 2008) has demonstrated, inclusion is in danger of becoming a cliché: a practice hijacked by standards and competition within education. Instead, schools should be places that affect change. It is to the tenets of inclusive education and critical pedagogy that we might turn to help re-energise such changes in schools.

Further reading

Armstrong, Armstrong and Barton (2000a). International contributions on inclusive education.

Christensen and Rizvi (1996). A key early text in the field of inclusive education.

Gabel (2002). A critical angle on critical pedagogy from disability studies.

Reiser and Mason (1992). A disability rights take on inclusive education.

Wedell (2008). A critical look back on 35 years of developments in inclusive and special education.

Notes

1 In contrast, Gerber (1996) sees IEPs as giving parents an unusually powerful role in modulating the school experience of their children.

2 Fanon (1993: 224) defines middle-class society as 'any society that becomes rigified in predetermined forms, forbidding all evolution, all gains, all progress, all discovery ... a closed society in which life has no taste, in which the air is tainted, in which ideas and men are corrupt'.

3 Standard Assessment Tests were introduced in Britain in 1988 in order to measure pupils' learning of the National Curriculum in schools and were intended to make schools and teachers accountable. However, as Wedell (2008) notes, such accountability meant that many schools have 'disapplied' (or pulled) students with SEN from these tests so as not to lower a school's SATs test results and, consequently, their place in league table rankings.

4 As Isaacs (1996: 33) puts it: 'an overemphasis on autonomy, freedom and constraint can easily suggest a metaphysics of individualism and an atomistic view of social reality.'

5 Even in the more collectivist and community-centred Nordic countries, Stromstad (2004) and Nes (2004) argue that a more 'rugged individualism' has appeared in recent years, which challenges these core principles.

6 This was a measure of excellence that was developed by the British government up until 2005 in which schools could apply for, and be recognised as, centres of educational excellence, (see www.standards.dfes.gov.uk/beaconschools).

7 One could almost choose any letter of the alphabet, add a 'D' to it and find a category defining a school-age child as a problem (Baker, 2002: 677).

TEN

Developments: *Critical Disability Studies*

****

Introduction

In this final chapter we will attend to the cross-cutting themes of the book, which connect disability studies with other important agendas of class, feminist, queer and postcolonial studies. Such intersections are at the heart of what we might term *critical* disability studies (McRuer, 2003; Davis, 2006b), where disability links together other identities as a moment of reflection that Davis (2002, 2006c) coins as *dismodernism,* and impairment and disability are interrogated as phenomena enacted at the levels of the psyche, culture and society. While critical disability studies might start with disability, they never end with it, remaining ever vigilant of political, ontological and theoretical complexity. And in order to analyse disablism we need to be mindful of the complementary hegemony of ablism. Critical disability studies contest dis/ablism.

Bodies (and minds) that matter

While some disability scholars want to keep a biological conception of the body alongside a dynamic sense of the relationship between these bodies and the social world (as we saw in Chapter 7 and as articulated by the Nordic relational model in Chapter 1), critical disability studies contest the idea that 'biology is destiny' (Linton, 1998a: 532), theorising the body's place in society and culture. This assists the queer feminist strategy of pulling the (male) homeless mind back into the body in order to think carefully about the close connection of private/public, individual/social, psyche/society and embodied/cultural worlds (Davis, 1997a). This unsettles the Cartesian split of body/mind (Chapter 5), which originally rejects the body as far too unruly for modernist rational discourse. Instead, we are encouraged to probe the body/mind as key sites for relational (Chapter 6), discursive (Chapter 7) and cultural inscription (Chapter 8). Theorists no longer suffer 'somatophobia' (fear of the body). Feminist writers such as Butler (1990, 1993), Haraway (1991), Gatens (1999) and Grosz (1999) have made the 'natural body' an untenable notion by opposing the idea that the (impaired) body is a brute, biological fact (see Chapter 7). Instead, the 'natural body' is understood as an artefact of liberal individualism and capitalist society: a phenomenon *materialised* through a host of self-actualising and becoming-fit practices through which we all strive to reach the standards of citizenship (Overboe, 2007a). Critical disability studies adopt similar understandings and take up the challenge of queer theories to highlight the limits of the straight, non-disabled body (McRuer, 2002: 224). For Overboe (2007a), the disabled body is a queer body, rejecting the stereotypical disabled-body-as-deficient and refiguring it as a place of becoming, reflection and production. Overboe describes his spasms (normatively and medically understood as a sign of the negative affliction of his Cerebral Palsy) as creative elements of his embodiment (queerly understood as productive, creative, physical attributes).

For Wilkerson (2002: 34), queer/disabled bodies are potential sites of pleasure, interpersonal connection and acceptance. Seemingly hard-wired (but actually heteronormatively constituted), masculine bodies can be queered (re-wired) by the experience of disability and impairment. Sparkes and Smith's (2002, 2003) work on the experiences of young men who have acquired spinal cord injuries (SCI) demonstrates very complex identity work. On becoming SCI, men spoke of losing old 'boys' friendships and the double bind of fighting to become 'whole' with 'incomplete bodies'. But, rather than simply being medical sociological accounts of 'biographical disruption' (see Chapter 4), their stories indicate that SCI does not inevitably cause a downward descent into the depressions of psychological adjustment (Chapter 6). Men spoke of their surprise at finding disability politics. For some, the solitary masculine relationships that they had prior to SCI had been replaced with more mutually inclusive and interdependent ones. Their 'new' bodies had prompted revision.

Disabled bodies call into question the 'giveness' of the 'natural body' and, instead, posit a corporeality that is fluid in its investments and meanings (Shildrick and Price, 1999a: 1). 'Disability', Killacky (2004: 62) comments, 'has given me real opportunities for wisdom. My connectivity to the world is deepening as I experience dependence on others.' Bodies are conceptualised not as solitary lacking entities (see Chapters 5 and 8) but as bodies of interconnection and production (Hickey-Moody, 2009: 75). The (disabled) body has a propensity to leak and overflow, blurring distinctions between self and other, with the potential to engulf (Shildrick and Price, 1999a). Disabled bodies expand and envelope in exciting ways. Theories of gendered, raced, sexed, classed and disabled bodies offer us critical languages for 'denaturalising impairment' (Donaldson, 2002: 112) – at the level of the individual (Chapter 5), psyche (Chapter 6), discourse (Chapter 7), culture (Chapter 8) and education (Chapter 9).

Thinking point: Cochlear implants, facial plastic surgery for children with the label of Down syndrome, cures for spinal injuries can be understood as 'body projects' with moral, ethical and political dimensions. Drawing on two or more chapters of this book, how would different disability studies perspectives make sense of these 'body projects'?

Queer feminists such as Davis (1997b) argue that we need to view surgery as a complex dilemma: problem and solution, a symptom of oppression and perceived act of empowerment, all in one. To recognise this duality ensures that we comprehend choice as always entailing compliance. Indeed, children and their families use 'new impairments' such as ADHD, Asperger's syndrome and Oppositional Defiance Disorder. For example, the slogan 'I'm not naughty, I'm Autistic' scrawled on the T-shirts of children so-labelled is a beneficial strategy to have in community settings. Conversely, though, labels risk categorising difference *only* through the powerful lens of biopower (Chapter 7). Furthermore, as Connell (2001) has demonstrated, while there is an 'epidemic of signification' around (disabled) bodies, most bodies are not white, not well fed and not living in rich countries. To ask what kinds of bodies we value has to take into account the majority of the world.

In *Bodies That Matter: On the Discursive Limits of Sex*, Butler (1993, see also 1999: 243) asked a number of questions, to which we could add linked questions to dis/ablism:

1. How, then, can we think through the matter of bodies as a kind of materialisation governed by regulatory norms in order to ascertain the workings of heterosexual hegemony in the formation of what qualifies as a viable body? *How are non-disabled bodies made more viable than disabled bodies?*
2. How does materialisation of the norm in bodily formation produce a domain of abjected bodies, a field of deformation, which, in failing to qualify as the fully human, fortifies those regulatory norms? *How do societal practices uphold the precarious higher status of non-disabled people through the abjection (rejection) of disabled people?*
3. What challenge does the abjected realm produce to a symbolic hegemony that might force a radical re-articulation of what qualifies as bodies that matter? *In what ways do disabled bodies rearticulate what qualifies as a body that matters?*

The first two questions have been addressed sociologically (Chapter 4), psychologically (Chapter 6), discursively (Chapter 7) and culturally (Chapter 8). The third question poses an exciting challenge for critical disability studies, which we take further in this chapter.

Self and others

Critical disability studies attend to the relational components of dis/ablism. For Ghai (2006: 128), feminist disability studies regard impairment as a 'material-semiotic phenomenon dependent upon one's relationships with others and their relationship with you'. This book engaged not just with the material realm of dis/ablism (Chapter 4) but also with semiotic (Chapters 7 and 8), educational (Chapter 9) and psychological processes (Chapters 5 and 6). A key task of Chapter 6 involved an interrogation of the boundaries of the (disabled) self and (non-disabled) other: to ask how the two are demarcated and to explore the kinds of boundary work that take place. Questions are asked about the individual that is valued by society (Chapter 5) and the ways in which culture reflects the insecurities of non-disabled society (Chapter 8). For Finkelstein (1997), disabled people are expected to occupy a 'bifurcated subjectivity': that combines the contradictory illusion of self-possessed autonomy (Chapter 5) with the expectation to act 'the crip' (Chapter 6). This contradiction marks the lives of people who fail to match up to the dominant other (Chapter 5):

> A woman is not simply alienated from her product, but in a deep sense does not exist as a subject, or even a potential subject, since she owes her existence as a woman to sexual appropriation. To be constituted by another's desire. (Haraway, 1991: 159)

For Haraway, acknowledging the discrepancy between the marginalised self and the antithetical dominant Other (Chapter 5) encourages the development of a distinct form of political consciousness: *the self-knowledge of a self-who-is-not*. Acknowledging this can be hard but emancipatory.

Thinking point:

'I was not born into disability secure in my manhood or comfortable breaking out of stereotypical male roles. What it meant to be a real man was deeply ingrained in me by the time I was 20. Fortunately, after many years of work, I am relatively free of socially imposed concepts of male sexuality and masculinity. Even at this juncture in my life, I sometimes wrestle with internalised notions of male roles as I prepare to stay home with our baby when my wife goes to work.' (Tepper, 1999: 41)

Questions: (1) Identify the discourses that Tepper is grappling with (Chapter 7). (2) Consider the extent to which Tepper's extract is an account of (a) the psychoemotional subject or (b) the social psychoanalytic subject (Chapter 6). (3) In what ways is Tepper describing his dealings with the imaginary and symbolic aspects of dis/ablism (Chapter 8)?

Critical disability studies open up spaces for rethinking self and other. The first seeks *transgression*, describing identities that shift norms, straddle standards and shake up the dis/ability distinction. To what extent is 'madness', for example, transgressive rather than diseased? Strands of psychoanalysis have long been committed to the ways in which 'the neurotic' and 'the hysteric' subvert conservative norms and offer superior ways of being (Donaldson, 2002: 100): a view held in the more surrealist writings of Lacan (Chapter 8) and developed by Deleuze and Guattari (1987) (see below). Mad Pride and Queer Crips reclaim labels for their creative potential (Chapter 7).

The second, *performativity*, explores how regulated selves might, nonetheless, offer embodied alternatives. Can the production of disability humour, often by disabled comedians, unsettle non-disablist norms (Mallett, 2007)? Is disability 'a gift' – not (necessarily) an act of God – but the promise of 'a deep ontology of learning' (Michalko, 2002: 153)? To what extent do disabled bodies, performing everyday tasks, disturb normative practices? When a disabled mother changes her kid's nappies with her teeth (see Reeve, 2008), does this unsettle normative notions of motherhood and expand conceptions of parenting? In what ways do disabled people, who draw on 24-hour personal assistance, trouble taken-for-granted ideas about independence (Chapter 5) and forms of care normally associated with the nuclear family (Wilkerson, 2002)?

The third, *affirmation*, recasts disability as a positive identity (Swain and French, 2000). This connects with queer: subversive, unruly and enabling aspects of being non-normative. To what extent do non-normative people subvert dull, rigid and unwelcoming heteronormative social settings? To what extent does liminality – a failure to fit particular social categories – open up possibly transformative ways for reconsidering social conventions (Chapter 8)? Do disabled children queer schools for the betterment of all children (Chapter 9)? In what ways does disability offer opportunities for what McKenzie (2009) terms *possability*: a neologism to describe the ways in which disabled children demand imaginative and responsive forms of educational provision. In what ways does disability stress the inherent vulnerabilities of *all* human beings? As Sable (2004: 78) observes: 'We may be so busy nursing our own vulnerabilities that we do not see anyone else's. The concept of "I'm not the only vulnerable one here" certainly would tend to make the playing field more level.'

Thinking point: How would acknowledging 'vulnerability' feed into the aims of critical pedagogy (Chapter 9)? Google 'Martha Nussbaum' and 'vulnerability' to help you answer this question.

Queer perverts the logic of the normative. Postcolonialism deconstructs the rationality of the occidental. Feminist disability studies unseat the certainties of the disabling *male*stream. These frameworks refute the standards of (ableist) culture, the myth of self-reliance and the isolationist individualism that condemns intersubjective relationships – such as care-taking or receipt – as signs of regressive dependency (Mintz, 2002: 167). Alliances can be made.

Studies of non-normative gay and lesbian families suggest that parents are put under enormous pressure to school their children in readiness for dealing with homophobia (Gabb, 2004, 2005a, 2005b). Similar tensions can be found in disabled families (McLaughlin et al., 2008). A question for both would be: how do these non-normative families create strategies for dealing with dis/ablism? In what ways do disabled families queer normative culture? How can queer and disabled families pool their resources? The study of disability is a study of its *alter ego*: ability. In this sense, critical disability studies deconstruct the 'hegemonic subject' – the able individual (Chapter 5) – and its foundational discourses (Chapter 7), cultural precedents (Chapter 8) and political origins (Chapter 1).

Thinking point: Queer makes for a politicised and contested space to talk about impairment and the body, not as simple biogenic concepts, but as fluid, ever-changing entities. Disability corrupts the body beautiful of gay, straight and normative:

'Wheelchair-bound', disabled and tragic? Hardly: 'I ride in style ... being a diva, it suits me' (Elkins, 2004: 24).

'Young, disabled and powerless'? No way: 'because of how small I am, people think I am actually older than I am, which is good – I get served drinks in bars', comments from a young man with restricted growth from www.rihsc.mmu.ac.uk/postblairproject.

In what ways do these accounts recast dis/ability as transgressive, performative and affirmative?

While celebrating queer, we must also keep in mind that the normative big Other has been placed out of bounds for many disabled people (Chapter 5 and 8). Motherhood, marriage and home-making are heteronormative roles that, when enacted by disabled women with others, may actually be seen as taking on a subversive quality (Mintz, 2002). Relationships are marked by the cultures in which they are enacted.

Discourses and institutions

> **Investigation reveals appalling neglect by NHS of people with learning disabilities**
>
> NHS and social care staff have been responsible for an appalling catalogue of neglect of people with learning disabilities, the health and local government ombudsman said today after an investigation into six 'distressing' deaths. They included the case of a 43 year-old man with Down's syndrome and epilepsy who starved for 26 days in Kingston hospital, Surrey, because he was unable to speak. (Carvel, J., The *Guardian*, 24 March 2009, p. 9)

Critical disability studies understand dis/ablism and impairment as being materialised in institutions of schools, long-stay hospitals, clinics, workplaces, universities, community groups, rehabilitation centres and families (Chapter 7). Institutions engender disability discourse (Corker and French, 1998) that can, quite literally, be a matter of life or death. This is particularly the case if you are economically, culturally and socially poor (Chapter 3).

Disability is understood because, according to Davis (1995: 11), the human diversity continuum of dis/ability is carved into oppositional poles of disability and ability. The contemporaneous exponential rise in the number of impairment labels – particularly in childhood – is akin to the labelling of women's mental health, the medicalisation of homosexuality and the pathologisation of 'non-WENAns' in the twentieth century. Questions need to be asked (of institutions) about the discursive construction of these new impairments, their location in the bodies/minds of individuals and why this might lead eventually to the neglect of these individuals. We need also to ask macroscopic questions around discourse (Chapters 4, 5 and 8).

Clearly, the privileging of one discursive position/social group over another creates discriminatory social institutions. Connor (2008) draws on a critical race theory (CRT) to interrogate the juridical position of disabled people. A CRT perspective recognises dis/ablism/racism as endemic, is sceptical of neutrality of law, insists on historical analysis of law, brings in perspectives of people of colour, is interdisciplinary, works to end racial oppression and asks how law recreates racism. Austin (1999) provides a queer analysis of law. He observes that it is based on and helps constitute the patriarchal family. In some states in the USA, gay and lesbian people are denied the opportunity of adopting children and the right to marry. Institutions are founded on laws that embrace compulsory heterosexuality (Rich, 1980), compulsory able-bodiedness (Wilkerson, 2002) and the patriarchal dividend (Connell, 2002). They therefore require constant deconstruction and critical disability studies need to analyse international law and its close relationship with the political economy (Hosking, 2008). The need for practitioners of these institutions to deconstruct their reactions to disabled people remains a key concern of critical disability studies.

Writing back

Critical disability studies are found in and outside academic research circles in cultural politics. Examples of this include the performing arts, film, music and poetry. As we saw in Chapters 1, 4 and 8 of this text, it is fundamentally important that disabled people revise as well as deconstruct dominant modes of cultural production in ways that give voice to their potentialities.

Llorens (2008a) provides an account of the poetry of survivors of mental health systems in Venezuela, suggesting that this poetry constitutes a form of writing back similar to that articulated by Tuhiwai-Smith (1999) in her call for decolonising methodologies. Non-disabled professionals have typically implemented research on survivors in similar ways to colonising methodologies described by Tuhiwai-Smith as, 'research has probed, recollected, appropriated and ultimately exploited the life experiences of other cultures in insensitive and offensive ways' (Llorens, 2008a: 3). There are clear overlaps between the writing back of postcolonial thinkers, the development of feminist stand/sitpoint theory (Stanley and Wise, 1993; Garland-Thomson, 2002), the queering of heteronormative research production (Vickers, 2008) and the emergence of participatory/emancipatory approaches to disability (Chapter 2). Writing back invites subjugated voices to re-enter cultural and political critique: deconstructing taken-for-granted imaginary and symbolic elements of everyday life (Chapter 8). Angela, for example, found herself increasingly broadening her own norms about appropriate behaviour through gradually accepting her disabled 'son's ways':

> He wants his clothes off, he wants them off and you have a right battle, and of course the older he gets, people might tolerate, but they might start and like, look and think he shouldn't be doing that ... I often think it's quite sad really 'cause I think you know, 'what's the harm?' But it is social rules at the end of the day isn't it, what kids have to sort of fit in to (from Goodley and McLaughlin, 2008)

Writing back from a valued position of one's own diversity, on one's own terms, reclaims the research agenda.

Thinking point: Visit the spoof website of the Institute for the Study of the Neurologically Typical (ISNT) (www.isnt.autistics.org/). *This website has been set up by people who typically would be labelled as having Autism or Asperger's syndrome but who identify themselves as 'neurologically atypical'. The website turns the tables on the 'neurologically typical' (normal) and provides the diagnostic descriptors for visitors to find out if they 'suffer' with this 'syndrome'. To what extent do you agree with the statement that 'ISNT queers the normative space of disability studies by drawing our attention to the value of being "neurologically atypical"*

> *(normatively described as 'Autism' and 'Asperger's syndrome') and the sorrows of being neurologically typical (what we would vaguely term 'normal')'?*

Lurie (2004: 84) describes queer as creating a new language. Writing back confronts the pathologising tendencies of research and, following Fanon (1993: 30), involves people 'freeing themselves of the arsenal of complexes that have been developed by an exploitative environment'. Crucial facets of writing back are to be found in relation to the re/storying of self (Chapter 6) and critical forms of pedagogy (Chapter 9).

Empire

Critical disability studies are aware of the inequities of globalisation. Hardt and Negri's *Empire* (2000) provides a means of bringing together analyses of globalisation, economic expansion of late capitalism, rapid developments in communication and the impact of biopower on the 'global citizen'. *Empire* is conceived of as a postcolonial and postmodern process, in which knowledge, particularly from the Global North, spreads across the globe in ways that are, potentially, imposed on, taken up or resisted by citizens in their local contexts. Hardt and Negri are Marxists in attitude and postmodernists by design. While interested in the ways in which powerful WENA nations police, govern and master the global economic and cultural stage – through the workings of supranational organisations such as the United Nations, the World Bank and the International Monetary Fund – they are also mindful of the ways in which less powerful nations, collectives and groups (what they term 'multitudes') may resist such inequities. Simultaneously, their ideas allow us to consider the ways in which citizens are subjected to big modern ideas (such as choice, competition, capitalism, meritocracy, science and medicine) while also holding on to more local concerns (such as mutuality, community, tradition and local expertise).

Hardt and Negri are clear that powerful nations and WENA ideas have the potential to demolish powerless nations and local concerns. But, their work might also be seen as an account of the kinds of community and activism that can emerge through and in response to the ideas of *Empire*. At the heart of *Empire* is the Foucauldian notion of *biopower* (Chapter 7). As we saw, the discourses of biopower are re/produced in the institutional regimes of family, school, healthcare and welfare setting, prison and workplace. These discourses are used to create our psychologies – our sense of our selves and others – our subjectivities. Through globalisation and the rapid expansion of the capitalist free market, it could be argued that all global citizens are more and more likely to come into contact with biopower. Ideas from psychiatry and psychology, for example, know no fixed boundaries as they are caught up in plural pan-national exchanges of information and communication. *Empire* refers to a *globalised biopolitical machine* (Hardt and Negri, 2000: 40), through which theories of subjectivity spread across the globe, infecting or affecting citizens in every corner of the world. The processes of biopower have in mind a preferred psychology and version of the self: healthy, rational, autonomous, educated, economically viable, self-governing and able – a self-contained individual. And if you don't fit, then *Empire* is ready to fix you. That said, Hardt and

Negri (2000) are mindful of the ways in which global citizens envisage other ways of being – through and against the practices of biopower – that are enabling to them.

Thinking point: Hardt and Negri (2000) consider the ways in which non-governmental organisations (NGOs), such as Oxfam, Médecins Sans Frontières and Amnesty, provide international aid in the development of nation states of the majority world, addressing issues such as poverty, literacy and disability. Following Chapter 7 – and considering the concepts of 'well being', 'healthy' and 'human rights' – visit the websites of Oxfam, Médecins Sans Frontières and Amnesty. To what extents do the aims of these organisations reflect the liberal philosophies and values of WENA countries? Why might it be important to promote these values across the globe? What are the potential dangers of such promotion?

Examples of *Empire* in the majority world include:

- the intervention of speech and language therapists in African countries;
- the application of the United Nations Convention on the Rights of the Child in Pakistan;
- the production of the Indian Human Development report (2009) available at http://ihds.umd.edu
- the implementation of the United Nation's Millennium Development Goals – the Millennium Development Goals in which states and NGOs have agreed, by 2015, to reduce extreme poverty and child mortality and fight AIDS;
- the development of self-advocacy and Independent Living principles in Malaysia (www.unitedvoice.com.my);
- the delivery of Disability Equality Training (devised in the UK) in the Asia Pacific (Kuno et al., 2008);
- a Balinese organisation of disabled people which declares its ambitions as moving from 'isolation to integration'. Funded by donors from Malaysia, Singapore and Europe, this registered charity provides an accessible village for disabled people to live and work in and has campaigned against the lack of physical access in Bali. The only non-disabled person employed by the organisation is the driver (www.senanghati.org).

These examples show that *Empire* can be *both* pacifying *and* productive (Hardt and Negri, 2000). The pacifying effects are related to the unproblematic rolling out of biopower that threatens to instil deficient understandings of disabled children (Goodley and Lawthom, 2010) and eradicate local enabling community practices. The UN Convention of the Rights of the Child aims to extend children's welfare, cultural and political rights, but also instils a culturally-specific notion of idealised child subjects and family forms (Burman, 2008: 53). Indian Human Development reports have, according to Ghai (2006), smuggled in archetypal Global North conceptions of impairment that do not fit readily with the Indian context. The extent to which disabled children are included in schools in the majority world is framed by bilateral and multinational donors from the minority world who fund and monitor the progress of the nations they patronise (see Gabel and Danforth, 2008b). One of the International Monetary Fund's loan requirements for Argentina has been the reduction to pensions and programmes for elderly people, many of whom are disabled (McRuer and Wilkerson, 2003: 3). *Empire* can damage local contexts.

The productive impacts are to be found when the self-contained individualism of *Empire* (Chapter 5) is used politically towards specific ends. The examples of *Empire* cited above use the language of self-contained individualism: of individual human rights, educational achievement through inclusion, independence, self-help. Understanding disability requires us to think carefully about the hybrid of local and global meanings, of tradition and *Empire*, of new forms of welfare, social services, politics, social class and social capital. Grech (2009a) makes an important observation when he connects disability studies and development studies in order to address the needs and ambitions of disabled people in poor countries. A key resource for development studies is the work of Sen (1985, 1999) and his capabilities approach. Grech argues that this approach reorients a focus on people and the ends they seek through Sen's separation of capabilities (the opportunities to lead a life one has reason to value) and functionings (what a person manages to do or be). Such an approach, in the context of *Empire*, examines the extent to which disabled people are denied or offered opportunities as the 'outcome of personal characteristics (for example, type of impairment), the individual's resources and environmental characteristics (physical, social, political, cultural and economic)' (Grech, 2009b: 779). NGOs therefore, need to ask to what extent they are expanding the human capabilities of disabled people through broadening their opportunities to obtain 'valued functionings, hence entailing a focus on peoples' basic achievements rather than goods or commodities' (Grech, 2009b: 779). Key to such interventions require NGOs working with the opportunities, resources and capabilities that might already exist within local communities (for example, forms of labour which are 'remunerated' by food rather than money, and kinship networks of care and support) rather than imposing WENA-based views of the citizenship (for example, paid labour and wage, and individualised packages of care offered by trained practitioners).

Miles (2000, 2002, 2006) and Grech (2008, 2009a, 2009b, 2009c) enunciate a postcolonial attitude against the rise of new disability discourses (developed in the Global North) and the potential dangers of transplanting them (in the Global South). Their work critiques Occidentalism (discourses emanating from the Metropole), which includes aspirations such as 'rights', 'independence' and 'individualism', and they remind us that if disability studies are to develop in ways that do not recreate colonialist pasts, then scholars and researchers have to be mindful of the fit of their theories in specific geographical places. Following Hardt and Negri (2000) and McKenzie (2009), effective politics, such as those displayed in South Africa, combine a call on the truth and rights discourse of *Empire* (that redress the impacts of colonisation) while also celebrating cultural specifics of distinct national communities (which enlarge notions of community and civic membership).

How we understand these complex meetings of global/local, North/South and new/traditional requires theoretical ideas that are in tune with fusion of these binaries. *Empire* takes as a given that all majority and minority world contexts are mixes of the old and new, the occidental and oriental, North and South. Cities of the Global South are mixed with the consumerism traditionally associated with the Global North (Burman, 2008: 187) and the sweatshops of Paris and New York rival those of Manila and Hong Kong (Hardt and Negri, 2000). Consequently, this raises interesting questions about how we not only understand dis/ablism but also respond to it: resistance.

Resistance: cyborgs and hybrids

Critical disability studies think differently about the unruly impaired body and mind. 'The disruptive child', 'the wheelchair-bound' and 'the intellectually disabled' are turned on their heads to become 'the productive child', 'the human-machine hybrid' and 'the distribution of intelligence' that is required of sustainable communities. The concepts of *hybrids and cyborgs* allow us to think about the potential of human beings in an increasingly technological (and postmodern) landscape. Cyborg is a concept associated with the work of Haraway (1991), who argues that by the late twentieth century, 'we are all chimeras, theorised and fabricated hybrids of machine and organism' (Haraway, 1991: 50).

Thinking point: The cyborg is a figurative view of our selves that is less caught up in the trappings of tradition and modernity (Burman, 2008). 'The cyborg can be taken as a metaphorical, actual or literal concept which relates to the enmeshing of technology and subjectivities; the blurring of organic and artificial forms of intelligence; the blending of national and global contexts; the mixing of human and machine.[1] It denotes the ways in which corporeal identities carry the marks of technological change' (Meekosha, 1998: 26). Cyborgs are 'spunky, irreverent and sexy: they accept with glee the ability to transgress old boundaries between machine and animal ... male and female, and mind and body' (Siebers, 2006: 178). To what extent can it be argued that disabled people and cyborgs are mutually inclusive concepts?

For Braidotti (2002) technology is at the heart of a colossal hybridisation of human and machine. These insights, hugely developed in feminist writings (Malacrida and Low, 2008), remain largely dormant in disability studies. This is understandable. The history of disability technology is one of normalisation, cure and rehabilitation (Chapter 1). But, at the turn of the twenty-first century, the postmodernisation of *Empire* (Hardt and Negri, 2000) has created new relationships with technology and science which deeply influence how we view of bodies.

> We are witnessing a new kind of human subjectivity – inter-subjectivity if you like – technological humans – hybrids, cyborgs, or monsters. What better place to extend our ideas about ableism and the production of disability than the subject of trans-humanism with all its incumbent issues around ontology, humanness and of course the place of technology. (Campbell, 2009: 35)

Olkin (2009: 23) provides a thoughtful starting point for thinking about the (disabled) body as cyborg:

> When I use crutches I feel connected to them as if they are one of my limbs. When I set them aside and get on the wheelchair I disconnect from the crutches and take on the wheelchair as part of me. I don't like anyone to move my crutches without my permission, or to lean on the arm of the wheelchair or rest their hand on the back of it unless it is someone I feel comfortable touching me.

Olkin captures the subjective qualities of being enabled by prosthetics of wheelchair and crutches, in which animate body and inanimate prosthetics become intertwined. Haraway (1991) and Braidotti (1994, 2002) speculate that the (disabled) body-as-cyborg is interfaced in infinite, polymorphous ways (Marks, 1999b: 14); an ironic figuration of the half-organic, half-machine (Shildrick and Price, 1999a: 11). The disabled body is already cyborg because it pushes at the margins of the idea of the embodied self (Shildrick and Price, 1999). The cyborg works to fray identities. Other examples of the cyborg might include: (1) disabled activists 'plugged into' the transnational disabled people's movement via the Internet; (2) assistive technologies that provide non-speakers with the opportunity to communicate; (3) differing levels of personal assistance required and managed by disabled people; and (4) the potency of the self-advocacy of individuals with the label of intellectual disabilities being realised through the collectivity of group membership.

The cyborg/disabled body is a sophisticated body, aware of its needs, its history and anticipating its future. The cyborg raises important questions about human rights (individual or collective), independence (or interdependence) and co-dependence. The cyborg makes us think about how we can interconnect with one another in inclusive ways. The distinction between human and machine, nature and society, self and other, able and disabled, all become hard to sustain. For Garland-Thomson (2002: 9), the cyborg is not a metaphorical invocation but a referent for the *actual* bodies of disabled people. We should not, as Reeve (2008) and Campbell (2009) urge, romanticise the cyborg. Many fusions of machine and human carry with them perfecting technologies (Baker, 2002) – genetic testing – and normalising practices (Shakespeare, 2006b) – unnecessary physiotherapy – that threaten the existence of disabled people. But cyborg captures the material interconnectedness of (disabled) bodies to social and technological worlds (Reeve, 2008) and, if used carefully, provides a vision of the future that transcends the limits of normalcy and allows those with disabled bodies to be seen as part of the range of beings that inhabit societies (Meekosha, 2008). The disabled person/cyborg is a vision of an interconnected future that blurs nature/technology and bodies/culture (Chapter 7).

This mixing of the given and the new resonates with the postcolonial concept of *hybridisation*. Bhabha's (1985) work on hybrids emerged out of writing about postcolonial contexts. He suggests that it is best to understand the postcolonial subject as a subject who fuses pre-, present and postcolonial practices through 'mimicry, hybridity and sly civility' (Bhabha, 1994: 21 cited by Sherry 2007: 19). The Indianised gospel, a British-born Pakistani identity, the glocalisation of a South-East Asian youth exemplify the appropriation and imitation of colonial *and* traditional cultural practices (see also Spivak, 1985: 253). The postcolonial subject is always hybridised. We can state similar things in relation to disability. The Temporarily Able Bodied is a hybrid – an able body that will *become* disabled. For Sherry (2007: 19), Bhabha's (1994) model of hybridisation 'stresses those in-between moments that initiate new sites of identity, new collaborations and new conflicts of one's identity'. The hybrid[2] draws attention to the weaving away, making sense of, experimenting nature of human subjectivity and relationships. This is captured well in Tepper's (1999: 40) description of 'doing sexuality' as a newly disabled man:

> Along the way I did a lot of experimentation, at times hurting others' feelings and getting my own feelings hurt too. I sought out every opportunity to express my sexuality and have it affirmed. ... I dated a nurse who cared for me in the ICU and then my primary care rehabilitation nurse while I was still at the hospital. ... (M)y male energy drove me to deal with my disability ... the women assumed I was *safe* ... the perennial friend. (Italics in original)

This account illuminates the hybridised ways in which Tepper makes sense of himself and others, through the contradictory discourses, attitudes and practices that abound around disability, masculinity and sexuality.[3] As Baker (2002) has argued, disabled people are subjectively colonised by a concern to be able to prove one's autonomy. They are, simultaneously, considered as non-normative and therefore perverse in the light of the normative (Wilkerson, 2002). The only way out of such assumptions lies in a complex interweaving of these contradictory discourses. Goodley (2007b) tried to make sense of the contradictory accounts of parents of their disabled babies and young children. For many of the parents in the study (see McLaughlin et al., 2008), they spoke with uncertainty about their children and disability:

> I'm not saying I'm embarrassed because I'm not ... perhaps it's because I've not accepted it myself yet, I don't know, I don't quite know what it is but ... some people aren't bothered about disability but I am, sometimes. (Rebecca Greenwood, cited in Goodley, 2007b: 155)

One interpretation of Rebecca's account is that she is struggling to talk about her child because there are good ('accepting') and bad ('bothered') ways of being a parent. Splitting parenting into two distinct ways of being would place Rebecca on the 'bad parent' side: a parent in denial. This interpretation is, following Deleuze and Guattari (1987), a mistake of modernist thinking, which insists on the segmentation of the human subject along binary lines (e.g. 'bothered bad' or 'accepting good' parent), centralised in linear ways by available discourses (e.g. medical or social models) and a key feature of psychoanalytic culture (see Chapters 6 and 8). The question they encourage us to ask is not which subject one should be (a bad or good parent), but how do we work with these binaries in the process of becoming (becoming-parent).

Indeed, if we read Rebecca's account carefully, it is full of uncertainties and contradictions: a hybridised account. When we understand parenting as a process of becoming and hybridisation, we are able to capture the subtle ways in which parents of disabled children engage with dis/ablism through understanding their children (and their own parenting) in ways that find moments of breakout: 'To hit a line of flight … challenging, not totally escaping, disabling strata of society' (Goodley, 2007b: 154):[4]

> I am coping. I do one thing at a time, one day at a time. I do not make huge plans, I don't expect certain things. If we overcome a hurdle then great but there'll be something else around the corner. (Cheryl Smith, in Goodley, 20007b: 155)
>
> I have this booklet written by the mother of a special needs child. It's called *Welcome to Holland*. She talks about the wonderful dreams we attach to pregnancy, birth and having the child and likens it to going on a journey to Italy. It's what you've always dreamt of, you get on the plane and you're all excited. And then you get on this plane after a couple of hours later or whatever, you've now landed in Holland. And you were expecting this fantastic place, Italy, and you're just so disappointed. But if you look carefully and don't let go of Italy, you'll see the beauty that's in Holland, the beautiful tulips, the canals. It will have certain things Italy may never have. You'll meet people that you wouldn't meet if you were going to Italy. And you might not get Italian wine but, hey, they've got some really good beer in Holland. (Rebecca Greenwood, in Goodley, 2007b: 155)

Hybridisation may well allow us to combine seemingly competing ideas, such as those around impairment (that we considered in Chapters 2 and 7) and the mixing of dis/ability binaries (referred to in Chapters 5 and 8). Indeed, that disabled people have politicised their lives suggests a collective ability to hybridise and *mimic* the conditions of normative culture (to show they 'really are independent', 'disabled but not stupid', 'people first not intellectually disabled'), while displaying *a sly civility* (Bhabha, 1985) that recognises the failings of normative culture by subverting common-sense ideas of what it means to be independent ('Who wants to be independent?', 'What's so good about work?', 'We all have some form of intellectual disabilities'). Cyborg and hybrid encapsulate the in-between-ness of life, offering possibilities for what Bhabha (1985) describes as the setting off of chains of alternative signifiers (see Chapter 8) or a transitional cultural space to play out fantasies, to disrupt categorisation (Burman, 2008). Perhaps at the heart of a critical disability studies are the appropriation of and resistance to various signifiers of disabling society and the making of new signifiers for the understanding and transformation of self, culture and society. The task is to attend to cultural particularities without sliding into romanticised ideas about 'the Other' (Burman, 2008: 203). Understanding disability in a twenty-first-century village or town, in say, South-East Asia and WENA, require us to think carefully about the hybridisation of local and global meanings, of tradition and *Empire*, of new forms of welfare, social services, politics, social class and social capital. For example, the 'social model of disability' makes complete sense to indigenous Malaysian families because they *already* think about disability as a gift from god and something that is dealt with by the whole community (Ling, 2007). Furthermore, those national contexts that celebrate an ensembled individualism (Chapter 5) might be well placed to respond collectively to dis/ablism. Hybrids demand analysis of the complex glocal response to dis/ablism. Hence, the self-advocacy movement of people with intellectual disabilities combines very real occidental concerns (human rights) while also challenging individualistic values (valuing interdependence rather than independence). Disability politics is necessarily hybridised.

Disability activisms

Critical disability studies look for emerging forms of disability activism in keeping with twenty-first-century politics. Where does disability activism go in this epoch of *Empire*? Hughes (2009) suggests that the politics of disability is at a crossroads. On one side we have the Disabled People's Movement, defined as 'social model stalwarts', that address structural exclusion. On the other side we have 'biological citizens', embodied health movements that embrace specialised medical and scientific knowledge associated with their 'condition'. Parkinson's Action Network and patients' action groups argue against stigmatisation but also organise thanatopolitically (Chapter 7), garnering support for biological solutions to health problems. The National Autistic Society campaigns against societal prejudice but champions forms of biomedical research and intervention (www.nas.org.uk/). Hughes concludes that we are witnessing a medicalised recolonisation of disability politics through biological citizenship. This raises huge questions about the direction that disability activism will follow at the start of the twenty-first century. Moreover, paraphrasing Richardson (2005: 525), the failure of governments to anticipate and respond to the vulnerabilities of excluded people, which are the direct result of economic neoliberal policies, have left NGOs to try to fill the gap. This has led to disability organisations becoming businesses, offering services to disabled people that have been lost through the rolling back of the state. This has created further divisions within disability activism from those described in Chapter 1.

On a more enabling note, technological forms of activism have narrowed the divide between disabled people in the Global North and South. While accepting the digital divide that still persists between poor and rich countries (and within countries between the technologically rich and poor), technology opens up possibilities for an externalisation of the self: an opening up of flows and communication (Lash, 2001). The potentiality is linked to four key concepts. The first, *the flattening of life*, envisages the fusion of world and things, thoughts and practices, reflexivity as practice, where information is produced as much for others as it is for ourselves. Hence, disability organisations in Indonesia can interface with disability organisations in Britain, sharing practice, developing disability awareness training, educating nondisabled people in the local and global contexts. The impact of blogging is clearly important and the uses of Web 2.0 and Web 3.0 technologies open up activism, critique and whistle-blowing. Though this brings risks with it (see, for example, the experience of Malaysian bloggers in 2007), it also provides an alternative media reportage and activism (evidenced, for example, by Peter Tan's disability activist blog from Malaysia, www.petertan.com/blog).

The second aspect, articulated by Lash (2001), relates to *technological forms of life*, most obviously in relation to the speed by which information can be passed on and shared. This allows us to think not so much about the narratives of past and present, but more about present and future. Key questions are raised, then, about the kinds of societies and citizens of future societies. For disabled people, this is crucial, in terms of configuring a place in the new technological age. Third, and related, is *stretch-out*. The imagined community is stretched-out and continuous. Hence, parents of disabled children, users identifying themselves as neurologically atypical, web users in search of companionship, can utilise the wide expanse of the web to, potentially, form subjective relationships, activism and intercourse.

Finally, the Internet may be seen as a *lifted-out space* – a generic or no particular space. The community for (non)disabled people is there to be imagined. In this sense, engagement with the virtual in many ways deconstructs fixed discourses of impairment and identity (Chapter 7). Nevertheless, we should remain mindful of what Hardt and Negri (2000: 299) describe as the oligopolistic aspects of the Internet: certain forms of knowledge and experts (e.g. medicalisation) still dominate the knowledge production of the Internet.

Profession(al)s allied to the community

A distinctive feature of the community living experiences of disabled people – compared with other minority groupings – is their involvement with a huge army of health and welfare professionals who 'continue to exercise significant power and control over disabled people' (Thomas, 2007: 59). Professional deployment will only increase in these times of *Empire*. Professionals are to be found in all aspects of social life that non-disabled people take for granted (including schools, jobs, transport, houses, public buildings and leisure) and disabled people are often barred from. Within these contexts are complex junctures of psyche, culture and society, through which disabled people find themselves disabled and professionals hold a key role:

> If society, through the technological revolution, now has the means to reintegrate its disabled people and if, as disabled people are saying, integration means taking control over one's own life and if disabled people do need continuing assistance from others, then the basis of the future helper/helped relationship has to undergo profound transformation. (Finkelstein, 1981c: 4)

Before conceptualising the role of the professional we need to foreground those disability cultures that have emerged through the self-organisation of disabled people. For Olkin (2009: 15–20), these cultures have a number of elements, including pride, a shared model of disability, emphasising the social and cultural experiences of disabled people, common concerns for civil rights and inclusive education, cultural production through the arts, music, humour and literature, disability norms that anticipate the needs of people, role models and expertise of disabled people that challenges the monopolisation of disability knowledge by non-disabled professionals. Recognising that people can have satisfying lifestyles as disabled people is a key starting assumption for professionals (Finkelstein and Stuart, 1996). A related assumption is that dis/ablism is not simply about disabled people but about wider environmental issues of marginalisation.

An ideal proposed by Finkelstein (1999a, 1999b) is the notion of the *profession allied to the community* (PAC). In contrast to professions allied to medicine, PACs refer to services and professionals that respond to and are led by the aspirations of disabled people and their representative organisations. The work of Centres for Independent Living offer a possibility for guiding the shaping of the PAC role precisely because they place control and choice in the hands of disabled people in terms of the services and assistance they require (Barnes and Mercer, 2006). Indeed, the Association of Disabled Professionals (www.adp.org.uk) recognises the growing expertise of disabled people in private and public arenas. Developing a PAC could bring into a production a 'virgin field of theory and practice through which professionals are re-engaged with the aspirations of disabled people' (Finkelstein, 1999b: 3). This virgin field incorporates critical disability studies and demands professionals to invest less time in pathological views of impairment and more in *challenging the conditions of dis/ablism*; 'in a more benign environment, one less attached to global diagnosis, their behaviours and judgements might be more effective' (Rosenhan, 1973: 258). Parker (1999a), Law (2007) and Llorens (2008b) draw attention to the emergence of narrative approaches to psychotherapy – a practice oft-associated with dis/ablism – that place politics at their centre, recuperating the political conditions of distress and oppression. Therapy is conceived not as an engagement with interiorities of distress, but more about opening up a democratic space for addressing the processes of (disabling) symbolisation into which people come to make sense of themselves and others (Bondi, 2005). This requires not only the 'client' redressing their own assumptions, but, crucially, professionals addressing their own acts of psychoemotional dis/ablism and demands of emotional labour (Chapter 6), pathologising forms of biopower (Chapter 7), disavowal (Chapter 8) and individualisation (Chapters 5 and 9) which underpin the understandings they hold of the people they are paid to enable. Part of this process of self-reflection could, Dunst (2008) argues, address the propensity of professionals to protect, control and routinise their practices around concerns with risk, health and safety. Instead, professionals should uphold the dignity of risk and emphasise the capacities of those with whom they work. A way forward for addressing their paranoid assessments of disabled people (Marks, 1999a) is to enable closer working relationships between professionals and organisations run by disabled people.

Critical disability studies take as their starting point the development of disability theory through the politicisation of dis/ablism. PAC would similarly adopt this viewpoint and seek to address, for example, the impacts of marketisation on service provision (Chapter 9) that fail an ever-growing number of labelled children. Such a focus raises important issues about citizenship and community contribution. Can we recognise and envisage contributions that are not narrowly defined in relation to paid work, consumerism and autonomy? What other forms of cultural contribution are offered by, for example, disability culture? How can the symbols of culture be changed to include diversity (Chapter 8)? Relatedly, the PAC would adopt a strong deconstructionist approach to the realities of impairment (Chapter 7), turning the gaze back at the potential or pitfalls of environmental responses to difference. This would involve practitioners and researchers working with disabled people in collaborative ways to identify those questions and social practices that should be addressed by research (Chapter 2) (see Table 10.1).

Table 10.1 Professionals allied to professionals or the community

Professional allied to professionals	Professional allied to the community
Individual, moral and medical models	Social, minority, cultural and relational models
Rehabilitation	Community regeneration
Disabled people are service users	Disabled people are expert citizens
Impairment	Intersections
Individual adjustment and repair	Systemic change and community cohesion
Attitudinal change	Ideological and structural change
Care and cure	Support and hope
Individual	Relational
Human beings	Cyborg and hybridised becomings
Participation	Emancipation
Health	Well being
Advocacy	Politicisation
Expertise	Collective empowerment
Deficit-model	Capacity-thinking
Service centred	Community centred
Alliances with other professionals and services	Alliance with organisations of disabled people and other political groups
Services culture	Community culture
WENA	Local/Glocal
Segregation	Inclusion
Rights, in/dependence and mastery	Rights, interdependence and vulnerability
Diagnosis	Recognition
Marketisation	Democratisation
Paid employment	Cultural and community contribution

Sources: Drawn on Rioux, 1994b; Finkelstein and Stuart, 1996; Oliver, 1996; Finkelstein, 1999a, 1999b; Garland-Thomson, 2002; Kagan, 2002; Kagan and Burton, 2002; and Dunst, 2008.

Conclusion

Critical disability studies connect the aspirations and ambitions of disabled people with transformative agendas of class, feminist, queer and postcolonial studies. My hope is that this book has encouraged you to draw on disability studies theory in ways that challenge dis/ablism at the levels of psyche, culture and society.

Notes

1 Haraway's (1991: 180–181) manifesto is captured in the following section:

> Bodies are maps of power and identity … cyborgs might consider more seriously the partial, fluid, aspects of sex and sexual embodiment. Gender might not be global identity after all, even if it has profound historical breadth and depth. … Cyborg imagery can suggest a way out of the maze of dualisms in which we have explained our bodies and our tools to ourselves. This is a dream not of a common language, but of a powerful infidel heteroglossia. It is an imagination of a feminist speaking in tongues to strike fear into the circuits of the supersaves of the new right. It means both building and destroying machines, identities, categories. … I would rather be a cyborg than a goddess.

2 Bhabha's (1985: 155–158) hybridity:

> Represents that ambivalent turn of the discriminated subject into the terrifying, exorbitant object of paranoid classification – a disturbing questioning of the images and presence of authority … the split screen of the self and its doubling, the hybrid … the hybrid object … retains the actual semblance of the authoritative symbol but revalues its presence by resisting it as signifier … the display of hybridity – its peculiar 'replication' – terrorizes authority with the ruse of recognition, its mimicry its mockery.

3 Further insight into this process of hybridisation is provided by Killacky (2004: 57), who reflects, on acquiring his impairment, that 'as someone who was quite phallocentric, I have been forced to reorient my sexuality'.

4 For further discussions of the application of Deleuze and Guattari's ideas in the development of critical disability studies, see Shildrick (2004), Shildrick and Price (2006), Goodley (2007a, 2007b), Roets et al. (2008) and the special issue on Deleuze of the *Journal of Literary and Cultural Disability Studies*, 3(3), 2009.

References

Aalten, A. (1997). Performing the body, creating culture. In K. Davis (ed.), *Embodied Practices: Feminist Perspectives on the Body*. (pp. 41–58). London: Sage.

Abberley, P. (1987). The concept of oppression and the development of a social theory of disability. *Disability, Handicap and Society*, 2 (1), 5–19.

Agamben, G. (1998). *Homo Sacer: Sovereign Power and Bare Life*. Stanford, CA: Stanford University Press.

Ainsworth, D. (2009). Aid organization hit by fall in value of the pound. *Third Sector*, 20 January 2009, 4.

Albrecht, G.L., Seelman, K. and Bury, M. (eds) (2001). *Handbook of Disability Studies*. London: Sage.

Allan, J. (1999). *Actively Seeking Inclusion: Pupils with Special Needs in Mainstream Schools*. London: Falmer.

Allan, J. (2004a). The aesthetics of disability as a productive ideology. In L. Ware (ed.), *Ideology and the Politics of (In)exclusion*. (pp. 38–46). New York: Peter Lang.

Allan, J. (2004b). Deterritorializations: putting postmodernism to work on teacher education and inclusion. *Educational Philosophy and Theory*, 36 (4), 417–432.

Allan, J. and Slee, R. (2008). Doing inclusive education research. In S. Gabel and S. Danforth (eds), *Disability and the International Politics of Education*. (pp. 141–163). New York: Peter Lang.

Allport, G.W. (1947). *The Use of Personal Documents in Psychological Science*. New York: Social Science Research Council.

Althusser, L. (1971). *Lenin and Philosophy and Other Essays*. London: New Left Books.

American Association on Mental Deficiency (1973). *Manual on Terminology and Classification in Mental Retardation*. Viewed 3 January 2010 at: http://openlibrary.org/b/OL14730742M/Manual_on_terminology_ and_ classification _in_ mental_ retardation.

Apple, M. (1982). *Education and Power*. Boston: Routledge & Kegan Paul.

Armstrong, F. (2002). The historical development of special education: humanitarian rationality or 'wild profusion of entangled events'?. *History of Education*, 31 (5), 437–450.

Armstrong, F., Armstrong, D. and Barton, L. (eds) (2000a). *Inclusive Education: Policy, Contexts and Comparative Perspectives*. London: David Fulton.

Armstrong, F., Armstrong, D. and Barton, L. (2000b). Introduction. In F. Armstrong, D. Armstrong and L. Barton (eds), *Inclusive Education: Policy, Contexts and Comparative Perspectives*. (pp. 1–11). London: David Fulton.

Armstrong, F., Belmont, B. and Verillon, A. (2002). 'Vive la difference?' Exploring context, policy and change in special education in France: developing cross-cultural collaboration. In F. Armstrong, D. Armstrong and L. Barton (eds), *Inclusive Education: Policy, Contexts and Comparative Perspectives*. (pp. 60–77). London: David Fulton.

Arthur, S. and Zarb, G. (1995a). *Measuring Disablement in Society: Working Paper 3. Disabled People and the Citizen's Charter*. Viewed 1 May 2009 at: www.leeds.ac.uk/disability-studies/archiveuk/Zarb/meas%20work%20paper%203.pdf.

Arthur, S. and Zarb, G. (1995b). *Measuring Disablement in Society: Working Paper 4. Barriers to Employment for Disabled People.* Viewed 1 May 2009 at: www.leeds.ac.uk/disability-studies/archiveuk/Zarb/barriers%20to%20employment.pdf.

Asch, S.E. (1951). Effects of group pressure upon the modification and distortion of judgment. In H. Guetzkow (ed.), *Groups, Leadership and Men.* (pp. 177–190). Pittsburgh, PA: Carnegie Press.

Aspis, S. (1997). Inclusion and exclusion. Paper presented at the Social History of Learning Disability Conference: 'Inclusion and Exclusion', The Open University, Walton Hall Milton Keynes, 10 December.

Aspis, S. (1999). What they don't tell disabled people with learning difficulties. In S. Corker and S. French (eds), *Disability Discourse.* (pp. 173–182). Buckingham: Open University Press.

Atkinson, D. (1989). Research interviews with people with mental handicaps. *Mental Handicap Research*, 1 (1), 75–90.

Atkinson, D. (ed.) (1993a). *Past Times: Older People with Learning Difficulties Look Back on Their Lives.* Buckingham: Open University Press.

Atkinson, D. (1993b). Relating. In P. Shakespeare, D. Atkinson and S. French (eds), *Reflecting on Research Practice: Issues in Health and Social Welfare.* (pp. 47–57). Buckingham: Open University Press.

Atkinson, D., Jackson, M. and Walmsley, J. (eds) (1997). *Forgotten Lives: Exploring the History of Learning Disability.* Plymouth: BILD.

Atkinson, D. and Williams, F. (eds) (1990). *'Know Me as I Am': An Anthology of Prose, Poetry and Art by People with Learning Difficulties.* Kent: Hodder & Stoughton in association with the Open University and MENCAP.

Atkinson, E. and DePalma, R. (2008). Using children's literature to challenge homophobia in primary schools. *Books for Keeps*, 169, 6–7.

Austin, G.W. (1999). Queering family law. *Australasian Gay and Lesbian*, 8, 49–67.

Azzopardi, A. (2000). Understanding disability politics in Malta: New directions explored. Unpublished masters thesis, University of Sheffield.

Azzopardi, A. (2003). Inclusive education and the denial of difference: Is this the Cotton era experience? Exploring whether the discourse of inclusive education has been hijacked by standards. *International Journal of Inclusive Education*, 7 (2), 159–174.

Azzopardi, A. (2007). *Career Guidance for Persons with Disability.* Valetta, Malta: Euro Guidance Malta.

Azzopardi, A. (2008). Reading stories of inclusion: engaging with different perspectives towards an agenda for inclusion. In S. Gabel and S. Danforth (eds), *Disability and the International Politics of Education.* (pp. 101–120). New York: Peter Lang.

Badza, A., Chakuchichi, A. and Chimedza, R. (2008). An analysis of inclusive education policy implementation in Zimbabwe: challenges for learner support. In S. Gabel and S. Danforth (eds), *Disability and the International Politics of Education.* (pp. 53–68). New York: Peter Lang.

Baker, B. and Campbell, F. (2006). Transgressing non-crossable borders: disability, law, schooling and nations. In S. Danforth and S. Gabel (eds), *Vital Questions in Disability Studies and Education.* (pp. 319–346). New York: Peter Lang.

Baker, B.M. (2002). The hunt for disability: the new eugenics and the normalization of schoolchildren. *Teachers College Record*, 104, 663–703.

Baker, C.E. (1983). Outcome equality or equality of respect: the substantive content of equal protection. *University of Pennsylvania Law Review*, 131 (3), 933.

Ball, S. (1990). Introducing Monsieur Foucault. In S. Ball (ed.), *Foucault and Education: Disciplines and Knowledge.* (pp. 1–8). London: Routledge.

Ballard, K. (2004). Ideology and the origins of exclusion: a case study. In L. Ware (ed.), *Ideology and the Politics of (In)exclusion.* (pp. 89–107). New York: Peter Lang.

Bardach, J.L. (2007). Discussion of Margrit Shildrick's 'dangerous discourses' as it relates to need for attitudinal change amongst the psychoanalytic community. *Studies in Gender and Sexuality*, 8 (3), 245–252.

Barker, C. (2008). Exceptional children, disability and cultural history in contemporary post-colonial fiction. Unpublished doctoral thesis, University of Leeds.

Barnes, C. (1990). *The Cabbage Syndrome: The Social Construction of Dependence*. London: Falmer Press.

Barnes, C. (1991). *Disabled People in Britain and Discrimination: A Case for Anti-Discrimination Legislation*. London: Hurst & Company, University of Calgary Press in Association with the British Council of Organisations of Disabled People.

Barnes, C. (1993). *Disabling Imagery and the Media: An Exploration of the Principles for Media Representations of Disabled People*. Halifax: Ryburn and The British Council of Organisations of Disabled People.

Barnes, C. (1995). *Measuring Disablement in Society: Hopes and Reservations*. Viewed 1 May 2009 at: www.leeds.ac.uk/disabilitystudies/archiveuk/Barnes/measuring%20dis.pdf.

Barnes, C. (1996). Disability and the myth of the independent researcher. *Disability and Society*, 11 (2), 107–110.

Barnes, C. (1998). The social model of disability: a sociological phenomenon ignored by sociologists. In T. Shakespeare (ed.), *The Disability Reader: Social Science Perspectives*. (pp. 65–78). London: Continuum.

Barnes, C. (1999). Disability studies: new or not so new directions. *Disability & Society*, 14 (4), 577–580.

Barnes, C. (2002). Introduction: disability, policy and politics. *Policy and Politics*, 30 (3), 311–318.

Barnes, C. (2004). Disability, disability studies and the academy. In J. Swain, S. French, C. Barnes and C. Thomas (eds), *Disabling Barriers, Enabling Environments* (2nd edition). (pp. 28–33). London: Sage.

Barnes, C. (2006). *Key Debates in Disability Studies*. Paper 4 of the Applying Disability Studies Seminar Series. Centre of Applied Disability Studies, University of Sheffield, 15 May.

Barnes, C. and Mercer, G. (eds) (1997a). *Doing Disability Research*. Leeds: The Disability Press.

Barnes, C. and Mercer, G. (eds) (1997b). *Exploring the Divide*. Leeds: The Disability Press.

Barnes, C. and Mercer, G. (2003). *Disability: Key Concepts*. Cambridge: Polity Press.

Barnes, C. and Mercer, G. (2006). *Independent Futures: Disability Services in the 21st Century*. Bristol: The Policy Press.

Barnes, C., Mercer, G. and Shakespeare, T. (1999). *Exploring Disability*. London: Polity Press.

Barnes, C., Oliver, M. and Barton, L. (eds) (2002). *Disability Studies Today*. Cambridge: Polity Press.

Barnes, C. and Roulstone, A. (eds) (2005). *Working Futures*. Bristol: The Policy Press.

Barton, L. (ed.) (2001). *Disability, Politics and the Struggle for Change*. London: David Fulton.

Barton, L. (2004a). The disability movement: some personal observations. In J. Swain, S. French, C. Barnes and C. Thomas (eds), *Disabling Barriers, Enabling Environments* (2nd edition). (pp. 285–290). London: Sage.

Barton, L. (2004b). The politics of special education: a necessary or irrelevant approach? In L. Ware (ed.), *Ideology and the Politics of (In)exclusion*. New York: Peter Lang.

Barton, L. (2005). *Special Educational Needs: An Alternative Look. A Response to Warnock M. 2005: Special Educational Needs – A New Look*. Viewed 1 January 2008 at: www.leeds.ac.uk/disability-studies/archiveuk/barton/Warnock.pdf.

Barton, L. and Oliver, M. (eds) (1997). *Disability Studies: Past Present and Future*. Leeds: The Disability Press.

Beckett, A.E. (2009). Challenging disabling attitudes, building an inclusive society: considering the role of education in encouraging non-disabled children to develop positive attitudes towards disabled people. *British Journal of Sociology of Education*, 30 (3), 317–329.

Begum, N. and Zarb, G. (1996). *Measuring Disablement in Society: Working Paper 5. Measuring Disabled People's: Involvement in Local Planning.* Viewed 25 April 2009 at: www.leeds.ac.uk/disability-studies/archiveuk/Begum/local%20planning.pdf.

Bell, S., Morrow, M. and Tastsogloul, E. (2000). Teaching in environments of resistance: towards a critical, feminist and antiracist pedagogy. In G. Sefa Dei and A. Calliste (eds), *Power, Knowledge and Antiracist Pedagogy.* Halifax, NS: Fernwood Publishing.

Beresford, P., Harrison, C. and Wilson, A. (2002). Mental health service users and disability: implications for future strategies. *Policy and Politics*, 30, 387–396.

Beresford, P. and Wilson, A. (2002a). Genes spell danger: mental health service users/survivors, bioethics and control. *Disability & Society*, 17 (5), 541–553.

Beresford, P. and Wilson, A. (2002b). Madness, distress and postmodernity: putting the record straight. In M. Corker and T. Shakespeare (eds), *Disability and Postmodernity.* (pp. 143–158). London: Cassell.

Bertaux, D. (ed.) (1981). *Biography and Society: The Life History Approach in the Social Sciences.* Beverly Hills, CA: Sage.

Beyer, S. (2009). Supported employment and benefits. Paper presented at the Office for Disability Issues Evidence Day, 19 November, London.

Bhabha, H.K. (1985). Signs taken for wonders: questions of ambivalence and authority under a tree outside Delhi, May 1817. *Critical Inquiry*, 12 (1), 144–165.

Bhabha, H. (1994). *The Location of Culture*. London: Routledge.

Bhavnani, K.K. and Phoenix, A. (1994). *Shifting Identities, Shifting Racisms: A Feminism and Psychology Reader*. London: Sage.

Biesta, G.J.J. (1998). Pedagogy without humanism: Foucault and the subject of education. *Interchange*, 29 (1), 1–16.

Billington, T. (2000). *Separating, Losing and Excluding Children: Narratives of Difference.* London: Routledge Falmer.

Billington, T. (2002). Children, psychologists and knowledge: A discourse analytic narrative. *Educational and Child Psychology*, 19 (3), 32–41.

Bjarnason, D.S. (2002). New voices in Iceland: parents and adult children – juggling supports and choices in time and space. *Disability & Society*, 17 (3), 307–326.

Bjarnason, D.S. (2004). *New Voices from Iceland: Disability and Young Adulthood.* New York: Nova Science.

Bjarnason, D.S. (2008). Private troubles or public issues? The social construction of the disabled baby in the context of social policy and social and technological changes. In S. Gabel and S. Danforth (eds), *Disability and the International Politics of Education.* (pp. 251–274). New York: Peter Lang.

Björnsdóttir, K. (2009). Resisting the reflection: social participation of young adults with intellectual disabilities. Unpublished PhD thesis, University of Iceland, Reykjavik.

Blackmore, T. (2006). Travels in a non-disabled world: disabled adults' experiences of inclusion in everyday settings. Paper presented at the British Disability Studies Association 3rd Annual Conference, Lancaster, 18–21 September.

Blackmore, T. (2009). Money. Paper presented at the UK Disabled Peoples' Council London Forum, Greenwich Association of Disabled People, 30 June.

Blackmore, T., Simmons, B. and Vakirtzi, E. (2006). Postmodernist rhizomatics and synergistic knowledge creation: The case for rejecting grand narratives in educational research. Paper presented at the British Disability Studies Association 3rd Annual Conference, Lancaster, 18–21 September.

Bocock, R. (1976). *Freud and Modern Society.* London: Van Nostrand Reinhold.

Bogard, W. (2000). Smoothing machines and the constitution of society. *Cultural Studies,* 14 (4), 269–294.

Bogdan, R. and Taylor, S. (1976). The judged not the judges: an insider's view of mental retardation. *American Psychologist*, 31, 47–52.

Bogdan, R. and Taylor, S.J. (1982). *Inside Out: The Social Meaning of Mental Retardation.* Toronto: University of Toronto Press.

Boggs, C. (1996). *Social Movements and Political Power.* Philadelphia, PA Temple University Press.

Bollas, C. (1987). *The Shadow of the Object: Psychoanalysis of the Unthought Known.* London: Free Association Press.

Bolt, D. (2009). Introduction: Literary disability studies in the UK. *Journal of Cultural and Literary Disability Studies,* 3 (3), 1–4.

Bondi, L. (2005). Making connections and thinking through emotions: between geography and psychotherapy. *Transactions of the Institute of British Geographers,* 30, 433–448.

Booth, T. (2002). Inclusion and exclusion policy in England: who controls the agenda? In F. Armstrong, D. Armstrong and L. Barton (eds), *Inclusive Education: Policy, Contexts and Comparative Perspectives.* (pp. 78–98). London: David Fulton.

Booth, T. and Booth, W. (1994). *Parenting Under Pressure: Mothers and Fathers with Learning Difficulties.* Buckingham: Open University Press.

Booth, T. and Booth, W. (1998). *Growing Up with Parents Who Have Learning Difficulties.* London: Routledge.

Boseley, J. (2006). 10 million girl fetuses aborted in India. The *Guardian,* 9 January, 13.

Boxall, K. (2002a). Individual and social models of disability and the experiences of people with learning difficulties. In D. Race (ed.), *Learning Disability: A Social Approach.* (pp. 209–226). London: Routledge.

Boxall, K. (2002b). Course that confronts barriers to inclusion. *Community Living,* 15 (4), 24–25.

Boxall, K., Carson, I. and Docherty, D. (2004). Room at the academy? People with learning difficulties and higher Education. *Disability & Society,* 19 (2), 99–112.

Braginsky, D. and Braginsky, B. (1971). *Hansels and Gretels: Studies of Children in Institutions for the Mentally Retarded.* New York: Holt, Reinhart and Winston.

Braidotti, R. (1994). *Nomadic Subjects: Embodiment and Sexual Difference in Contemporary Feminist Theory.* New York: Columbia University Press.

Braidotti, R. (2002). *Metamorphoses: Towards a Materialist Theory of Becoming.* Cambridge: Polity Press.

Braithwaite, J. and Mont, D. (2008). Disability and poverty: a survey of World Bank poverty assessments and implications. SP Discussion Paper No. 0805. Viewed on 11 November at: web.worldbank.org/WBSITE/EXTERNAL/TOPICS/EXTSOCIALPROTECTION/EXTDISABILITY/0,,contentMDK:20193783~menuPK:419389~pagePK:148956~piPK:216618~theSitePK:282699,00.html#Pub.

Brandon, T. (2008). Is being fat the new disability? Keynote address to the Research Institute of Health and Social Change Annual Conference, Manchester Metropolitan University, 13–17 June.

Branson, J., Miller, D. and Branson, K. (1988). An obstacle race: a case study of a child's schooling in Australia and England. *Disability, Handicap and Society,* 3 (2), 101–118.

Bratlinger, E.A. (2001). Poverty, class and disability: historical, social and political perspectives. *Focus on Exceptional Children,* 33 (7), 1–24.

Bratlinger, E.A. (2004). Ideologies discerned, values determined: getting past the hierarchies of special education. In L. Ware (ed.), *Ideology and the Politics of (In)exclusion.* (pp. 11–31). New York: Peter Lang.

Brechin, A., Liddiard, P. and Swain, J. (eds) (1981). *Handicap in a Social World: A Reader.* Sevenoaks, Kent: Hodder & Stoughton.

Breggin, P.R. (1991). *Toxic Psychiatry: Why Therapy, Empathy and Love Must Replace the Drugs, Electroshock, and Biochemical Theories of the 'New Psychiatry'.* New York: St Martin's Press.

Brown, H. and Craft, A. (eds) (1989). *Thinking the Unthinkable: Papers on Sexual Abuse and People with Learning Difficulties.* London: Family Planning Association.

Brown, H. and Smith, H. (eds) (1992). *Normalisation: A Reader for the Nineties.* London: Routledge.

Burke, L. (2009). Novels and the problem of life itself: the role of literary discourse in contemporary bioethical debate. Paper presented at the Disability Research Forum, Manchester Metropolitan University, 20 January.

Burman, E. (ed.) (1990). *Feminists and Psychological Practice.* London: Sage.

Burman, E. (1994). *Deconstructing Developmental Psychology.* London: Routledge.

Burman, E. (ed.) (1998). *Deconstructing Feminist Psychology.* London: Sage.

Burman, E. (2008). *Developments: Child, Image, Nation.* London: Routledge.

Burman, E. and Parker, I. (eds) (1993a). *Discourse Analytic Research: Repertoires and Readings of Texts in Action.* London: Routledge.

Burman, E. and Parker, I. (1993b). Introduction – discourse analysis: the turn to the text. In E. Burman and I. Parker (eds), *Discourse Analytic Research: Repertoires and Readings of Texts in Action.* (pp. 1–12). London: Routledge.

Burrell, G. and Morgan, G. (1979). *Sociological Paradigms and Organisational Analysis: Elements of the Sociology of Corporate Life.* London: Heinemann.

Butler, J. (1990). *Gender Trouble: Feminism and the Subversion of Identity.* London: Routledge.

Butler, J. (1993). *Bodies That Matter: On the Discursive Limits of Sex.* London: Routledge.

Butler, J. (1999). Bodies that matter. In J. Price and M. Shildrick (eds), *Feminist Theory and the Body.* (pp. 235–245). Edinburgh: Edinburgh University Press.

Campbell, F.K. (2008a). Refusing able(ness): a preliminary conversation about Ableism. *M/C – Media and Culture,* 11 (3).

Campbell, F.K. (2008b). Exploring internalized Ableism using critical race theory. *Disability & Society,* 23 (2), 151–162.

Campbell, F.K. (2009). *Contours of Ableism: Territories, Objects, Disability and Desire.* London: Palgrave Macmillan.

Campbell, J. and Oliver, M. (1996). *Disability Politics: Understanding Our Past, Changing Our Future.* London: Routledge.

Campling, J. (1981). *Images of Ourselves: Women with Disabilities Talking.* London: Routledge & Kegan Paul.

Chamberlin, J. (1990). The ex-patients' movement: where we've been and where we're going. *Journal of Mind and Behaviour,* 11 (3), 323–336.

Chander, J. (2008). The role of residential schools in shaping the nature of the advocacy movement of the blind in India. In S. Gabel and S. Danforth (eds), *Disability and the International Politics of Education.* (pp. 201–224). New York: Peter Lang.

Chappell, A. (1992). Towards a sociological critique of the normalisation principle. *Disability & Society,* 7 (1), 35–51.

Chappell, A. (1998). Still out in the cold: people with learning difficulties and the social model of disability. In T. Shakespeare (ed.), *The Disability Reader: Social Science Perspectives.* (pp. 211–220). London: Cassell.

Chappell, A., Goodley, D. and Lawthom, R. (2000). Connecting with the social model: the relevance of the social model of disability for people with learning difficulties. *British Journal of Learning Disabilities,* 29, 45–50.

Charlton, J. (1998). *Nothing about Us without Us: Disability, Oppression, and Empowerment.* Berkeley, CA: University of California Press.

Charlton, J. (2006). The dimensions of disability oppression. In L. Davis (ed.), *The Disability Studies Reader* (2nd edition). (pp. 217–229). New York: Routledge.

Charmaz, K. (1995). The body, identity and self: adapting to impairment. *Sociological Quarterly,* 35 (4), 657–680.

Charmaz, K. (2004). Premises, principles and practices in qualitative research: revisiting the foundations. *Qualitative Health Research,* 14 (7), 976–993.

Chasseguet-Smirgel, J. and Grunberger, B. (1986). *Freud or Reich: Psychoanalysis and Illusion.* (Trans C. Pajaczowska). London: Free Association Books.

Chataika, T. (2007). Inclusion of disabled students in higher education in Zimbabwe: from idealism to reality – a social ecosystem perspective. Unpublished PhD thesis, University of Sheffield.

Chimedza, R., Badza, A. and Chakuchichi, D. (2008). An analysis of the impact of advocacy and disability rights on the quality of life of people with disabilities in Zimbabwe. In S. Gabel and S. Danforth (eds), *Disability and the International Politics of Education.* (pp. 165–176). New York: Peter Lang.

Chinn, D. (2006). All parents together: professionals talk about parents with developmental disabilities. Paper presented at the British Disability Studies Association 3rd Annual Conference, Lancaster, 18–21 September.

Christensen, C. (1996). Disabled, handicapped or disordered: what's in a name? In C. Christensen, and F. Rizvi (eds), *Disability and the Dilemmas of Education and Justice.* (pp. 63–78). Buckingham: Open University Press.

Christensen, C. and Rizvi, F. (eds) (1996). *Disabilty and the Dilemmas of Education and Justice. Buckingham.* Open University Press.

Clough, P. and Barton, L. (eds) (1995). *Making Difficulties: Research and the Construction of Special Educational Needs.* London: Paul Chapman.

Clough, P. and Barton, L. (eds) (1998). *Articulating with Difficulty: Research Voices in Special Education.* London: Paul Chapman.

Clough, P. and Corbett, J. (2000). *Theories of Inclusive Education: A Students' Guide.* London: Paul Chapman.

Clough, P. and Nutbrown, C. (2002). *A Students' Guide to Methodology.* London: Sage.

Connell, R.W. (2001). Bodies, intellectuals and world society. In N. Watson and S. Cunningham-Burley (eds), *Reframing the Body.* London: Palgrave.

Connell, R.W. (2002). *Gender.* Cambridge: Polity Press.

Connor, D.J. (2008). Not so strange bedfellows: the promise of disability studies and critical race theory. In S. Gabel and S. Danforth (eds), *Disability and the International Politics of Education.* (pp. 201–224). New York: Peter Lang.

Corbett, J. (1991). So, who wants to be normal? *Disability, Handicap, and Society,* 6 (3), 259–260.

Corbett, J. and Slee, R. (2002). An international conversation on inclusive education. In F. Armstrong, D. Armstrong and L. Barton (eds), *Inclusive Education: Policy, Contexts and Comparative Perspectives.* (pp. 133–146). London: David Fulton.

Corker, M. (1998). *Deaf and Disabled or Deafness Disabled.* Buckingham: Open University Press.

Corker, M. (1999). Differences, conflations and foundations: the limits to 'accurate' theoretical representation of disabled people's experience? *Disability & Society,* 14 (5), 627–642.

Corker, M. (2001). Sensing disability. *Hypatia,* 16 (4), 34–52.

Corker, M. and French, S. (eds) (1998). *Disability Discourse.* Buckingham: Open University Press.

Corker, M. and Shakespeare, T. (eds) (2002). *Disability/Postmodernity: Embodying Disability Theory.* London: Continuum.

Cregan, K. (2006). *The Sociology of the Body.* London: Sage.

Cromby, J. and Nightingale, D.J. (eds) (1999). *Social Constructionist Psychology: A Critical Analysis of Theory and Practice.* Buckingham: Open University Press.

Crossley, N. (1995). Merleau-Ponty, the elusive body and carnal knowledge. *Body and Society,* 1 (1), 43–63.

Crow, L. (1996). Including all of our lives: renewing the social model of disability. In C. Barnes and G. Mercer (eds), *Exploring the Divide.* (pp. 55–72). Leeds: The Disability Press.

Curt, B. (pseud.) (1994). *Textuality and Tectonics: Troubling Social and Psychological Science.* Buckingham: Open University Press.

Danforth, S. (2008). Using metaphors to research the cultural and ideological construction of disability. In S. Gabel and S. Danforth (eds), *Disability and the International Politics of Education.* (pp. 385–400). New York: Peter Lang.

Darder, A., Baltodano, M.P. and Torres, R.D. (eds) (2009). *The Critical Pedagogy Readers* (2nd edition). New York: Routledge.

Darder, A. and Torres, R.D. (2009). After race: an introduction. In A. Darder, M.P. Baltodano and R.D. Torres (eds), *The Critical Pedagogy Reader* (2nd edition). (pp. 1–22). New York: Routledge.

Davis, K. (ed.) (1997a). *Embodied Practices: Feminist Perspectives on the Body.* London: Sage.

Davis, K. (1997b). Embodying theory: beyond modernist and postmodernist readings of the body. In K. Davis (ed.), *Embodied Practices: Feminist Perspectives on the Body.* (pp.1–23). London: Sage.

Davis, L.J. (1995). *Enforcing Normalcy: Disability, Deafness, and the Body.* New York: Verso.

Davis, L.J. (ed.) (1997). *The Disability Studies Reader.* London: Routledge.

Davis, L.J. (2002). *Bending over Backwards: Disability, Dismodernism and other Difficult Positions.* New York: New York University Press.

Davis, L.J. (ed.) (2006a). *The Disability Studies Reader* (2nd edition). New York: Routledge

Davis, L.J. (2006b). Preface to the second edition. In L.J. Davis (ed.), *The Disability Studies Reader* (2nd edition). (pp. viii–xv). New York: Routledge.

Davis, L.J. (2006c). The end of identity politics and the beginning of dismodernism: on disability as an unstable category. In L.J. Davis (ed.), *The Disability Studies Reader* (2nd edition). (pp. 231–242). New York: Routledge.

Deleuze, G. and Guattari, F. (1987). *A Thousand Plateaus: Capitalism and Schizophrenia.* London: Continuum.

Devlieger, P., Renders, F., Froyen, H. and Wildiers, K. (2006b). *Blindness and the Multi-Sensorial City.* Antwerp: Garant.

Devlieger, P., Rusch, F. and Pfeiffer, D. (2003). *Rethinking Disability: The Emergence of New Definitions, Concepts and Communities.* Antwerp: Garant.

Devlieger, P., Van Hove, G. and Renders, F. (2006a). Disability cosmology: the practice of making disability worlds. *Journal of Psychology in Africa*, X, 85–93.

Dexter, L.A. (1956). Towards a sociology of the mentally defective. *American Journal of Mental Deficiency*, 61, 10–16.

DfES (2001). Special Educational Needs Code of Practice. Accessed 18 March 2010 at: www.teachernet.gov.uk/_doc/3724/SENCodeofPractice.pdf.

Disabled-World.com (2009). *Disability: Facts and Statistics.* Viewed 3 March 2009 at: www.disabled-world.com/disability/statistics.

Docherty, D., Hughes, R., Phillips, P., Corbett, D., Regan, B., Barber, A., Adams, P., Boxall, K., Kaplan, I. and Izzidien, S. (2005). This is what we think. In D. Goodley and G. Van Hove (eds), *Another Disability Reader? Including People with Learning Difficulties.* (pp. 17–30). Antwerp: Garant.

Donaldson, E. (2002). The corpus of the madwoman: toward a feminist disability studies theory of embodiment and mental illness. *NWSA Journal*, 14 (3), 95–119.

DPI (1982). *Proceedings of the First World Congress.* Singapore: Disabled People's International.

Duckett, P.S. (1998). What are you doing here? 'Non disabled' people and the disability movement: a response to Fran Branfield. *Disability & Society*, 13 (4), 625–628.

Dunst, C. (2008). Participatory opportunities, capacity building processes and empowerment actions. Keynote presentation to Intellectual Disability Conference – empowering people with intellectual disabilities, their families and supporters: reflections on research and practice, Park Building, University of Portsmouth 12–13 September.

Dwyer, P. (2004). *Understanding Social Citizenship: Issues for Policy and Practice.* Bristol: The Policy Press.

Eagleton, T. (1983). *Literary Theory: An Introduction.* Oxford: Blackwell.

Edgerton, R.B. (1967). *The Cloak of Competence: Stigma in the Lives of the Mentally Retarded.* Berkeley, CA: University of California Press.

Edgerton, R.B. (1976). *Deviance: A Cross-cultural Perspective.* London: Benjamin/Cummings.

Edgerton, R.B. (ed.) (1984a). *Lives in Process: Mentally Retarded Adults in a Large City*. Monograph No. 6. Washington, DC: American Association on Mental Deficiency.

Edgerton, R.B. (1984b). The participant-observer approach to research in mental retardation. *American Journal of Mental Deficiency*, 88 (5), 498–505.

Edgerton, R.B. and Bercovici, S. (1976). The cloak of competence: years later. *American Journal of Mental Deficiency*, 80 (5), 485–497.

Edwards, D. (1995). Sacks and psychology. *Theory and Psychology*, 5 (3), 579–596.

Edwards, D. (1999). Emotion discourse. *Culture and Psychology*, 5 (3), 271–291

Edwards, D., Ashmore, M. and Potter, J. (1995). Death and furniture: the rhetoric, politics, and theology of bottom line arguments against relativism. *History of the Human Sciences*, 8 (2), 25–49.

Elkins, H. (2004). Nasty habits. In B. Guter and J. Killacky (eds), *Queer Crips: Disabled Gay Men and their Stories*. (pp. 23–28). New York: Haworth Press.

Emerson, E. (2009). 'Resilience' and the behavioural and emotional well-being of children with intellectual disabilities. Paper presented at the Office for Disability Issues Evidence Day, London, 19 November.

Emerson, E., Shahtahmasebi, S., Lancaster, G. and Berridge, D. (2009). Poverty trajectories of families supporting a disabled child. Paper presented at the Office for Disability Issues Evidence Day, London, 19 November.

Erevelles, N. (2005). Understanding curriculum as normalizing text: disability studies meets curriculum theory. *Journal of Curriculum Studies,* 37 (4), 421–439.

Erickson, E.H. (1959). *Identity and the Life Cycle*. New York: International Universities Press.

Fanon, F. (1993). *Black Skins, White Masks* (3rd edition). London: Pluto Press.

Feher-Gurewich, J. (2001). Lacan in America. *Journal of European Psychoanalysis*, 12(13), 1–5. Viewed 20 November 2008 at: www.psychomedia.it/jep.

Ferguson, P.M., Ferguson, D.L. and Taylor, S.J. (eds) (1992). *Interpreting Disability: A Qualitative Reader*. New York: Teachers College Press.

Fernald, W.E. (1912). The burden of feeble-mindedness. *Journal of Psychoasthenics*, 17, 87–111.

Ferri, B.A. (2008). Inclusion in Italy: what happens when everyone belongs. In S. Gabel and S. Danforth (eds), *Disability and the International Politics of Education*. (pp. 41–52). New York: Peter Lang.

Fine, M. and Asch, A. (eds) (1988).*Women with Disabilities: Essays in Psychology, Culture and Politics*. Philadelphia, PA: Tempe University Press.

Finkelstein, J. (1997). Chic outrage and body politics. In K. Davis (ed.), *Embodied Practices: Feminist Perspectives on the Body*. (pp. 150–169). London: Sage.

Finkelstein, V. (1981a). To deny or not to deny disabilities. In A. Brechin, P. Liddiard and J. Swain, (eds), *Handicap in a Social World*. (pp. 31–38). London: Hodder & Stoughton.

Finkelstein, V. (1981b). Disability and the helper/helped relationship: an historical view. In A. Brechin, P. Liddiard and J. Swain (eds), *Handicap in a Social World*. (pp. 12–22). London: Hodder & Stoughton.

Finkelstein, V. (1981c). *Disability and Professional Attitudes*, RADAR Conference Proceedings. NAIDEX '81, 21–24 October. Viewed 13 January 2008 at: www.leeds.ac.uk/disability-studies/archiveuk.

Finkelstein, V. (1997). Outside, 'Inside Out'. *Coalition*, April, 30–36.

Finkelstein, V. (1999a). A profession allied to the community: the disabled people's trade union. In E. Stone (ed.), *Disability and Development: Learning from Action and Research on Disability in the Majority World*. (pp. 21–24). Leeds: The Disability Press.

Finkelstein, V. (1999b). Professions allied to the community (PACS II). Viewed 20th September 2005 at: www.leeds.ac.uk/disability-studies/archive.

Finkelstein, V. (2001). A personal journey into disability politics. Paper presented at the Leeds University Centre for Disability Studies, October.

Finkelstein, V. (2004). Representing disability. In J. Swain, S. French, C. Barnes and C. Thomas (eds), *Disabling Barriers, Enabling Environments* (2nd edition). (pp. 13–20). London: Sage.

Finkelstein, V. and French, S. (1993). Towards a psychology of disability. In J. Swain, V. Finkelstein, S. French and M. Oliver (eds), *Disabling Barriers – Enabling Environments*. (pp. 26–33). London: Sage.

Finkelstein, V. and Stuart, O. (1996). Developing new services. In G. Hales (ed.), *Beyond Disability: Towards an Enabling Society*. (pp. 165–172). London: Sage.

Finlay, L. and Langdridge, D. (2007). Embodiment. In W. Hollway, H. Lucy and A. Phoenix (eds), *Social Psychology Matters*. (pp. 9–23). Maidenhead and Milton Keynes: Open University Press.

Foucault, M. (1973a). *The Birth of the Clinic: An Archaeology of Medical Perception*. (Trans A.M. Sheridan). New York: Pantheon Books.

Foucault, M. (1973b). *Madness and Civilisation: A History of Insanity in the Age of Reason*. (Trans R. Howard). New York: Vintage/Random House.

Foucault, M. (1977). *Discipline and Punish: The Birth of the Prison*. (Trans R. Howard). New York: Pantheon Books.

Foucault, M. (1978). *The History of Sexuality, Volume I*. New York: Vintage.

Foucault, M. (1983). The subject and power. In H.L. Dreyfus and P. Rabinov (eds), *Michael Foucault: Beyond Structuralism and Hermeneutics*. (pp. 208–223). Chicago: University of Chicago Press.

Fox, A.M. and Lipkin, J. (2002). Re(Crip)ting feminist theater through disability theater: selections from the DisAbility Project. *NWSA Journal*, 14 (3), 78–98.

Fox, D. and Prilleltensky, I. (eds) (1997). *Critical Psychology: An Introduction*. London: Sage.

Fox-Keller, E. (1962). *Reflections on Gender and Science*. New Haven, CT: Yale University Press.

Frank, A. (1994). Reclaiming an orphan genre: the first-person narrative of illness. *Literature and Medicine*, 13 (1), 1–21.

Frank, A. (1995). *The Wounded Storyteller: Body, Illness and Ethics*. Chicago: University of Chicago Press.

Frank, A. (2000). Illness and autobiographical work: dialogue as narrative destabilization. *Qualitative Sociology*, 23 (1), 135–155.

Frank, A. (2005). What is dialogical research, and why should we do it? *Qualitative Health Research*, 15 (7), 964–974.

Freidman-Lambert, P. (1984). How would you like it? *Entourage*, 2 (2), 15–17.

French, S. (1993). Can you see the rainbow? In J. Swain, V. Finkelstein, S. French and M. Oliver (eds), *Disabling Barriers–Enabling Environments*. (pp. 69–77). London: Sage.

Frosh, S. (1987). *The Politics of Psychoanalysis: An Introduction*. London: Macmillan.

Fukushima, S. (2009). The deafblind and disability studies. Keynote address to the Disability and Economy: Creating a Society for All conference, hosted by Research on Economy and Disability, the University of Tokyo, in association with Manchester Metropolitan University, Manchester, 29–30 April.

Gabb, J. (2004). 'I could eat my baby to bits': passion and desire in lesbian mother–children love. *Gender, Place and Culture*, 11 (3), 399–415.

Gabb, J. (2005a). Lesbian M/Otherhood: strategies of familial-linguistic management in lesbian parent families. *Sociology of Health & Illness*, 39 (4), 585–603.

Gabb, J. (2005b). Locating lesbian parent families: everyday negotiations of lesbian motherhood in Britain. *Gender, Place and Culture*, 12 (4), 419–432.

Gabel, S. (2001). I wash my face with dirty water: narratives of disability and pedagogy. *Journal of Teacher Education*, 52, 31–47.

Gabel, S. (2002). Some conceptual problems with critical pedagogy. *Curriculum Inquiry*, 32 (2), 177–201.

Gabel, S. (2006). Disability studies and inclusive education: negotiating tensions and integrating research, policy and practice. Paper presented at 2nd International City Conference of Disability Studies on Disability Studies in Education, Michigan State University. Viewed 1 April 2008 at: www.edr1.educ.msu.edu/DSEConf/SusanGabel.htm.

Gabel, S.L. and Chander, J. (2008). Inclusion in Indian education. In S. Gabel and S. Danforth (eds), *Disability and the International Politics of Education*. (pp. 69–80). New York: Peter Lang.

Gabel, S. and Danforth, S. (eds) (2008a). *Disability and the International Politics of Education.* New York: Peter Lang.

Gabel, S. and Danforth, S. (2008b). Foreword. In S. Gabel and S. Danforth (eds), *Disability and the International Politics of Education.* (pp. i–ix). New York: Peter Lang.

Gabel, S. and Peters, S. (2004). Presage of a paradigm shift? Beyond the social model of disability toward resistance theories of disability. *Disability & Society*, 19 (6), 585–600.

Gabriel, M. (1985). Compliance, conversion and the Asch paradigm. *European Journal of Social Psychology*, 14 (4), 353–368.

Gallagher, J.J. (1976). The sacred and profane uses of labeling. *Mental Retardation*, 14, 3–7.

Garland-Thomson, R. (ed.) (1996). *Freakery: Cultural Spectacles of the Extraordinary Body.* New York: New York University Press.

Garland-Thomson, R. (1997). *Extraordinary Bodies: Figuring Physical Disability in American Literature and Culture.* New York: Columbia University Press.

Garland-Thomson, R. (2002). Integrating disability, transforming feminist theory. *NWSA Journal*, 14, (3), 1–32.

Garland-Thomson, R. (2005). Feminist disability studies. *Signs: Journal of Women in Culture and Society*, 30 (2), 1557–1587.

Gatens, M. (1999). Power, bodies and difference. In J. Price and M. Shildrick (eds), *Feminist Theory and the Body.* (pp. 227–234). Edinburgh: Edinburgh University Press.

Gerber, M. (1996). Reforming special education: beyond 'inclusion'. In C. Christensen and F. Rizvi (eds), *Disability and the Dilemmas of Education and Justice.* (pp. 156–174). Buckingham: Open University Press.

Gergen, K.J. (2001). Psychological science in a postmodern world. *American Psychologist*, 56 (10), 803–813.

Gerrschick, T. (2000). Toward a theory of disability and gender. *Signs*, 25 (4), 1263–1268.

Ghai, A. (2002). Disabled women: an excluded agenda for Indian feminism. *Hypatia: A Journal of Feminist Philosophy*, 17 (3), 49–66.

Ghai, A. (2006). *(Dis)embodied Form: Issues of Disabled Women.* Delhi: Shakti Books.

Gillman, M., Swain, J. and Heyman, B. (1997). Life history or 'care history': the objectification of people with learning difficulties through the tyranny of professional discourses. *Disability & Society*, 12 (5), 675–694.

Giroux, H. (2003). Public pedagogy and the politics of resistance: notes on a critical theory of educational struggle. *Educational Philosophy and Theory*, 35 (1), 5–16.

Giroux, H. (2004). Critical pedagogy and the postmodern/modern divide: towards a pedagogy of democratisation. *Teacher Education Quarterly*, Winter, 31–47.

Giroux, H. (2009). Critical theory and educational practice. In A. Darder, M.P. Baltodano and R.D. Torres (eds), *The Critical Pedagogy Reader* (2nd edition). (pp. 27–56). New York: Routledge.

Gjonca, E., Tabassum, F. and Breeze, E. (2009). Socioeconomic differences in physical disability in older age. *Journal of Epidemiology and Community Health*, 63, 928–935.

Gleeson, B. (1999a). *Geographies of Disability.* London: Routledge.

Gleeson, B. (1999b). Beyond goodwill: the materialist view of disability. *Social Alternatives*, 18 (1), 11–17.

Goffman, E. (1961). *Asylums.* New York: Doubleday.

Goffman, E. (1963). *Stigma: Some Notes on the Management of Spoiled Identity.* Harmondsworth: Penguin.

Goggin, G. (2008). Innovation and disability. *M/C Journa*l, 11 (3), np.

Goldberg, E.M. and Morrison, S.L. (1963). Schizophrenia and social class. *The British Journal of Psychiatry*, 109, 782–802.

Gonzales, C. (2004). Rolling on. In B. Guter and J. Killacky (eds), *Queer Crips: Disabled Gay Men and their Stories.* (pp. 51–56). New York: Haworth Press.

Goodley, D. (2000). *Self-advocacy in the Lives of People with Learning Difficulties: The Politics of Resilience*. Maidenhead: Open University Press.

Goodley, D. (2001). 'Learning difficulties', the social model of disability and impairment: challenging epistemologies. *Disability & Society* 16 (2), 207–231.

Goodley, D. (2004). Who is disabled? Exploring the scope of the social model of disability. In J. Swain, S. French, C. Barnes and C. Thomas (eds), *Disabling Barriers, Enabling Environments*. (2nd edition). (pp. 118–124). London: Sage.

Goodley, D. (2007a). Towards socially just pedagogies: deleuzoguattarian critical disability studies. *International Journal of Inclusive Education*, 11 (3), 317–334.

Goodley, D. (2007b). Becoming rhizomatic parents: Deleuze, Guattari and disabled babies. *Disability & Society*, 22 (2), 145–160.

Goodley, D., Hughes, B. and Davis, L. (2011). *Disability and Social Theory*. London: Palgrave Macmillan.

Goodley, D. and Lawthom, R. (2005a). Epistemological journeys in participatory action research: alliances between community psychology and disability studies. *Disability & Society*, 20, (2), 135–152.

Goodley, D. and Lawthom, R. (eds) (2005b). *Disability and Psychology: Critical Introductions and Reflections*. London: Palgrave.

Goodley, D. and Lawthom, R. (2005c). Disability studies and psychology: new allies. In D. Goodley, and R. Lawthom (eds), *Psychology and Disability: Critical Introductions and Reflections*. (pp. 1–16). London: Palgrave.

Goodley, D. and Lawthom, R. (2010). Disability and empire: making sense of disability in changing economic times. *International Journal of Inclusive Education*.

Goodley, D., Lawthom, R., Clough, P. and Moore, M. (2004). *Researching Life Stories: Method, Theory and Analyses in a Biographical Age*. London/New York: Routledge Falmer.

Goodley, D. and McLaughlin, J. (2008). Community practices. In J. McLaughlin, D. Goodley, E. Clavering and P. Fisher, *Families Raising Disabled Children: Enabling Care and Social Justice*. London: Palgrave.

Goodley, D. and Moore, M. (2000). Doing disability research: activist lives and the academy. *Disability & Society*, 15 (6), 861–882.

Goodley, D. and Rapley, M. (2001). How do you understand learning difficulties: towards a social theory of 'impairment'. *Mental Retardation*, 39 (3), 229–232.

Goodley, D. and Rapley, M. (2002). Changing the subject: postmodernity and people with learning difficulties. In M. Corker and T. Shakespeare (eds), *Disability/Postmodernity: Embodying Disability Theory*. London: Continuum.

Goodley, D. and Roets, G. (2008). The (be)comings and goings of developmental disabilities: The cultural politics of 'impairment'. *Discourse: Studies in the Cultural Politics of Education*, 29 (2), 239–255.

Goodley, D. and Runswick-Cole, K. (2010). Emancipating play: dis/abled children, development and deconstruction. *Disability & Society*.

Goodley, D. and Tregaskis, C. (2006). Storying disability and impairment: retrospective accounts of disabled family life. *Qualitative Health Research*, 16 (4), 630–646.

Goodwin, J. (1982). *Sexual Abuse: Incest Victims and their Families*. Bristol: John Wright.

Gorman, R. (2009). Time out: a life narrative approach to ADHD, racialization, and gender nonconformity. Paper presented to the Society for Disability Studies Conference, Tucson, Arizona, 17–20 June.

Graham, L. and Slee, R. (2008). Inclusion? In S. Gabel and S. Danforth (eds), *Disability and the International Politics of Education*. (pp. 81–100). New York: Peter Lang.

Grech, S. (2008). Living with disability in rural Guatemala: exploring connections and impacts on poverty. *International Journal of Disability, Community & Rehabilitation*, 7 (2), (online).

Grech, S. (2009a). Disability in the folds of poverty: exploring connections and transitions in Guatemala: draft Chapter 2. Unpublished doctoral thesis, Manchester Metropolitan University.

Grech, S. (2009b). Disability, poverty and development: critical reflections on the majority world debate, *Disability & Society*, 24, (6), 771–784.

Grech, S. (2009c). Disability in the majority world: critical reflections on poverty, development and the western-centric disability studies. Paper presented to the Disability Research Forum, Manchester Metropolitan University, 20 January.

Greenop, D. (2009). Self-care: a narrative and dialogic study of adults with cystic fibrosis. Unpublished PhD thesis, Liverpool John Moores.

Greenwald, A.G. (1980). The totalitarian ego: fabrication and revision of personal history. *American Psychologist*, 35, 603–618.

Groce, N. (1992). 'The Town Fool': an oral history of a mentally retarded individual in a small town society. In P.M. Ferguson, D.L. Ferguson and S.J. Taylor (eds), *Interpreting Disability: A Qualitative Reader*. (pp. 175–196). New York: Teachers College Press.

Groome, R. (2007). Being nomad: an investigation into the causality of depression. Viewed 3 September 2008 at: www.topoi.net/place6/depression.html.

Grosz, E. (1994). *Volatile Bodies: Toward a Corporeal Feminism*. London: Routledge.

Grosz, E. (1999). Psychoanalysis and the body. In J. Price and M. Shildrick (eds), *Feminist Theory and the Body*. (pp. 267–272). Edinburgh: Edinburgh University Press.

Gustavsson, A. (2004). The role of theory in disability research: springboard or strait-jacket? *Scandinavian Journal of Disability Research,* Special Issue: *Understanding Disability*, 6 (1), 55–70.

Hahn, H. (1988a). The politics of physical differences: disability and discrimination. *Journal of Social Issues*, 44, 39–47.

Hahn, H. (1988b). Can disability be beautiful? *Social Policy*, 18 (winter), 26–31.

Haraway, D. (1991). *Simians, Cyborgs and Women: The Reinvention of Nature*. London: Free Association Books.

Hardt, M. and Negri, A. (2000). *Empire*. Cambridge, MA: Harvard University Press.

Hardy, K. (2008). Blind kids are right to learn. *Special Supplement on Development*, The *Guardian*, 21 November, 1–11.

Hare Mustin, R.T. and Marecek, J. (1992). The meaning of difference: gender theory, postmodernism and psychology. J.S. Bohan (ed.), *Seldom Heard, Rarely Heard: Women's Place in Psychology*. (pp. 227–235). Boulder, CO: Westview Press.

Harré, R. (1984). *Personal Being*. Cambridge, MA: Harvard University Press.

Harwood, V. and Humphrey, N. (2008). Taking exception: discourses of exceptionality and the invocation of the ideal. In S. Gabel and S. Danforth (eds), *Disability and the International Politics of Education*. (pp. 371–384). New York: Peter Lang.

Hasler, F. (1993). Developments in the disabled people's movement. In J. Swain, V. Finkelstein, S. French and M. Oliver (eds), *Disabling Barriers – Enabling Environments*. London: Sage.

Henriques, J., Hollway, W., Urwin, C., Venn, C. and Walkerdine, V. (1984). *Changing the Subject: Psychology, Social Regulation and Subjectivity*. London: Methuen.

Herndon, A. (2002). Disparate but disabled: fat embodiment and disability studies. *NWSA Journal*, 14 (3), 120–137.

Hevey, D. (1992). *The Creatures Time Forgot: Photography and Disability Imagery*. London: Routledge.

Hewitt, S. (2004). Sticks and stones in a boy. In B. Guter and J. Killacky (eds), *Queer Crips: Disabled Gay Men and Their Stories*. (pp. 117–120). New York: Haworth Press.

Hickey-Moody, A. (2006). Folding the flesh into thought. *Angelaki: Journal of the Theoretical Humanities*, 11 (1), 189–193.

Hickey-Moody, A. (2009). *Unimaginable Bodies: Intellectual Disability, Performance and Becomings*. Rotterdam: Sense Publishers.

HMSO (1995). *Disability Discrimination Act.* London: HMSO.

Hochschild, A.R. (1983). *The Managed Heart: Commercialisation of Human Feeling.* Berkeley, CA: University of California Press.

Hodge, N. (2006). Disabling families: how parents experience the process of diagnosing autism spectrum disorders. Unpublished EdD thesis, Sheffield Hallam University.

Hodgkins, S.L. and Bailey, S. (2006). 'I use my disability, I try and make the most of it if that makes much sense' and 'I know that I can't walk but I can still see, if you took my eyes away I'd kill myself': disclosure and the dilemmatic nature of disability ideology and subject positioning. Paper presented at the British Disability Studies Association 3rd Annual Conference, Lancaster, 18–21 September.

Hollway, W. (2007). Self. In W. Hollway, H. Lucy and A. Phoenix (eds), *Social Psychology Matters.* Maidenhead: Open University Press.

Hollway, W. and Jefferson, T. (2000). *Doing Qualitative Research Differently: Free Association, Narrative and the Interview Method.* London: Sage.

hooks, b. (1989). Black women and feminism. *Trouble and Strife,* 15 (Summer), 42–46.

Hosking, D. (2008). The theory of critical disability theory. Paper presented at the Disability Studies Association 4th International Disability Studies Conference, University of Lancaster, Lancaster, UK, 2–4 September.

House, H. and Loewenthal, L. (2008). *Against and for CBT: Towards a Constructive Dialogue?* Ross-on-Wye: PCCS Books.

Howe, K. (1996). Educational ethics, social justice and children with disabilities. In C. Christensen, and F. Rizvi (eds), *Disability and the Dilemmas of Education and Justice.* (pp. 46–62). Buckingham: Open University Press.

Hughes, B. (1999). The constitution of impairment: modernity and the aesthetic of oppression. *Disability & Society,* 14 (2), 155–172.

Hughes, B. (2000). Medicine and the aesthetic invalidation of disabled people. *Disability & Society,* 15 (3), 555–568.

Hughes, B. (2002a). Disability and the body. In C. Barnes, L. Barton and M. Oliver (eds), *Disability Studies Today.* (pp. 58–76). Cambridge: Polity Press.

Hughes, B. (2002b). Invalidated strangers: impairment and the cultures of modernity and post-modernity. *Disability & Society,* 17, (5), 571–584.

Hughes, B. (2004). Disability and the body. In J. Swain, S. French, C. Barnes and C. Thomas (eds), *Disabling Barriers, Enabling Environments* (2nd edition). (pp. 63–68). London: Sage.

Hughes, B. (2009). Disability activisms: social model stalwarts and biological citizens. *Disability & Society,* 24 (6), 677–688.

Hughes, B. and Paterson, K. (1997). The social model of disability and the disappearing body: towards a sociology of 'impairment'. *Disability & Society,* 12 (3), 325–340.

Hughes, B. and Paterson, K. (2000). Disabled bodies, In P. Hancock et al. (eds), *The Body, Culture and Society: An Introduction.* (pp. 29–44). Buckingham: Open University Press.

Hunt, P. (1966). A critical condition. In P. Hunt (ed.), *Stigma: The Experience of Disability.* (pp. 145–149). London: Geoffrey Chapman.

Husaini, A. (2009). The impact of inclusion on individuals with a cognitive disability: a United Arab Emirates perspective. Unpublished Phd thesis, University of Sheffield.

Illich, I., McKnight, J. and Zola, I.K. (1977). *Disabling Professions.* London: Marion Boyars Publishers.

Isaacs, P. (1996). Disability and the education of persons. In C. Christensen and F. Rizvi (eds), *Disability and the Dilemmas of Education and Justice.* (pp. 27–45). Buckingham: Open University Press.

Jarman, M. (2008). Disability studies ethics: theoretical approaches for the undergraduate classroom. *Review of Disability Studies,* 4, 5–13.

Jung, K.E. (2002). Chronic illness and educational equity: the politics of visibility. *NWSA Journal,* 14 (3), 178–200.

Kagan, C. (2002). Making the road by walking it. Inaugural professorial lecture, Manchester Metropolitan University, 30 January.

Kagan, C. and Burton, M. (2002). Community psychology: why this gap in Britain? *History and Philosophy of Psychology,* 4 (2), 10–23.

Kennedy, M. (1996). *Thoughts about Self-advocacy.* Article with Bonnie Shoultz, Viewed 1 January 1995 at: www.soeweb.syr.edu.

Killacky, J.R. (2004). Careening toward Kensho: ruminations on disability and community. In B. Guter and J. Killacky (eds), *Queer Crips: Disabled Gay Men and Their Stories.* (pp. 57–62). New York: Haworth Press.

Kitchin, R. (2001). Using participatory action research approaches in geographical studies of disability: some reflections. *Disability Studies Quarterly,* 21(4), 61–69.

Kittay, E.F. (1999a*). Loves Labour: Essays on Women, Equality and Dependency.* New York: Routledge.

Kittay, E.F. (1999b). Not my way, Sesha, your way slowly: 'maternal thinking' in the raising of a child with profound intellectual disabilities. In J. Hanisberg and S. Ruddick (eds), *Mother Troubles: Rethinking Contemporary Maternal Dilemmas.* (pp. 147–161). Boston, MA: Beacon Press.

Kittay, E.F. (2001). When caring is just and justice is caring: justice and mental retardation. *Public Culture,* 13 (3), 557–579.

Kittay, E.F. (2006). Thoughts on the desire for normality. In E. Parens (ed.), *Surgically Shaping Children: Technology, Ethics and the Pursuit of Normality.* (pp. 90–112). Baltimore, MD: The Johns Hopkins University Press.

Kitzinger, C. (1987). *The Social Construction of Lesbianism.* London: Sage.

Klotz, J. (2003). The cultural concept: anthropology, disability studies and intellectual disability. Paper presented to the Disability Studies and Research Institute Symposium, University of Sydney, Australia, May.

Koch, T. (2008). Is Tom Shakespeare disabled? *Journal of Medical Ethics,* 34, 18–20.

Koegel, P. (1981). Life history: a vehicle towards a holistic understanding of deviance. *Journal of Community Psychology,* 9, 162–176.

Koegel, P. (1986). You are what you drink: evidence of socialised incompetence in the life of a mildly retarded adult. In L.L. Langness and H.G. Levine (eds), *Culture and Retardation.* (pp. 47–63). Dordrecht: Kluwer/D. Reidel.

Kristiansen, K. and Traustadóttir, R. (eds) (2004). *Gender and Disability Research in the Nordic Countries.* Lund: Studentlitterature.

Kristiansen, K., Vehmas, S. and Shakespeare, T. (eds) (2008). *Arguing about Disability: Philosophical Perspectives.* London and New York: Routledge.

Kuhn, T.S. (1968). *The Structure of Scientific Revolutions.* Chicago: University of Chicago Press.

Kuno, K., Carr, L. and Darke, P. (2008). *Training Them and Us: A Guide to Social Equality for Society.* Kuala Lumpur: Utasan Publications.

Lacan, J. (1977). *Ecrits: A Selection.* New York: W.W. Norton.

Langdon, T.L. (2009). Meeting with Difference on the Street: Walking with Crutches and Bumping into Others. Paper presented at Society for Disability Studies Conference, 17 to 20 June 2009 in Tucson, Arizona.

Langdridge, D. (2007). *Phenomenological Psychology: Theory, Research and Method.* Harlow: Pearson Education.

Langness, L.L. and Levine, H.G. (eds) (1986a). *Culture and Retardation.* Dordrecht: Kluwer/D. Reidel.

Langness, L.L. and Levine, H.G. (1986b). Introduction. In L.L. Langness and H.G. Levine(eds), *Culture and Retardation.* (pp. 1–18). Dordrecht: Kluwer/D. Reidel.

Larson, E. (1998). Reframing the meaning of disability to families: the embrace of paradox. *Social Science & Medicine,* 47 (7), 865–875.

Lash, S. (2001). Technological forms of life. *Theory, Culture and Society*, 18 (1), 105–120.

Lather, P. (1986). Research as praxis. *Harvard Educational Review*, 56 (3), 257–277.

Lavia, J. (2007). Postcolonialism as aspiration: articulating a theory of hope. Paper presented at the Social Change and Well-Being Research Centre, seminar series, Manchester Metropolitan University, 28 November.

Law, I. (2007). Self as research. Unpublished PhD thesis, Manchester Metropolitan University.

Lawson, M. (1991). A recipient's view. In S. Ramon (ed.), *Beyond Community Care: Normalisation and Integration Work*. (pp. 62–84). London: Macmillan, in association with MIND Publications.

Lawthom, R. and Goodley, D. (2005). Community psychology: towards an empowering vision of disability. *The Psychologist*, 18 (7), 423–425.

Le Bon, G (1896). *The Crowd: A Study of the Popular Mind*. New York: The Macmillan Co. Viewed 13 April 2007 at: www.etext.virginia.edu/etcbin/toccer-new2?id=BonCrow.sgm&images=images/modeng&data=/texts/english/modeng/parsed&tag=public&part=all.

Levine, H.G. and Langness, L.L. (1986). Conclusions: themes in an anthropology of mild mental retardation. In L.L. Langness and H.G. Levine (eds), *Culture and Retardation*. (pp. 191–206). Dordrecht: Kluwer/D. Reidel.

Levinson, F. and Parritt, S. (2005). Against stereotypes: experiences of disabled psychologists. In D. Goodley and R. Lawthom (eds), *Disability and Psychology: Critical Introductions and Reflections*. (pp. 111–122). Basingstoke: Palgrave.

Lewis, B. (2006). Mad fight: psychiatry and disability activism. In L. Davis (ed.), *The Disability Studies Reader* (2nd edition). (pp. 339–354). New York: Routledge.

Liberatos, P., Link, B.G. and Kelsey, J.L. (1988). The measurement of social class in epidemiology. *Epidemiological Reviews*, 10, 87–121.

Lindeman, G. (1997). The body of gender differences. In K. Davis (ed.), *Embodied Practices: Feminist Perspectives on the Body*. (pp. 73–92). London: Sage.

Ling, H.K. (2007). *Indigenising Social Work: Research and Practice in Sarawak*. Petaling Jaya, Malaysia: Strategic Information and Research Development Centre.

Linton, S. (1998a). Disability studies/not disability studies. *Disability & Society*, 13 (4), 525–539.

Linton, S. (1998b). *Claiming Disability: Knowledge and Identity*. New York: New York University Press.

Linton, S. (2006a). Reassigning meaning. In K. Davis (ed.), *The Disability Studies Reader* (2nd edition). (pp. 161–172). New York: Routledge.

Linton, S. (2006b). *My Body Politic: A Memoir*. Ann Arbor, MI: University of Michigan Press.

Lipsky, D. and Gartner, A. (1996). Equity requires inclusion: the future for all students with disabilities. In C. Christensen and F. Rizvi (eds), *Disability and the Dilemmas of Education and Justice*. (pp. 145–155). Buckingham: Open University Press.

Llorens, M. (2008a). Psychology of oppression and exclusion – poetry talks back to psychiatry: four poetic retellings of psychiatric experience. Unpublished Masters thesis, Manchester Metropolitan University.

Llorens, M. (2008b). Psychotherapy and politics – political resistance and intimacy: dilemmas, possibilities and limitations. Unpublished Masters thesis, Manchester Metropolitan University.

Lloyd, M. (1992). Does she boil an egg? Towards a feminist model of disability. *Disability, Handicap and Society*, 7 (2), 157–166.

Longman, P. and Umansky, L. (eds) (2001). *The New Disability History: American Perspectives (History of Disability)*. New York: New York University Press.

Loomba, A. (2001). *Colonialism/Postcolonialism*. London: Sage.

Lurie, S. (2004). Loving you, loving me. In B. Guter and J. Killacky (eds), *Queer Crips: Disabled Gay Men and Their Stories*. (pp. 83–86). New York: Haworth Press.

Lynn, M. (2004). Inserting the 'race' into critical pedagogy: an analysis of 'race-based epistemologies'. *Educational Philosophy and Theory*, 36 (2), 153–165.

Lynn, M. (2006). Race, culture and the education of African Americans. *Educational Theory*, 56 (1), 107–119.

Lyotard, J.-F. (1979). *The Postmodern Condition: A Report on Knowledge.* Manchester: Manchester University Press.

MacMillan, D.L. (1977). *Mental Retardation in School and Society.* Boston, MA: Little Brown and Co.

Mafrica, F. and Fodale, V. (2007). Down subjects and Oriental population share several specific attitudes and characteristics. *Medical Hypothesis*, 69 (2), 438–440.

Malacrida, C. and Duguay, S. (2009). 'The AISH review is a big joke': contradictions of policy participation and consultation in a neo-liberal context. *Disability & Society*, 24 (1), 19–32.

Malacrida, C. and Low, J. (eds) (2008). *Sociology of the Body: A Reader.* Oxford: Oxford University Press.

Mallett, R. (2007). Critical correctness: exploring the capacities of contemporary Disability criticism. Unpublished PhD thesis, University of Sheffield.

Manion, M.L. and Bersani, H.A. (1987). Mental retardation as a western sociological construct. *Disability, Handicap and Society*, 2 (3), 213–245.

Marks, D. (1999a). *Disability: Controversial Debates and Psychosocial Perspectives.* London: Routledge.

Marks, D. (1999b). Dimensions of oppression: theorizing the embodied subject. *Disability & Society*, 14 (5), 611–626.

Marks, D. (2002). Some concluding notes. Healing the split between psyche and social: constructions and experiences of disability. *Disability Studies Quarterly*, 22 (3), 46–52.

Martin, J., Meltzer, H. and Elliot, D. (1988). *Report 1: The Prevalence of Disability among Adults.* London: HMSO.

Martin, J. and White, A. (1988). *Report 2: The Financial Circumstances of Disabled Adults in Private Households.* London: HMSO.

Marx, K. (1845). Theses on Feuerbach. In K. Marx and F. Engels (eds), *Selected Works.* (pp. 55–60). London: Lawrence & Wishart.

Marx, K. and Engels, F. (1832/1962). *The German Ideology.* Moscow: Progress Publishers.

Masschelein, J. and Simons, M. (2005). The strategy of the inclusive education apparatus. *Studies in Philosophy and Education*, 24 (2), 117–138.

Masson, J. (1989). *Against Therapy.* London: William Collins.

Mckeever, P. and Miller, K.L. (2004). Mothering children with disabilities: A Bourdieusian interpretation of maternal practices. *Social Science and Medicine*, 59 (6), 1177–1191.

McKenzie, J.A. (2009). Constructing the intellectually disabled person as a subject of education: a discourse analysis using Q-methodology. Unpublished PhD thesis, Rhodes University, South Africa.

McLaren, P. (2009). Critical pedagogy: a look at major concepts. In A. Darder, M.P. Baltodano and R.D. Torres (eds), *The Critical Pedagogy Reader* (2nd edition). (pp. 69–96). New York: Routledge.

McLaughlin, J. and Goodley, D. (2008). Seeking and rejecting certainty: exposing the sophisticated lifeworlds of parents of disabled babies. *Sociology*, 42 (2), 317–335.

McLaughlin, J., Goodley, D., Clavering, E. and Fisher, P. (2008). *Families Raising Disabled Children: Enabling Care and Social Justice.* London: Palgrave.

McRuer, R. (2002). Critical investments: AIDS, Christopher Reeve, and queer/disability studies. *Journal of Medical Humanities*, 23 (3/4), 221–237.

McRuer, R. (2003). As good as it gets: queer theory and critical disability. *GLQ: A Journal of Lesbian and Gay Studies*, 9 (1–2), 79–105.

McRuer, R. (2006). Compulsory able-bodiedness and queer/disabled existence. In L. Davis (ed.), *The Disability Studies Reader* (2nd edition). (pp. 301–308). New York: Routledge.

McRuer, R. and Wilkerson, A. (2003). Cripping the (queer) nation. *GLQ: A Journal of Lesbian and Gay Studies*, 9 (1–2), 1–23.

Meekosha, H. (1998). Superchicks, clones, cyborgs, and cripples: cinema and messages of bodily transformations. *Social Alternatives*, 18 (1), 24–28.

Meekosha, H. (2002). Virtual activist? Women and the making of identities of disability. *Hypatia*, 17 (3), 67–88.

Meekosha, H. (2004). Drifting down the Gulf Stream: navigating the cultures of disability studies. *Disability & Society*, 19 (7), 721–733.

Meekosha, H. (2008). Contextualizing disability: developing southern theory. Keynote presentation, Disability Studies Association 4th conference, Lancaster,. 2–4 September.

Meekosha, H. and Jakubowicz, A. (1996). Disability, participation, representation and social justice. In C. Christensen and F. Rizvi (eds), *Disability and the Dilemmas of Education and Justice.* (pp. 79–95). Buckingham: Open University Press.

Mercer, J.R. (1973). *Labelling the Mentally Retarded: Clinical and Social System Perspectives on Mental Retardation.* Los Angeles: University of California Press.

Mercogliano, C. (2009). Canaries in the coal mine. In S. Timimi and J. Leo (eds), *Rethinking ADHD.* (pp. 382–397). London: Palgrave.

Merleau-Ponty, M. (1962). *The Phenomenology of Perception.* London: Routledge.

Michalko, R. (2002). *The Difference that Disability Makes.* Philadelphia, PA: Temple University Press.

Michalko, R. (2008). DoubleTrouble. In S. Gabel and S. Danforth (eds), *Disability and the International Politics of Education.* (pp. 401–416). New York: Peter Lang.

Miles, M. (2000). Disability on a different model: glimpses of an Asian heritage. *Disability & Society*, 15 (4), 603–618.

Miles, M. (2002). *Community and Individual Responses to Disablement in South Asian Histories: Old Traditions, New Myths? Online document.* Viewed 15 December 2008 at: www.independentliving.org/docs3/miles2002a.html.

Miles, M. (2006). *Social Responses to Disability and Poverty in Economically Weaker Countries: Research, Trends, Critique, and Lessons Usually Not Learnt. Annotated Bibliography of Modern and Historical Material. Online document.* Viewed 15 December 2008 at: www.independentliving.org/docs/miles200603.html.

Miller, J.A. (2008). *Objects in the Analytic Experience.* Viewed 9 September 2008 at: www.lacan.com/lacaniancompass9miller.htm.

Mintz, S.B. (2002). Invisible disability: Georgina Kleege's *Sight Unseen*. In K.Q. Hall (eds), *Feminist Disability Studies.* Special issue, *NWSA Journal*, 14 (3), 155–177.

Mitchell, D. and Snyder, S. (eds) (1997). *The Body and Physical Difference: Discourse of Disability.* New York: Verso.

Mitchell, D. and Snyder, S. (2006). Narrative prosthesis and the materiality of metaphor. In L. Davis (ed.), *The Disability Studies Reader* (2nd edition). (pp. 205–216). New York: Routledge.

Mitchell, J. (1974). *Psychoanalysis and Feminism.* New York: Pantheon Books.

Mohit, A. (2000). Disability in India: family responsibility of social change? Signs of a gradual paradigm shift. *Disability World*, 4. Viewed 16 June 2009 at http://www.disabilityworld.org/Aug-Sept2000/International/India.html.

Moloney, P. and Kelly, P. (2004). Beck never lived in Birmingham: why CBT may be a less useful treatment for psychological distress than is often supposed. *Clinical Psychology*, 34 (February), 4–11.

Moore, M., Beazley, S. and Maelzer, J. (1998). *Researching Disability Issues.* Buckingham: Open University Press.

Morris, C. (1972). *The Discovery of the Individual, 1050–1200.* London: Camelot Press.

Morris, J. (1991). *Pride against Prejudice: Transforming Attitudes to Disability.* London: The Women's Press.

Morris, J. (1992). Personal and political: a feminist perspective on researching physical disability. *Disability, Handicap and Society*, 7 (2), 157–166.

Morris, J. (1993a). Gender and disability. In J. Swain, V. Finkelstein, S. French and M. Oliver (eds), *Disabling Barriers – Enabling Environments.* London: Sage.

Morris, J. (1993b). *Independent Lives: Community Care and Disabled People*. London: Macmillan.

Morris, J. (ed.) (1996). *Encounters with Strangers: Feminism and Disability*. London: The Women's Press.

Munford, R. (1994). The politics of care-giving. In M. Rioux and M. Bach (eds), *Disability Is Not Measles: New Directions in Disability*. (pp. 265–287). Ontario: L'Institut Roeher.

Murray, P. and Penman, J. (eds) (1996). *Let Our Children Be: A Collection of Stories*. Sheffield: Parents with Attitude.

Nagi, S.Z. (1976). An epidemiology of disability among adults in the United States. *Millbank Memorial Fund Quarterly: Health and Society*, 54, 439–468.

Naidoo, P. (2009). An analysis of the experiences of children with cerebral palsy in therapeutic horse-riding. Unpublished PhD thesis, University of KwaZulu-Natal, South Africa.

Ngcobo, J. and Muthukrishna, N. (2008). Teachers' dominant discourses of inclusion and disability: a case study at a semi-rural township school in the province of KwaZulu-Natal, South Africa. In S. Gabel and S. Danforth (eds), *Disability and the Politics of Education: An International Reader*. (pp. 53–68). New York: Peter Lang Publishers.

Nes, K. (2004). Quality versus equality? Inclusive politics in Norway at century's end. In L. Ware (ed.), *Ideology and the Politics of (In)exclusion*. (pp. 27–36). New York: Peter Lang.

Newman, F. and Holzman, L. (1993). *Lev Vygotsky: Revolutionary Scientist*. London: Routledge.

Nicholson, H. (1928). *The Development of Biography*. New York: Harcourt Brace.

Nikander, P. (1995). The turn to the text: the critical potential of discursive social psychology. *Nordiske Udkast*, 2, 3–15.

Nind, M. (2008). Learning difficulties and social class: exploring the intersection through family narratives. *International Studies in Sociology of Education*, 18 (2), 87–98.

Nisbet, R. (1976). *Sociology as an Art Form*. London: Heinemann.

Nkweto-Simmonds, F. (1999). My body, myself: how does a black woman do sociology. In J. Price and M. Shildrick (eds), *Feminist Theory and the Body*. (pp. 50–63). Edinburgh: Edinburgh University Press.

Noll, S. and Trent, J.W. (2004). *Mental Retardation in America*. New York: New York University Press.

Nunkoosing, K. and Haydon, M. (2008). 'I am verbally aggressive to other people: I am unwilling to listen to reason'. A critical discourse analysis of referrals to a community learning disability team. Paper presented to intellectual disability conference – empowering people with intellectual disabilities, their families and supporters: reflections on research and practice, Park Building, University of Portsmouth, 12–13 September.

Oakley, A. (1981). Interviewing women: a contradiction in terms. In H. Roberts (ed.), *Doing Feminist Research*. (pp. 30–61). London: Routledge.

O'Brien, J. (1987). A guide to life style planning: using the Activities Catalogue to integrate services and natural support systems. In B.W. Wilson and G.T. Bellamy (eds), *The Activities Catalogue: An Alternative Curriculum for Youth and Adults with Severe Disabilities*. (pp. 104–110). Baltimore, MD: Brookes.

O'Brien, P. and Sullivan, M. (1997). *Human Services: Towards Partnership and Support*. Palmerston North, New Zealand: Dunmore Press.

O'Brien, P. and Sullivan, M. (2005). *Allies in Emancipation: Shifting from Providing Services to Being of Support*. Melbourne: Thomson Dunmore Press.

Office for National Statistics (2009). Self-coded version on the NS-SEC. Viewed 11 November 2009 at: www.ons.gov.uk/about-statistics/classifications/current/ns-sec/self-coded/index.html.

Oliver, K. (2007). Innocence, perversion and Abu Ghraib. *Philosophy Today*, Fall, 343–356.

Oliver, K. and Edwin, S. (eds) (2002). *Between the Psyche and the Social: Psychoanalytic Social Theory*. Maryland: Rowman and Littlefield Publishers Inc.

Oliver, M. (1983). *Social Work with Disabled People*. Basingstoke: Macmillan.

Oliver, M. (1990). *The Politics of Disablement*. Basingstoke: Macmillan.

Oliver, M. (1992). Changing the social relations of research production. *Disability, Handicap and Society*, 7 (2), 101–114.

Oliver, M. (1993a). What's so wonderful about walking? Inaugural professorial lecture, University of Greenwich, London.

Oliver, M. (1993b). Conductive education: if it wasn't so bad it would be funny. In J. Swain, V. Finkelstein, S. French and M. Oliver (eds), *Disabling Barriers – Enabling Environments.* (pp. 69–74). London: Sage.

Oliver, M. (1996). *Understanding Disability: From Theory to Practice.* London: Macmillan.

Oliver, M. (1998). Final accounts and the parasite people. In M. Corker and S. French (eds), *Disability Discourse.* (pp. 183–191). Buckingham: Open University Press.

Oliver, M. and Barnes, C. (1997). All we are saying is give disabled researchers a chance. *Disability & Society*, 12 (5), 811–813.

Oliver, M. and Zarb, G. (1989). The politics of disability: a new approach. *Disability, Handicap and Society*, 4 (3), 221–239.

Oliver, M., Zarb, G., Silver, M., Moore, M. and Salisbury, V. (1988). *Walking into Darkness: The Experience of Spinal Cord Injury.* Basingstoke: Macmillan.

Olkin, R. (2001). Disability-affirmative therapy. *Spinal Cord Injury Psychosocial Process*, 14 (1), 12–23.

Olkin, R. (2002). Could you hold the door for me? Including disability in diversity. *Cultural Diversity and Ethnic Minority Psychology*, 8 (2), 130–137.

Olkin, R. (2003). Women with physical disabilities who want to leave their partners: a feminist and disability-affirmative perspective. *Women and Therapy*, 26 (3/4), 237–246.

Olkin, R. (2008). Physical or systemic disabilities. In J. Worell and C. Goodheart (eds). *Handbook of Girls' and Women's Psychological Health.* (pp. 94–102). New York: Oxford University Press.

Olkin, R. (2009). *Women with Physical Disabilities Who Want to Leave Their Partners: A Feminist and Disability-affirmative Perspective.* California School of Professional Psychology and Through the Looking Glass, Co.

Olkin, R. and Pledger, C. (2003). Can disability studies and psychology join hands? *American Psychologist*, 58 (4), 296–304.

Orford, J. (1992). *Community Psychology: Theory and Practice.* Chichester: John Wiley & Sons.

Overboe, J. (2007a). Disability and genetics: affirming the bare life (the state of exception). *Genes and Society: Looking Back on the Future*, Special Issue of *Canadian Review of Sociology*, 44 (2), 219–235.

Overboe, J. (2007b). Vitalism: subjectivity exceeding racism, sexism, and (psychiatric) ableism. *Intersecting Gender and Disability Perspectives in Rethinking Postcolonial Identities*, Special issue of *Wagadu, Journal of Transnational Women's and Gender Studies*, 7, 1–34.

Parker, I. (1989). Discourse and power. In J. Shotter and K.J. Gergen (eds), *Texts of Identity.* (pp. 56–69). London: Sage.

Parker, I. (1992). *Discourse Dynamics: Critical Analysis for Social and Individual Psychology.* London: Routledge.

Parker, I. (1993). *Lacan: Psychoanalysis and Society Sourse Notes.* Manchester: Manchester Metropolitan University.

Parker, I. (1997). *Psychoanalytic Culture.* London: Sage.

Parker, I. (1999a). *Deconstructing Psychotherapy.* London: Sage.

Parker, I. (1999b). Against relativism in psychology, on balance. *History of the Human Sciences*, 12 (4), 61–78.

Parker, I. (2003). Discursive resources in the discourse unit. *Discourse Analysis Online*, 1 (1). Viewed 8 June 2008 at: www.extra.shu.ac.uk/daol.

Parker, I. (2007). *Revolution in Psychology: Alienation to Emancipation.* London: Pluto Press.

Parker, I. and the Bolton Discourse Network (1999). *Critical Textwork: An Introduction to Varieties of Discourse and Analysis.* Buckingham: Open University Press.

Parker, I., Georgaca, E., Harper, D., McLaughlin, T. and Stowell-Smith, M. (1995). *Deconstructing Psychopathology.* London: Sage.

Parker, I. and Shotter, J. (eds) (1990). *Deconstructing Social Psychology.* London: Routledge.

Parsons, T. (1951). *The Social System.* London: Routledge & Kegan Paul.

Paterson, K. and Hughes, B. (1999). Disability studies and phenomenology: the carnal politics of everyday life. *Disability & Society*, 14 (5), 597–610.

Perreault, M. (2004). Acting for others, acting for myself. In B. Guter and J. Killacky (eds), *Queer Crips: Disabled Gay Men and Their Stories*. (pp. 103–106). New York: Haworth Press.

Peters, S. and Chimdeza, R. (2000). Conscientization and the cultural politics of education: a radical minority perspective. *Comparative Education Review*, 44 (3), 245–271.

Peters, S., Wolbers, K. and Dimling, L. (2008). Reframing global education from a disability rights movement perspective. In S. Gabel and S. Danforth (eds), *Disability and the International Politics of Education*. (pp. 291–310). New York: Peter Lang.

Pfeiffer, D. and Yoshida, K. (1995). Teaching disability studies in Canada and the USA. *Disability & Society*, 10 (4), 475–500.

Phillips, S.D. (2009). 'There are no invalids in the USSR!' A missing Soviet chapter in the new disability history. *Disability Studies Quarterly*, 29 (3), 1–35.

Pledger, C. (2003). Discourse on disability and rehabilitation issues. *American Psychologist*, 58, 279–312.

Pledger, C. (2004). Disability paradigm shift. *American Psychologist*, 59, 275–276.

Potter, J. (2005). Making psychology relevant. *Discourse and Society*, 16 (5), 739–747.

Potter, J. and Wetherell, M. (1987). *Discourse and Social Psychology*. London: Sage.

Potter, J. and Wetherell, M. (1995). Discourse analysis. In J. Smith, R. Harré and L. Langenhove (eds), *Rethinking Methods in Psychology*. (pp. 80–92). London: Sage.

Potts, M. and Fido, R. (1991). *A Fit Person to be Removed: Personal Accounts of Life in a Mental Deficiency Institution*. Plymouth: Northcote House.

President's Committee on Mental Retardation. (1970). The six hour mentally retarded child. A Report. Viewed 3 January 2010 at: http://openlibrary.org/b/OL14741990M/Six-hour_retarded_child.

Price, J. (2007). Engaging disability. *Feminist Theory*, 8 (1), 77–89.

Price, J. and Shildrick, M. (eds) (1999). *Feminist Theory and the Body*. Edinburgh: Edinburgh University Press.

Priestley, M. (1998). Constructions and creations: idealism, materialism and disability theory. *Disability & Society*, 13 (1), 75–94.

Priestley, M. (1999). *Disability Politics and Community Care*. London: Jessica Kingsley.

Priestley, M. (ed.) (2001). *Disability and the Life Course: Global Perspectives*. Cambridge: Cambridge University Press.

Quinlan, K., Bowleg, L. and Faye Ritz, S. (2008). Virtually invisible women: women with disabilities in mainstream psychological theory and research. *Review of Disability Studies*, 4, 4–17.

Race, D., Boxall, K. and Carson, I. (2005). Towards a dialogue for practice: reconciling social role valorisation and the social model of disability. *Disability & Society*, 20 (5), 507–521.

Rapley, M. (2004). *The Social Construction of Intellectual Disability*. Cambridge: Cambridge University Press.

Rapley, M. and Antaki, C. (1996). A conversation analysis of the 'acquiescence' of people with learning disabilities. *Journal of Community and Applied Social Psychology*, 6, 207–227.

Rapley, M. and Ridgway, J. (1998). Quality of life talk and the corporatisation of intellectual disability. *Disability & Society*, 13 (3), 451–471.

Rauscher, L. and McClintock, M. (1997). Ableism curriculum design. In M. Adams, L.A. Bell and P. Griffin (eds), *Teaching for Diversity and Social Justice*. (pp. 198–230). London: Routledge.

Read, J. (2000). *Disability, the Family, and Society: Listening to Mothers*. Buckingham: Open University Press.

Reeve, D. (2002). Negotiating psycho-emotional dimensions of disability and their influence on identity constructions. *Disability & Society*, 17 (5), 493–508.

Reeve, D. (2004). Counselling and disabled people: help or hindrance? In J. Swain, S. French, C. Barnes and C. Thomas (eds), *Disabling Barriers, Enabling Environments* (2nd edition). (pp. 233–238). London: Sage.

Reeve, D. (2005). Towards a psychology of disability: the emotional effects of living in a disabling society. In D. Goodley and R. Lawthom (eds), *Disability and Psychology: Critical Introductions and Reflections* (pp. 94–107.) London: Palgrave.

Reeve, D. (2006). Am I a real disabled person or someone with a dodgy arm? A discussion of psycho-emotional disablism and its contribution to identity constructions. Paper presented at the British Disability Studies Association 3rd Annual Conference, Lancaster, 18–21 September.

Reeve, D. (2007). *Homo sacer* and zones of exception: metaphors for the contemporary experience of disablism? Paper presented at the Nordic Network of Disability Research Conference, Stockholm, April.

Reeve, D. (2008). Negotiating disability in everyday life: the experience of psycho-emotional disablism. Unpublished PhD thesis, Lancaster.

Reindal, S.M. (1999). Independence, dependence, interdependence: some reflections on the subject and personal autonomy. *Disability & Society*, 14 (3), 353–367.

Reiser, R. and Mason, M. (1992). *Disability Equality in the Classroom: A Human Rights Issue.* London: Disability Equality in Education.

Rich, A. (1980). Compulsory heterosexuality and lesbian existence. *Signs, Women: Sex and Sexuality*, 5 (4), 631–660.

Richardson, D. (2005). Desiring sameness? The rise of neoliberal politics of normalization. *Antipode*, 37 (3), 515–535.

Rioux, M. (1994a). New directions and paradigms: disability is not measles. In M. Rioux and M. Bach (eds), *Disability Is Not Measles: New Directions in Disability.* (pp. 1–8). Ontario: L'Institut Roeher.

Rioux, M. (1994b). Towards a concept of equality of well being: overcoming the social and legal construction of inequality. In M. Rioux and M. Bach (eds), *Disability Is Not Measles: New Directions in Disability*. (pp. 67–108). Ontario: L'Institut Roeher.

Rioux, M. and Bach, M. (eds) (1994). *Disability Is Not Measles: New Directions in Disability.* Ontario: L'Institut Roeher.

Rizvi, F. and Lingard, B. (1996). Disability, education and the discourses of justice. In C. Christensen and F. Rizvi (eds), *Disability and the Dilemmas of Education and Justice.* (pp. 9–26). Buckingham: Open University Press.

Roach, A.T. (2004). In search of a paradigm shift: what can disability studies contribute to school psychology? *Disability Studies Quarterly*, 23 (3/4), np.

Robertson, S. (2004). Men and disability. In J. Swain, S. French, C. Barnes and C. Thomas (eds), *Disabling Barriers, Enabling Environments* (2nd edition). (pp. 75–80). London: Sage.

Roets, G., Goodley, D. and Van Hove, G. (2007). Narrative in a nutshell: sharing hopes, fears and dreams with self-advocates. *Intellectual and Developmental Disabilities (Mental Retardation)*, 45 (5), 323–334.

Roets, G., Reinaart, R., Adams, M. and Van Hove, G. (2008). Looking at lived experiences of self-advocacy through gendered eyes: becoming femme fatale with/out 'intellectual disabilities'. *Gender & Education*, 20 (1), 15–29.

Roets, G., Van de Perre, D., Van Hove, G., Schoeters, L. and De Schauwer, E. (2004). One for all – All for one! An account of the joint fight for human rights by Flemish Musketeers and their Tinker Ladies. *British Journal of Learning Disabilities*, 32 (2), 54–64.

Rose, D. (1995). Official social classifications in the UK. *Social Research Update, July 1995*, University of Surrey, Guildford.

Rose, J. (1986). *Sexuality in the Field of Vision*. London: Verso.

Rose, N. (1979). The psychological complex: mental measurement and social administration. *Ideology & Consciousness*, 4, 5–68.

Rose, N. (1985). *The Psychological Complex: Psychology, Politics and Society in England 1869–1939.* London: Routledge & Kegan Paul.

Rose, N. (2001). The politics of life itself. *Theory, Culture & Society*, 18 (6), 1–30.

Rosenhan, D.L. (1973). On being sane in insane places. *Science*, 179, 250–258.

Roulstone, A. (1998). *Enabling Technology: Disabled People, Work and New Technology.* Buckingham: Open University Press.

Roulstone, A. and Balderston, S. (2009). Is violence, murder and harassment against disabled people really hate crime? Paper presented at the Office for Disability Issues Evidence Day, London, 19 November.

Rudberg, M. (1997). The researching body: the epistemophilic body. In K. Davis (ed.), *Embodied Practices: Feminist Perspectives on the Body.* (pp. 182–202). London: Sage.

Runswick-Cole, K. (2007). 'The tribunal was the most stressful thing, more stressful than my son's diagnosis or behaviour': the experiences of families who go to the special educational needs and disability tribunal (sendist). *Disability & Society*, 22 (3), 315–328.

Ryan, J. and Thomas, F. (1987). *The Politics of Mental Handicap.* London: Free Association Press.

Ryan, S. (2005). People don't do odd, do they? Mothers making sense of the reactions of others to their learning disabled children in public places. *Children's Geographies*, 3 (3), 291–305.

Sable, A. (2004). How to find love with a fetishist. In B. Guter and J. Killacky (eds), *Queer Crips: Disabled Gay Men and Their Stories.* (pp. 65–82). New York: Haworth Press.

Sachs, R. (2008). *Disability support services, Montgomery College.* Viewed 5 January 2009 at: www.mc.md.us/departments/dispsvc/diversity.htm.

Salvage, A. and Zarb, G. (1995a). *Measuring Disablement: Working Paper 1: Disabled People and Public Transport.* Viewed 1 May 2009 at: www.leeds.ac.uk/disability-studies/archiveuk/Salvage/meas%20work%20paper%201.pdf.

Salvage, A. and Zarb, G. (1995b). *Measuring Disablement in Society: Gaining Access: Disabled People and the Physical Environment.* Viewed 30 April 2009 at: www.leeds.ac.uk/disability-studies/archiveuk/Salvage/meas%20work%20paper%202.pdf.

Sampson, E.E. (1977). Psychology and the American ideal. *Journal of Personality and Social Psychology*, 35 (11), 767–782.

Sampson, E.E. (1985). The decentralisation of identity: toward a revised concept of personal and social order. *American Psychologist*, 40 (11), 1203–1211.

Sampson, E.E. (1988). The debate on individualism: indigenous psychologies of the individual and their role in personal and societal functioning. *American Psychologist*, 43 (1), 15–22.

Sampson, E.E. (1993). Identity politics: challenges to psychology's understanding. *American Psychologist*, 48 (12), 1219–1230.

Samuels, E. (2002). Critical divides: Judith Butler's body theory and the question of disability. *NWSA Journal*, 14 (3), 58–76.

Sapsford, R. (ed.), (1998). *Theory and Social Psychology.* London: Sage.

Sayce, L. (2000). *From Psychiatric Patient to Citizen: Overcoming Discrimination and Social Exclusion.* London: Macmillan.

Sen, A. (1985). *Commodities and Capabilities.* Amsterdam: North-Holland.

Sen, A. (1999). *Development as Freedom.* Oxford: Oxford University Press.

Scheff, T.J. (1974). Labelling theory of mental illness. *American Sociological Review*, 39, 444–452.

Shah, S. (2005). *Career Success of Disabled High-Flyers.* London: Jessica Kingsley.

Shakespeare, T. (1993). Disabled people's self-organisation: a new social movement? *Disability, Handicap and Society*, 8 (3), 249–264.

Shakespeare, T. (1997a). Cultural representation of disabled people: dustbins for disavowal? In L. Barton and M. Oliver (eds), *Disability Studies: Past, Present and Future.* Leeds: The Disability Press.

Shakespeare, T. (1997b). Rules of engagement: changing disability research. In L. Barton and M. Oliver (eds), *Disability Studies: Past, Present and Future.* Leeds: The Disability Press.

Shakespeare, T. (2000). *Help.* London: Venture Press.

Shakespeare, T. (2006a). *Disability Rights and Wrongs.* London: Routledge.

Shakespeare, T. (2006b). The blooming of a hundred flowers: activism, academia, and the disability studies challenge. Keynote presentation at the Disability Studies Association 3rd Annual Conference, Lancaster, 18–21 September.

Shakespeare, T. (2009). It's the economy, stupid! The ironic absence of class analysis in British disability studies. Keynote presentation at the Disability and Economy: Creating a Society for All Conference, hosted by Research on Economy and Disability, the University of Tokyo in association with Manchester Metropolitan University, 29–30 April.

Shakespeare, T., Gillespie-Sells, K. and Davies, D. (1996). *The Sexual Politics of Disability.* London: Cassells.

Shakespeare, T. and Watson, N. (1997). Defending the social model. *Disability & Society*, 12 (2), 293–300.

Shakespeare, T. and Watson, N. (2001a). The social model of disability: an outdated ideology? Exploring theories and expanding methodologies. *Research in Social Science and Disability*, 2, 9–28.

Shakespeare, T. and Watson, N. (2001b). Making the difference: disability, politics, recognition. In G. Albrecht, C. Searle and M. Bury (eds), *International Handbook of Disability Studies.* (pp. 546–654). London: Sage.

Shen, Q., McCabe, H. and Chi, Z. (2008). Disability education in the People's Republic of China: tradition, reform, and outlook. In S. Gabel and S. Danforth (eds), *Disability and the International Politics of Education.* (pp. 177–200). New York: Peter Lang.

Shepherd, A. (1966). One body. In P. Hunt (ed.), *Stigma: The Experience of Disability.* (pp. 40–53). London: Geoffrey Chapman.

Sherry, M. (2000). Hate crimes against disabled people. *Social Alternatives*, 19 (4), 23–30.

Sherry, M. (2004). Overlaps and contradictions between queer theory and disability studies. *Disability & Society*, 19 (7), 769–783.

Sherry, M. (2006). *If I Only Had a Brain: Deconstructing Brain Injury*. London: Routledge.

Sherry, M. (2007). *(Post)Colonising disability*. Special issue of *Wagadu, Journal of Transnational Women's and Gender Studies*, 4 (Summer), 10–22.

Shield, S.A. (1992). Functionalism, Darwinism and the psychology of women: a study in social myth. In J.S. Bohan (ed.), *Seldom Seen, Rarely Heard.* (pp. 79–106). Boulder, CO: Westview Press.

Shildrick, M. (2004). Queering performativity: disability after Deleuze. *SCAN: Journal of Media Arts Culture*, 1 (3), 1–6. Viewed 2 January 2008 at: www.scan.net.au/scan/journal/display.php?journal_id=36.

Shildrick, M. (2007a). Dangerous discourse. Anxiety, desire and disability. *Studies in Gender & Sexuality*, 8 (3), 221–244.

Shildrick, M. (2007b). A response to Bardach and Hannabach. *Studies in Gender & Sexuality*, 8 (3), 263–268.

Shildrick, M. and Price, J. (1999a). Openings on the body: a critical Introduction. In J. Price and M. Shildrick (eds), *Feminist Theory and the Body.* (pp. 1–14). Edinburgh: Edinburgh University Press.

Shildrick, M. and Price, J. (1999b). Breaking the boundaries of the broken body. In J. Price and M. Shildrick (eds), *Feminist Theory and the Body.* (2nd edition), (pp. 432–444). Edinburgh: Edinburgh University Press.

Shildrick, M. and Price, M. (2005/2006). Deleuzian connections and queer corporealities: shrinking global disability, *Rhizomes*, 11/12. Viewed 28 February 2007 at: www.rhizomes.net/issue11/shildrickprice/ index.html.

Shilling, C. (2005). *The Body in Culture, Technology and Society*. London: Sage.

Shor, I. (2009). What is critical literacy? In A. Darder, M.P. Baltodano and R.D. Torres (eds), *The Critical Pedagogy Reader* (2nd edition). (pp. 282–304). New York: Routledge.

Shuttleworth, R. (2000). The search for sexual intimacy for men with cerebral palsy. *Sexuality and Disability*, 18 (4), 263–282.

Shuttleworth, R. (2002). Defusing the adverse context of disability and desirability as a practice of the self for men with cerebral palsy. In M. Corker and T. Shakespeare (eds), *Disability and Postmodernity.* (pp. 112–126). London: Cassell.

Shuttleworth, R. and Grove, H. (2008). A critical literature review of sexuality and disability. Paper presented at the Disability Studies Association 4th conference, Lancaster, September.

Sibley, D. (2003). Geography and psychoanalysis: tensions and possibilities. *Social & Cultural Geography*, 4 (3), 391–399.

Siebers, T. (2006). Disability in theory: from social constructionism to the new realism of the body. In K. Davis (ed.), *The Disability Studies Reader* (2nd edition). (pp. 173–184). New York: Routledge.

Sigelman, C.K., Budd, E.C., Spanhel, C.L. and Schoenrock, C.J. (1981a). When in doubt, say yes: acquiescence in interviews with mentally retarded persons. *Mental Retardation*, 19 (April), 53–58.

Sigelman, C.K., Budd, E.C., Spanhel, C.L. and Schoenrock, C.J. (1981b). Asking questions of retarded persons: a comparison of yes-no and either-or formats. *Applied Research in Mental Retardation*, 2, 347–357.

Sigelman, C.K., Budd, E.C., Winer, J.L., Schoenrock, C.J. and Martin, P.W. (1982). Evaluating alternative techniques of questioning mentally retarded persons. *American Journal of Mental Deficiency*, 86 (5), 511–518.

Sigelman, C.K., Schoenrock, C.J., Spanhel, C.L., Hromas, S.G., Winer, J.L., Budd, E.C. and Martin, P.W. (1980). Surveying mentally retarded persons: responsiveness and response validity in three samples. *American Journal of Mental Deficiency*, 84 (5), 479–486.

Silvers, A. (1995). Reconciling equality to difference: caring (f)or justice for people with disabilities. *Hypatia*, 10 (1), 30–38.

Sinason, V. (1992). *Mental Handicap and the Human Condition*. London: Free Association Books.

Skrtic, T.M. (ed.) (1995). *Disability and Democracy: Reconstructing (Special) Education for Postmodernity*. New York: Teachers College Press.

Slee, R. (1996). Disability, class and poverty: school structures and policising identities. In C. Christensen and F. Rizvi (eds), *Disability and the Dilemmas of Education and Justice*. (pp. 96–188). Buckingham: Open University Press.

Slee, R. (1997). Imported or important theory? Sociological interrogations of disablement and special education. *British Journal of Sociology of Education*, 18 (3), 407–419.

Slee, R. (2004). Meaning in the service of power. In L. Ware (ed.), *Ideology and the Politics of (In) exclusion*. New York: Peter Lang.

Smith, B. and Sparkes, A.C. (2004). Men, sport, spinal injury and narrative: an analysis of metaphors and narrative types. *Disability & Society*, 19 (6), 613–626.

Smith, B. and Sparkes, A.C. (2005). Men, sport, spinal cord injury and narratives of hope. *Social Science & Medicine*, 61 (5), 1095–1105.

Smith, P. (2008). Cartographies of eugenics and special education: a history of the (ab)normal. In S. Gabel and S. Danforth (eds), *Disability and the International Politics of Education*. (pp. 417–432). New York: Peter Lang.

Snyder, S.L. and Mitchell, D.T. (2001). Re-engaging the body: disability studies and the resistance to embodiment. *Public Culture*, 13 (3): 367–389.

Snyder, S.L. and Mitchell, D.T. (2006). *Cultural Locations of Disability*. Chicago: University of Chicago Press.

Sparkes, A.C. and Smith, B. (2002). Sport, spinal cord injuries, embodied masculinities, and narrative identity dilemmas. *Men and Masculinities*, 4 (3), 258–285.

Sparkes, A.C. and Smith, B. (2003). Men, sport, spinal cord injury and narrative time. *Qualitative Research*, 3 (3), 295–320.

Spender, D. (1982). *Women of Ideas – and What Men Have Done to Them* (2nd edition, 1988). London: Routledge.

Spivak, G.C. (1985). Three women's texts and a critique of imperialism. *Critical Inquiry*, 12 (1), 243–261.

Stanley, L. and Wise, S. (1993). *Breaking Out Again: Feminist Ontology and Epistemology*. London: Routledge.

Stannett, P. (2005). Disabled and graduated: barriers and dilemmas for the disabled psychology graduate. In D. Goodley and R. Lawthom (eds), *Disability and Psychology: Critical Introductions and Reflections*. (pp. 71–83). London: Palgrave.

Stevens, B. (2008). Managing unruly bodies: public policy and disability sexuality. *Review of Disability Studies*, 4 (4), 15–22.

Stone, E. (ed.) (1999). *Disability and Development: Learning from Action and Research on Disability in the Majority World.* Leeds: The Disability Press. Viewed May 2008 at: www.leeds.ac.uk/disability-studies/archiveuk/stone/intro.pdf.

Stone, E. and Priestley, M. (1996). Parasites, pawns and partners: disability research and the role of non-disabled researchers. *British Journal of Sociology*, 47 (4), 699–716.

Stramondo, J. (2009). Fear, anxiety, and authentic understanding of disability: a Heideggerian examination. Paper presented at the Society for Disability Studies Conference, Tucson, Arizona, 17–20 June.

Stratford, B. (1991). Human rights and equal opportunities for people with mental handicap – with particular reference to Down's Syndrome. *International Journal of Disability, Development & Education*, 38 (1), 3–13.

Stromstad, M. (2004). Accounting for the ideology and politics in the development of inclusive practice in Norway. In L. Ware (ed.), *Ideology and the Politics of (In)exclusion.* (pp. 146–165). New York: Peter Lang.

Stuart, O. (1993). Double oppression: an appropriate starting point? In J. Swain, V. Finkelstein, S. French and M. Oliver (eds), *Disabling Barriers – Enabling Environments.* London: Sage.

Swain, J., Finkelstein, V., French, S. and Oliver, M. (eds) (1993). *Disabling Barriers – Enabling Environments.* London: Sage.

Swain, J. and French, S. (2000). Towards an affirmation model of disability. *Disability & Society*, 15 (4), 569–582.

Syme, S.L. and Berkman, L.F. (1976). Social class, susceptibility and sickness. *American Journal of Epidemiology*, 104 (1), 1–8.

Taylor, S.J. and Bogdan, R. (1984). *Introduction to Qualitative Research Methods: The Search for Meanings* (2nd edition). New York: John Wiley & Sons.

Taylor, S.J. and Bogdan, R. (1989). On accepting relationships between people with mental retardation and non-disabled people: towards an understanding of acceptance. *Disability, Handicap & Society*, 4 (1), 21–37.

Taylor, S.J. and Bogdan, R. (1992). Defending illusions: the institution's struggle for survival. In P.M. Ferguson, D.L. Ferguson and S.J. Taylor (eds), *Interpreting Disability*. New York: Teachers Press College.

Tepper, M.S. (1999). Letting go of restrictive notions of manhood: male sexuality, disability and chronic illness. *Sexuality and Disability*, 17 (1), 37–52.

Terzi, L. (2004). The social model of disability: a philosophical critique. *Journal of Applied Philosophy*, 21 (3), 141–157.

Thomas, C. (1999). *Female Forms: Experiencing and Understanding Disability.* Buckingham: Open University Press.

Thomas, C. (2001a). Feminism and disability: the theoretical and political significance of the personal and the experiential. In L. Barton (ed.), *Disability, Politics and the Struggle for Change.* (pp. 48–58). London: David Fulton.

Thomas, C. (2001b). The body and society: some reflections on the concepts 'disability' and 'impairment'. In N. Watson and S. Cunningham-Burley (eds), *Reframing the Body.* (pp. 47–62). London: Palgrave.

Thomas, C. (2004). How is disability understood? An examination of sociological approaches. *Disability & Society*, 19 (6), 569–583.

Thomas, C. (2007). *Sociologies of Disability, 'Impairment', and Chronic Illness: Ideas in Disability Studies and Medical Sociology.* London: Palgrave.

Thomas, C. (2008). Disability: getting it 'right'. *Journal of Medical Ethics*, 34, 15–17.

Thomas, D. (1982). *The Experience of Mental Handicap.* London: Methuen.

Thomas, G. and Loxley, A. (2001). *Deconstructing Special Education and Constructing Inclusion.* Buckingham: Open University Press.

Timimi, S. (2002). *Pathological Child Psychiatry and the Medicalization of Childhood.* Hove and New York: Brunner-Routledge.

Timimi, S. (2005). *Naughty Boys: Antisocial Behaviour, ADHD and the Role of Culture.* London: Palgrave.

Titchkosky, T. (2003). *Disability, Self and Society.* Toronto: University of Toronto Press.

Titchkosky, T. (2008). I got trouble with my reading: an emerging literacy. In S. Gabel and S. Danforth (eds), *Disability and the International Politics of Education.* (pp. 337–352). New York: Peter Lang.

Tobbell, J. and Lawthom, R. (2005). Dispensing with labels: enabling children and professionals to share a community of practice. *Educational and Child Psychology*, 22 (3), 89–97.

Todd, L. (2005). Enabling practice for professionals: the need for practical post-structuralist theory. In D. Goodley and R. Lawthom (eds), *Disability and Psychology: Critical Introductions and Reflections.* Basingstoke: Palgrave.

Tomlinson, S. (1982). *A Sociology of Special Education.* London: Routledge.

Tøssebro, J. (2002). Leaving the individual out: practical and logical problems. Paper presented at a Plenary Symposium 'Understanding Disability: The UK Social Model and the Nordic Relational Approach' at the 6th NNDR Conference, Disability Research, Theory and Practice, Reykjavík, Iceland, 22–24 August.

Tøssebro, J. (2004). Understanding disability: introduction to the special issues of SJDR. *Scandinavian Journal of Disability Research*, Special Issue of *Understanding Disability*, 6 (1), 3–7.

Traustadóttir, R. (1991). Mothers who care: gender, disability and family life. *Journal of Family Issues*, 12 (2), 221–228.

Traustadóttir, R. (1995). A mother's work is never done: constructing a 'normal' family life. In S.J. Taylor, R. Bogdan and Z.M. Lutfiyya (eds), *The Variety of Community Experience: Qualitative Studies of Family and Community Life.* Baltimore, MD: Brookes Publishing.

Traustadóttir, R. (1999). Gender, disability and community life: toward a feminist analysis. In H. Bersani (ed.), *Responding to the Challenge: Current Trends and International Issues in Developmental Disabilities.* Cambridge, MA: Brookline Books.

Traustadóttir, R. (2004a). Disability studies: a Nordic perspective. Keynote lecture, British Disability Studies Association conference, Lancaster, 26–28 July.

Traustadóttir, R. (2004b). A new way of thinking: exploring the intersection of disability and gender. In K. Kristjaensen and R. Traustadóttir (eds), *Gender and Disability Research in the Nordic Countries* (pp. 49–71). Lund: Studentlitterature.

Traustadóttir, R. (2006a). Disability studies: a Nordic perspective. Paper presented at the Applying Disability Studies Seminar Series, Centre of Applied Disability Studies, University of Sheffield, May.

Traustadóttir, R. (2006b). Families of disabled children: an international perspective. Keynote address. Enabling Practices of Care and Support for Parents with Babies with Disabilities: End of Award Conference, University of Newcastle, Newcastle, June.

Tregaskis, C. (2004). *Constructions of Disability: Researching the Interface between Disabled and Non-Disabled People.* London: Routledge.

Tremain, S. (2000). Queering disability studies. *Sexuality and Disability*, 18 (4), 291–299.

Tremain, S. (2001). On the government of disability. *Social Theory and Practice*, 27 (4), 617–636.

Tremain, S. (2002). On the subject of impairment. In M. Corker and T. Shakespeare (eds), *Disability/Postmodernity: Embodying Disability Theory.* (pp. 32–47). London: Continuum.

Tremain, S. (ed.) (2005a). *Foucault and the Government of Disability.* Ann Arbor, MI: University of Michigan Press.

Tremain, S. (2005b). Foucault, governmentality and critical disability theory. In S. Tremain (ed.), *Foucault and the Government of Disability.* (pp. 1–25). Ann Arbor, MI: University of Michigan Press.

Tremain, S. (2006a). On the government of disability: Foucault, power and the subject of impairment. In K. Davis (ed.), *The Disability Studies Reader* (2nd edition). (pp. 185–196). New York: Routledge.

Tremain, S. (2006b). Reproductive freedom, self-regulation, and the government of impairment in Utero. *Hypatia*, 21 (1), 35–53.

Troyna, B. and Vincent, C. (1996). 'The ideology of expertism': the framing of special education and racial equality policies in the local state. In C. Christensen and F. Rizvi (eds), *Disability and the Dilemmas of Education and Justice*. (pp. 131–144). Buckingham. Open University Press.

Tuhiwai-Smith, L. (1999). *Decolonizing Methodologies: Research and Indigenous Peoples*. New York: St Martin's Press.

Turner, B. (2008). *The Body and Society* (3rd edition). London: Sage.

Turner, J.L. (1983). Secrets, artifice and semblance: forms and functions of naturally occurring fantasy in the lives of mentally retarded adults. Paper presented at the 107th Annual Meeting of the American Association on Mental Deficiency, June, Dallas, Texas.

UNESCO (1990). *World Declaration on Education for All*. Viewed 6 March 2010 at: www.unesco.org/education/pdf/JOMTIE_E.PDF.

UNESCO (1994). *Salamanca Statement and Framework for Action on Special Needs Education*. Viewed 6 March 2010 at: www.unesco.org/education/pdf/SALAMA_E.PDF.

United Nations (1982). *United Nations World Programme of Action concerning Disabled People*. Viewed 3 March 2010 at: www.un.org/documents/ga/res/37/a37r052.htm.

United Nations (1993). *Standard Rules on the Equalisation of Opportunities for Persons with Disabilities*. Viewed 3 March 2010 at: www.un.org/esa/socdev/enable/dissre00.htm.

United Nations (2007). *The Convention on the Rights of Persons with Disabilities*. Viewed 6 March 2010 at: www.un.org/disabilities/default.asp?id=150.

United Nations Department of Economic and Social Affairs (2009). *The United Nations Department of Economic and Social Affairs: Disability*. Viewed 3 March 2009 at: www.asil.org/rio/desa.html.

United Nations Department of Public Information (2008). *Backgrounder: Disability Treaty Closes a Gap in Protecting Human Rights*. Viewed 3 March 2009 at: www.un.org/disabilities/default.asp?id=476.

UPIAS (1976). *Fundamental Principles of Disability*. London: Union of the Physically Impaired Against Segregation.

Ussher, J. (1991). *Women's Madness: Misogyny or Mental Illness?* London: Harvester Wheatsheaf.

Van Hove, G., Roets, G. and Goodley, D. (2005). Disability studies: about relationships, power and knowing as form of participation. In D. Goodley and G. Van Hove (eds), *Another Disability Studies Reader: Including People with Learning Difficulties*. (pp. 185–197). Antwerp: Garant.

Van Hove, G., Roets, G., Mortier, K., De Schauwer, E., Leroy, M. and Broekaert, E. (2008). Research in inclusive education as a possible opening to disability studies in education. In S. Gabel and S. Danforth (eds), *Disability and the International Politics of Education*. (pp. 121–140). New York: Peter Lang.

Varela, R. (1978). Self-advocacy and changing attitudes. In G. Richman and P. Trohanis (eds), *Public Awareness Viewpoints*. (pp. 27–36). Chapel Hill, NC: University of North Carolina Press.

Vehmas, S. (2008). Philosophy and science: the axes of evil in disability studies? *Journal of Medical Ethics*, 43, 21–23.

Vehmas, S. and Mäkelä, P. (2008a). The ontology of disability and impairment: a discussion of the natural and social features. In K. Kristiansen, S. Vehmas and T. Shakespeare (eds), *Arguing about Disability: Philosophical Perspectives*. (pp. 42–56). London and New York: Routledge.

Vehmas S. and Mäkelä, P. (2008b). A realist account of the ontology of impairment. *Journal of Medical Ethics*, 43, 93–95.

Venn, C. (1984). The subject of psychology. In J. Henriques, W. Hollway, C. Urwin, C. Venn and V. Walkerdine, *Changing the Subject: Psychology, Social Regulation and Subjectivity*. (pp. 115–147). London: Methuen.

Venn, C. (2001). *Occidentalism: Modernity and Subjectivity*. London: Sage.

Vernon, A. (1999). The dialectics of multiple identities and the disabled people's movement. *Disability & Society*, 14 (3), 385–398.

Vickers, M. (2008). How queer! insider research in educational settings. Paper presented at the Social Change and Well-being Seminar series, Manchester Metropolitan University, 6 February.

Vislie, (2003). From integration to inclusion: focusing on global trends and changes in the Western European societies. *European Journal of Special Needs Education*, 18, 17–35.

Vlachou, A. (1997). *Struggles for Inclusion: An Ethnographic Study.* Buckingham: Open University Press.

Vlachou-Balafouti, A. and Zoniou-Sideris, A. (2002). Greek policy practices in the area of special/inclusive education. In F. Armstrong, D. Armstrong and L. Barton (eds), *Inclusive Education: Policy, Contexts and Comparative Perspectives.* (pp. 27–41). London: David Fulton.

Walkerdine, V. (1993). Beyond developmentalism. *Theory and Psychology*, 3 (4), 451–469.

Walmsley, J. (1997). Including people with learning difficulties: theory and practice. In L. Barton and M. Oliver (eds), *Disability Studies: Past, Present and Future* . (pp. 18–42). Leeds: The Disability Press.

Ware, L. (2002). Sunflowers, enchantment and empires: reflections on inclusive education in the United States. In F. Armstrong, D. Armstrong and L. Barton (eds), *Inclusive Education: Policy, Contexts and Comparative Perspectives.* (pp. 42–59). London: David Fulton.

Ware, L. (ed.) (2004a). *Ideology and the Politics of (In)exclusion.* New York: Peter Lang.

Ware, L. (2004b). Introduction. In L. Ware (ed.), *Ideology and the Politics of (In)exclusion.* (pp. 1–12). New York: Peter Lang.

Ware, L. (2009). Writing, identity and the other: dare we do disability studies? In A. Darder, M.P. Baltodano and R.D. Torres (eds), *The Critical Pedagogy Reader (*2nd edition). (pp. 397–476). New York: Routledge.

Warnock, M. (2005). *Special Educational Needs: A New Look.* London: Philosophy of Education Society of Great Britain.

Warnock Committee (1978). *Special Educational Needs.* The Warnock Report. London: Department of Schools and Education.

Waterman, D. (2004). Hustlers: a buyer's guide. In B. Guter and J. Killacky (eds), *Queer Crips: Disabled Gay Men and Their Stories.* (pp. 7–12). New York: Haworth Press.

Watson, N. (2002). Well, I know this is going to sound very strange to you, but I don't see myself as a disabled person: identity and disability. *Disability & Society*, 17 (5), 509–529.

Watson, N., Riddell, S. and Wilkinson, H. (eds) (2003). *Disability, Culture and Identity.* London: Prentice Hall.

Wedell, K. (2008). Confusion about inclusion: patching up or system change? *British Journal of Special Education*, 35 (3), 127–135.

Weiss, G. (1999). The durée of the techno-body. In E. Grosz (ed.), *Becomings: Explorations in Time, Memory and Futures.* (pp. 161–175). New York: Cornell University Press.

Wendell, S. (1996). *The Rejected Body: Feminist Philosophical Reflections on Disability.* New York: Routledge.

Whitemore, R., Langness, L. and Koegel, P. (1986). The life history approach to mental retardation. In L. Langness and H. Levine (eds), *Culture and Retardation.* (pp. 1–18). Dordrecht: Kluwer/D. Reidel.

Whitney, C. (2006). Intersections in identity–identity development among queer women with disabilities. *Sexuality and Disability*, 24 (1), 39–52.

Wilkerson, A. (2002). Disability, sex radicalism and political agency. *NWSA Journal*, 14 (3), 33–57.

Wilkinson, S. and Kitzinger, C. (eds) (1995). *Feminism and Discourse: Psychological Perspectives.* London: Sage.

Williams, C. (2003). Sky service: the demands on emotional labor in the airline industry. *Gender, Work and Organisation*, 10 (5), 513–551.

Williams, P. and Shoultz, B. (1982). *We Can Speak for Ourselves.* London: Souvenir Press.

Wilton, R.D. (2003). Locating physical disability in Freudian and Lacanian psychoanalysis: problems and prospects. *Social and Cultural Geography*, 4 (3), 369–389.

Wolfensberger, W. (1972a). *Citizen Advocacy for the Handicapped, Impaired and Disadvantaged: An Overview.* Washington, DC: President's Committee on Mental Retardation.

Wolfensberger, W. (1972b). *Normalization: The Principle of Normalization in Human Services.* Toronto: Leonard Crainford.

Wolfensberger, W. (1981). The extermination of handicapped people in World War II Germany. *Mental Retardation,* 19, 1–7.

Wolfensberger, W. (1987). Values in the funding of social services (a Commentary Paper). *American Journal of Mental Deficiency,* 92 (2), 141–143.

Wong, S.I. (2002). At home with Down syndrome and gender. *Hypatia,* 17 (3), 89–117.

Woodhill, G. (1994). The social semiotics of disability. In M.H. Rioux and M. Bach (eds), *Disability Is Not Measles: New Research Paradigms in Disability.* (pp. 201–216). Ontario: L'Institut Roeher Institute.

Woollet, A. and Marshall, H. (1997). Young women's accounts of their bodies in relation to autonomy and independence. In K. Davis (ed.), *Embodied Practices: Feminist Perspectives on the Body.* (pp. 27–40). London: Sage.

World Health Organisation (2001). *International Classification of Functioning, Disability and Health.* Geneva: World Health Organisation.

Wright Mills, C. (1970). *The Sociological Imagination.* Oxford: Oxford University Press.

Yarmol, K. (1987). Pat Worth–Self-Advocate par excellence. *Entourage,* 2 (2), 26–29.

Yates, S., Dyson, S. and Hiles, D. (2008). Beyond normalisation and impairment: theorising subjectivity in learning difficulties – theory and practice. *Disability & Society,* 23 (3), 247–258.

Yeo, S.L. (2006). Self-advocacy in Malaysia. Unpublished Masters thesis, University of Malaysia, Kuala Lumpur.

Young, I.M. (1990). *Justice and the Politics of Difference.* Princeton, NJ: Princeton University Press.

Zaidi, A. and Burchardt, T. (2009). Extra costs of living for disabled people and implications for poverty. Paper presented at the Office for Disability Issues Evidence Day, London, 19 November.

Zarb, G. (1992). On the road to Damascus: first steps towards changing the relations of disability research production. *Disability, Handicap and Society,* 7 (2), 125–138.

Žižek, S. (1997). The big Other doesn't exist. *Journal of European Psychoanalysis,* 5, 1–5. Viewed 5 August 2008 at: www.psychomedia.it/jep.

Žižek, S. (2006). Is psychoanalysis really outmoded? Apropos the 150th Anniversary of Freud's birth. *Journal of European Psychoanalysis,* 23 (2), 1–5. Viewed 5 August 2008 at: www.psychomedia.it/jep.

Zola, I. (1982). *Ordinary Lives: Voices of Disability and Disease.* Cambridge, MA/Watertown: Apple-wood Books.

Index

please note that page references to Figures and Tables will be in *italic* print